THE LONG TWENTIETH CENTURY

The Great Divergence
Hegemony, Uneven Development, and Global Inequality

Edited by
JOMO K. S.

OXFORD
UNIVERSITY PRESS

OXFORD

UNIVERSITY PRESS

YMCA Library Building, Jai Singh Road, New Delhi 110001

Oxford University Press is a department of the University of Oxford. It furthers
the University's objective of excellence in research, scholarship, and education
by publishing worldwide in

Oxford   New York
Auckland   Cape Town   Dar es Salaam   Hong Kong   Karachi
Kuala Lumpur   Madrid   Melbourne   Mexico City   Nairobi
New Delhi   Shanghai   Taipei   Toronto

With offices in
Argentina   Austria   Brazil   Chile   Czech Republic   France   Greece
Guatemala   Hungary   Italy   Japan   Poland   Portugal   Singapore
South Korea   Switzerland   Thailand   Turkey   Ukraine   Vietnam

Oxford is a registered trade mark of Oxford University Press
in the UK and in certain other countries

Published in India
by Oxford University Press, New Delhi

ISBN-13: 978-0-19-567386-9
ISBN-10: 0-19-567386-7

Typeset in Garamond in 10/12 by Jojy Philip
Printed at Pauls Press, New Delhi 110 020
Published by Oxford University Press
YMCA Library Building, Jai Singh Road, New Delhi 110 001

Contents

Tables, Figures, and Maps

Contributors

MARIA SERENA I. DIOKNO
Professor of History; former Academic Vice President, University of the Philippines, Diliman, Philippines; SEASREP (Southeast Asian Studies Exchange Program) Council, Manila. Executive Committee, SEPHIS.

BILL FREUND
Professor of Economic History, University of Natal, Durban, South Africa.

JOMO KWAME SUNDARAM
Assistant Secretary General for Economic Development, Department of Economic and Social Affairs, United Nations. Former Professor, Applied Economics Department, University of Malaya, Kuala Lumpur; former Senior Visiting Research Fellow, Asia Research Institute, National University of Singapore; Founder Chair, Executive Committee, IDEAs (International Development Economics Associates).

JOSÉ ANTONIO OCAMPO
United Nations Under-Secretary General for Economic and Social Affairs, New York; former Executive Secretary of the Economic Commission for Latin America and the Caribbean (ECLAC).

PRABHAT PATNAIK
Professor, Centre for Economic Studies and Planning, Jawaharlal Nehru University, New Delhi, India; Editor, *Social Scientist*.

SUMIT SARKAR
Professor, Department of History, Delhi University, Delhi, India.

LANCE VAN SITTERT
Senior Lecturer, Department of Historical Studies, University of Cape Town, Cape Town, South Africa.

FARUK TABAK
Ertegün Chair in Modern Turkish Studies, Walsh School of Foreign Service, Georgetown University.

1

Introduction

Jomo K. S.

The end of the Cold War has been followed by the unchallenged ascendance of USA to a position of global military superiority, though this has not necessarily guaranteed corresponding political hegemony, let alone comparable economic dominance. The events following 11 September 2001, especially the invasion and conquest of Afghanistan and then Iraq, have further reduced the remaining fetters on 'empire talk', especially in the Anglophone West. Not surprisingly, considering the circumstances of its emergence, this new discourse has tended to be driven by military and political interests. This general neglect of economic dimensions has hardly been compensated for by occasional references to economic—usually resource, and especially petroleum—considerations. Economic analysis is rarely enhanced when such discussions are drawn into the discourse of conspiracy theories, rather than more systemic considerations.

Contemporary context for discussion of imperialism and empire is remarkably different from the situation at the beginning of the last century when John Hobson and others first debated imperialism. In some respects, post-Second World War imperialism has been significantly different from the pre-war colonial empires. While elements of continuity have been captured by the term 'neo-colonial', aspects of discontinuity were recognized by early uses of the term 'post-colonial'. The contemporary revival of academic interest in empire and imperialism has been occasioned by recent political developments. It arose after the apparent victory of the West in the Cold War, the demise of the Soviet Union and existing 'state socialisms' as well as the consolidation of US military 'hyper-power'. This political triumph is often linked to the rise of a 'neo-liberal' economic ideology including an enthusiasm for economic liberalization, including its transnational or cross-border aspects often termed globalization. US hegemony became unambiguous after the Second World War, with Bretton Woods, the Cold War and the Marshall Plan, rather than 'gunboat diplomacy' or its contemporary and later equivalents. The long record of US military and other interventions abroad for over two centuries (Go 2004) and US colonialism since the Spanish–American war at the end of the nineteenth century do not in themselves negate the many novel aspects of post-war US hegemony, which has also changed significantly over the last six decades. Recent attempts to rethink contemporary imperialism on more 'post-modern' and 'post-colonial' lines—for example, in terms of 'network hegemony' and transnational corporate collusion (Hardt and Negri 2000)—should not obscure the changing realities of US hegemony, especially after the end of the Cold War.

But the immediate impulse for current 'empire talk' is the changed world situation after 11 September 2001. As is well known, the 'war on terror' has been invoked to legitimize the military invasions of Afghanistan and Iraq. Greater international belligerence is partially reflected in growing US unilateralism in world affairs. Clearly, these are interesting times where many old alliances, especially those built during the Cold War, are under stress and new coalitions are being put together, recast, and occasionally even abandoned in response to fast changing circumstances. Most importantly, this new situation has given rise to fresh justifications for assertion of imperial dominance, in the form of direct unilateral occupation (even if by the rarely fully specified 'coalition of the willing') or involving some multilateral administration (NATO or UN).

In recent decades, the academic study of imperialism in the West turned from the economic and the political to previously neglected cultural dimensions, largely under the influence of Edward Said (1979, 1993) and the 'post-colonial' stream of 'post-modernism'. Following the end of the Cold War, the ascendance of the 'neo-conservatives' during the presidency of George W. Bush and the 'war on terror' following 9/11 have resulted in dramatic developments and the emergence of new advocates of a US empire. Some of the better known 'neo-con' proponents include Max Boot, Robert Cooper, Dinesh D'Souza, Robert Kagan, Charles Krauthammer, Bernard Lewis, Sebastian Mallaby, Daniel Pipes, Richard Perle, and Paul Wolfowitz, many associated with the late Leo Strauss, the Project for a New American Century, and other influential quasi-academic advocacy initiatives.

Supporters of a greater US imperial role also include those, like Niall

Ferguson (2002, 2004), who have argued that British imperialism was benign and progressive—as previously argued by imperial apologists such as David Fieldhouse—and that US imperialism will be even more humane. For them, imperialism was clearly beneficial to both imperialists as well as the subjugated. Ferguson (2002) insists that the British empire in the late nineteenth and early twentieth centuries 'enhanced global welfare' by promoting 'the free movement of goods, capital, and labour' and imposing 'western norms of law, order, and governance around the world.'

Ferguson's rose-tinted, selective, and caricatured version of British imperial history implies that such consequences of imperialism were self-evidently beneficial and desirable, and should be acknowledged accordingly by the typically unappreciative conquered. Also, his assumption of a relatively homogenous empire does not recognize that his presumed benefits were actually rather unevenly and inconsistently spread, with significant variations over time and space. Nor does he consider the very varied, often unintended, consequences and implications of similar institutions, policies, and initiatives in different contexts. Imperial investments in infrastructure tended to follow or even lead profitable private investment opportunities, while social spending (for instance, on schools or public health) generally reflected colonial interests and needs, or responded to anti-colonial agitation, especially towards the end of empire.

To be sure, the consequences of imperialism were very varied over time, in various parts of the world, and for different groups of people, and it is likely that some of those conquered became better off as a consequence. But Ferguson argues that the colonized were generally better off due to imperialism, thanks to its essentially benign and modernizing nature. According to him, even decolonization was a consciously made sacrifice by an almost selfless British imperialism to defeat other malevolent imperialisms during the Second World War.

Drawing from his analysis of the British imperial experience, Ferguson (2004) reiterates the importance of imperial will and the need for the US to overcome remaining qualms to ensure success for the massive long-term commitment required for the imperial effort. Noting that the US has long been expansionist (also see Williams 1993, Go 2004)—albeit in rather distinct ways, not least due to its national origins as a settler colony—Ferguson urges the American leadership to rise to the challenges and responsibilities of its unchallenged imperial role. Drawing principally from a paternalistic selective portrayal of the post-colonial sub-Saharan African condition, he insists that a new US imperialism will be best for the entire post-colonial world. This is bolstered by his racist, but no less superficial picture of the Middle East as a culturally 'dysfunctional civilization of clashes', another school-boyishly clever wordplay with no serious analytical content.

To be sure, Ferguson's contempt is not only reserved for non-Western or non-European societies, cultures, and economies. Europe too is hopeless due to its diversity, self-preoccupation, weakness, social democratic concerns (with planning and welfare), sloth and aging population. Revealingly, he believes Europe's fast-growing Muslim population will prevent it from taking on the 'white man's burden'. Needless to say, the United Nations is hopeless to Ferguson. Through this mix of culturally chauvinistic and imperial apologia, Ferguson's policy conclusions betray his Thatcherite intellectual formation.

IMPERIALISM: CONTINUITY AND CHANGE[1]

With undisputed US global hegemony since the fall of the Berlin Wall, and especially after the US-led invasion and occupation of Afghanistan and Iraq, there has been a recent resurgence of 'empire talk' in the Anglophone West (Barber 2003, Ferguson 2004, Ikenberry 2004, Johnson 2004, Mann 2003, Todd 2003). However, while contemporary, interesting and important, much of this discourse is largely irrelevant to our concerns here as they focus almost exclusively on military and political aspects, largely divorced from the realm of the economic beyond occasional mention of 'resource wars', especially over the control of petroleum supplies, which some consider to be the basis for 'commodity money' in the present period. This is not to suggest that the political and the military are unrelated to the economic, but only to underscore the limited attention to economic aspects in recent 'empire talk'.

Most theories of imperialism accept that international economic interests could not be secured without coercion, or at least the threat of its exercise. After all, 'the object was not that Britain should sustain the Empire, but that the Empire should sustain Britain'; Whitehall oversaw 'what was in effect a self-generating and self-financing system—an empire on the cheap' (Louis and Robinson 1994: 463-4). 'Victorian imperialism withdrew from countries as reliable economic links and national organizations emerged—while it extended into others in need of development. Such was the genius of British free trade imperialism' (Louis and Robinson 1994: 495). The system relied on deals with client rulers who helped secure British power locally to their own advantage. Imperial preferences

---

[1] The following discussion draws heavily on the literature on the continuity of empire in the second half of the twentieth century, especially after decolonization, especially Louis and Robinson (1994).

encouraged trade within the sterling area, resulting in significant net capital inflows over the mid-nineteenth century, which contributed greatly to capital accumulation for the Industrial Revolution.

While London undoubtedly intermediated significant capital exports through much of the late nineteenth century into the early twentieth century, especially to the settler colonies, seeing London as the source of capital transfers ignores the massive wealth transfers on both the current and capital accounts from much of its empire, including British India, the West Indies, sub-Saharan Africa and Southeast Asia. Colonialism was clearly profitable, albeit unevenly so. Right after the Second World War, export earnings from British Malaya alone exceeded those of the rest of the empire while Britain itself also relied on net capital inflows from the US.

During the Cold War after the Second World War, the former British Empire was soon transformed into an Anglo-American sphere of influence, and then, with the further decline of the UK, into a predominantly US sphere of influence. Marshall Plan aid as well as other economic and strategic support offset the otherwise unbearable burden of perpetuating British power abroad. Thus, British imperial power was largely sustained with US support. More generally, Western Europe—and its empires— depended heavily on US aid. The British and French Empires were supported, ostensibly to save the Free World from communism, as the Americans sought to transform former European colonial into 'neo-colonial' client regimes.

But, unlike the Europeans, the US preferred 'independence' and covert influence to outright colonialism, but prioritized anti-communism over anti-colonialism. Thus, US anti-colonialism did not extend to informal empire, and instead sought to replace colonialism with informal control, especially by the US and its closest allies. Independence was thus to be granted to extend imperial influence and to better secure Anglo-American economic and strategic interests. After all, imperial preferences and financial controls had given way to a freer world economy and colonial controls were clearly no longer indispensable for metropolitan prosperity.

After the disastrous attempt to make sterling convertible in July 1947 led to a run on the pound and exhausted precious US credit resources, the pressures to decolonize became overwhelming. Increasingly, however, US Cold War considerations began to coincide with British imperial interests. UK and US officials soon agreed that Britain's colonies must move to self-government or independence as soon as possible while preserving economic and political links to the West. After the Suez debacle in 1956, the British followed the US preference for decolonization in favour of pro-Western allies with liberal economic policies the need to contain resistance and to bolster local collaborators influenced the pace of imperial retreat. Successor national regimes which would secure UK and US economic and strategic assets were cultivated and supported with American help.

Thus, the British relied increasingly heavily on the Americans to secure the post-colonial imperial order. 'The new world order needed a good deal of old-fashioned imperial and financial intervention.' As formal empires were dismantled, 'the thraldom of international economy remains. There was no conspiracy to take over the Empire. American influence expanded by imperial default and nationalist invitation...Such was the imperialism of decolonization' (Louis and Robinson 1994: 495).

US DOMINANCE AND VULNERABILITY

David Dapice (2003) has argued that 'No nation can dominate for long when its very economic health, much less its ability to project power, is based on the cooperation of those supposedly dominated'. He concludes that 'without greater economic strength, the future of US hegemony is likely to be either shorter or more nuanced than either the friends or critics of the US realize'. While these observations are important, they ignore the economic history of imperialism, which has rarely been characterized by the consistently relatively undiminished economic strength of hegemons.

Some critical observers have been stressing the vulnerability and imminent collapse of US hegemony for various reasons for decades. For many others, however, the US economy today remains stronger and more dynamic than its two major economic rivals, which may say more about Europe and Japan than about the US. Japan has remained moribund after more than a decade of virtual stagnation subsequent to its disastrous financial 'big bang'. Meanwhile, Europe has been fettered by its Growth and Stability Pact, increasingly considered to have deprived it of anti-deflationary monetary policy instruments.

Nevertheless, the emerging view of the US as a 'hyper-power' may not fully take into account the country's economic vulnerabilities. For example, the US's 'twin deficits' on its fiscal and current account balances as well as electoral considerations have compromised US positions on trade liberalization, for example its 2002 steel tariffs and agricultural subsidies which ensured retention of a Republican Congress and Senate. Tariffs and subsidies continue despite their rejection by the WTO dispute settlement process and the massive devaluation of the US dollar in 2002–3, further strengthening the impression of US unilateralism and unwillingness to submit to the rule of (international) law. The US also relies on an average of over USD 1.3 billion of capital inflows each day to finance its imports and the resulting current account deficit. Royalties from intellectual property rights and financial services account for an increasingly greater share of its foreign exchange earnings.

With the demise of the gold standard, the US dollar increasingly became accepted as the universal store of value and medium of exchange. The emergence and consolidation of a de facto 'dollar standard' has not been entirely smooth. European scepticism from the late 1960s mounted greater pressure on the greenback, leading to the US dollar devaluation in 1971 with Nixon's unilateral renunciation of US obligations under the Bretton Woods system set up in 1944 in anticipation of a post-war Pax Americana. Later, the September 1985 Plaza Accord dollar devaluation—following Paul Volcker's US Fed high interest rate deflationary interventions which then precipitated the sovereign debt crises of the 1980s—did not succeed in rectifying the large US current account deficit with Japan. Instead, subsequent capital inflows to the US have since financed the US current account deficits with East Asia that followed.

In recent decades, the strength of the greenback has been increasingly propped up by vast imports of capital from the rest of the world, rather than by the strength of US exports (today, intellectual property rights are the largest and fastest growing major export earner for the US). Ironically, much of these capital inflows to the US have come from East Asia itself, that is, East Asian exporters have been earning US dollars, which have been used by their governments to buy US Treasury bonds or otherwise invest in the US. Almost half of all US Treasury bonds are held as reserves by foreign central banks, principally in East Asia. During the 1990s, many central banks were encouraged to sell down their gold holdings, but only to replace them with even more US Treasury bonds. Most of these foreign central banks are unlikely to sell these bonds for fear of weakening their own currencies, which are invariably pegged in some way to the greenback.

The Bretton Woods system of fixed exchange rates tied to gold and the US dollar has been replaced by a system of flexible exchange rates since the early 1970s. But the demise of the Bretton Woods system in 1971 did not mean an end to the internationalization of the greenback and the build-up of US liabilities abroad. The virtual 'dollar standard'—implicit in pegging the value of the greenback to the price of gold—was thus 'freed' of its gold reference. Without the Bretton Woods system's framework, political hegemony and confidence have become all the more important. Globalization in this context and the seeming demise of systemic alternatives (often associated with the existence of the Soviet Union) have also served to strengthen the new arrangements.

US dollar hegemony has meant that economic growth abroad increases demand for dollar assets. As central banks increase money supply, they also want to hold more dollar assets in reserve to support their currencies. With globalization, the disproportionate rise in short-term cross-border transactions requires even more dollars to cover such dealings. Thus, the world economy is increasingly hostage to US monetary policy as the Federal Reserve determines world liquidity. The generally deflationary stance of the US Fed thus combines with the European Growth and Stability Pact and the Bank of Japan's historically deflationary monetary policy to conspire against more rapid economic growth globally, ostensibly to avoid the likely attendant inflation.

But the evolution of this system has also meant that global liquidity is dependent on acceptance—by both sides—of foreigners building up claims on US assets. After all, dollar bills or Treasury bonds abroad imply promises by the US Treasury to eventually pay up. In the meantime, the increase of such liabilities could eventually undermine confidence in their value. But the irony, of course, is that the world cannot afford to risk the US reversing these trends, without threatening a global liquidity crunch.

Not surprisingly, US creditors gain from this de facto dollar standard. Already, over half of all dollar bills in circulation are to be found abroad. The rest of the world exports to America, and must settle for less in return for the 'privilege' of securing dollars to sustain international liquidity. Most US government borrowing is now being financed from abroad, mainly by the central banks of China, Japan, and other East Asian economies. Meanwhile, US gross federal debt as a share of GDP is projected to be USD 8.1 trillion, or 767.5 per cent of GDP in the 2005 fiscal year, the highest ever since the Second World War (Weisbrot 2004), limiting its capacity to undertake more costly financial commitments.

As noted earlier, political developments since 11 September 2001 have had rather serious implications for economic globalization. Most importantly, more assertive US 'unilateralism', apparently under the influence of so-called 'neo-conservatives', continues to profoundly transform international relations and institutions, including those involved in international economic governance such as the International Monetary Fund (IMF), World Bank (WB) and the World Trade Organization (WTO). While the Zionist and selectively liberal democratic agenda of the 'neo-conservatives' is clear, their actual influence in the Bush conservative camp as well as its economic implications are still changing and unclear in the run-up to the 2004 US presidential election.

However, the 'neo-conservatives' are not the only ones who seek to consolidate and further US world domination. This is reflected, for example, by the 'sovereigntist' discourse which preceded the ascendance of

George W. Bush to become the 43rd president of the US in late 2000. Spiro (2000) notes that the 'new sovereigntism' is not isolationist in the sense of opposing international engagement, but rather insists on the exclusive right for the US to pick and choose those international conventions and laws that serve its interests, which have mainly been those furthering economic globalization and hence US corporate interests. These 'new sovereigntists' include ostensible liberals such as Michael Ignatieff who has argued that, 'Being an imperial power ... means enforcing such order as there is in the world and doing so in the American interest'.

Meanwhile, official development assistance (ODA) as a share of GNP continued to decline from 0.49 per cent in 1992 to 0.29 per cent in 2001, instead of rising to the 1970 Pearson Commission target of 0.7 per cent. The US contribution had dropped to 0.09 per cent in 2001 before US President George W. Bush promised at Monterrey in March 2002 to raise its contribution by half over five years, that is, to around 0.13 per cent[2] by 2007. Weisbrot (2004) and others suggest that the US government simply cannot afford the costs of empire, but such accounting overlooks the economic gains of empire, including its self-financing capacity, as evident in the deployment of petroleum revenues from post-Saddam Iraq.

Recent developments, especially after the invasion of Iraq, suggest that ODA, or aid and such disbursements are likely to be even more politicized and conditional than ever. It is well known that Israel has long been the largest recipient of US aid by far, with Egypt second since Camp David in the 1970s. After the defeat of the Taliban government, the 2003 US Budget failed to make any provisions for Afghanistan until a hasty amendment providing USD300 million was made on the floor of the US Congress to a country that had been at war since the late 1970s and was bombed extensively after 9/11.

The last quarter century, associated with globalization and liberalization, has been associated with much lower growth than the three decades after Second World War. The evidence points to increased economic volatility, growing international economic inequalities, reduced aid flows and other contradictory economic developments favouring transnational corporate (especially financial) ascendance. In this new era of unchallenged and seemingly un-challengeable US hyper-power, many existing multilateral institutions including the United Nations system, and even NATO are being reshaped.

---

[2] With Israel and Egypt at the top of the US recipients' list by far, one should not be surprised that it was left to Japan to pay the bills for the last Gulf War or for the rebuilding of Cambodia a decade ago, or to others to pay for rebuilding Afghanistan after the regime change in Kabul last year.

GLOBALIZATION, GROWTH, AND INEQUALITY

After the preceding review of hegemony and globalization in the modern period, we now turn to a brief historical review of the emerging evidence of changing global economic inequality. In his breath-taking survey of world economic history, Maddison (2001) suggests little significant inter-regional inequality a millennium ago. He suggests that Europe had re-gressed economically during the first Christian Era (CE) millennium, with GDP per capita higher in Asia excluding Japan ($450), Japan ($425) and even Africa ($416) than in Europe ($400) around 1000 CE. He suggests that growth paths began to diverge a millennium ago from a situation of almost world income equality; he estimates that the international ratio of the highest to the lowest GDP per capita by region rose from 1.1 in 1000 CE to 19.8 in 1998. Europe moved ahead of the rest around 1100 CE with the Renaissance in Italy, led by Venice, with development already quite widespread five centuries ago.

According to Maddison, inequality began to emerge after the beginning of the European Renaissance in the twelfth century, especially after West-ern Europe took off about five centuries ago. What is now Italy, led, during the first two-thirds of the sixteenth century, only to be overtaken by Holland (see Bagchi's chapter in the companion volume) around 1564. The UK overtook Holland around 1836 after growth accelerated there, more than half a century after the beginning of the Industrial Revolution around 1760. At the beginning of the twentieth century, around 1904, the US overtook the UK, and remains the world leader to the present. Maddison (2001: 126, Table 3–1b; also see Sharpe 2003: 24, Figure 2) shows disparities or 'divergence' accelerating from around 1820, arguably due to empire. Around 1870, the ratio of highest GDP per capita to lowest GDP per capita by region increased even faster, until around 1950 to be temporarily reversed during the post-World War II 'Golden Age'.

During the Golden Age of post-war capitalism, the disparities declined almost as sharply until around 1973, when they begin to rise again, even more dramatically than during the eight decades before 1950. The tempo-rary reversal during 1950–73 was largely due to per capita GDP growth in Asia (excluding Japan) outpacing such growth in the West. From a situation of near global equality a millennium ago (1.1:1 in 1000 CE), the inequality ratio reached 19: 1 in 1998! While China was ahead of Europe a millennium ago, average output per capita had fallen to less than half by 1820 and to a low of 7.3 per cent of the Western European level in 1973, before recovering to 17.4 per cent in 1998. Maddison also gives some hints of the economic welfare impact of imperialism, for instance, between 1850 and 1900, the per capita income of Indians fell by 50 per cent!

Drawing on Maddison's (1995) earlier work and their own estimates, Bourguignon and Morrisson (2001) show that the Gini coefficient of world income inequality increased by 30 per cent between 1820 and 1992. They argue that world income inequality has increased more or less continuously since the beginning of the nineteenth century until the Second World War, but suggest that inequality subsequently stabilized or increased more slowly. Although most of the early increase in this inequality was due to intra-country differences in the early nineteenth century, inequality was mainly due to inter-country and interregional differences by the end of the twentieth century (also see Milanovic 1999). It appears that more rapid international economic integration is correlated with these accelerated increases in the international and interregional aspects of overall world income inequality.

As is well known, much of the South experienced slower economic growth in the last two decades of the twentieth century compared to the previous two decades—except in significant parts of Asia which have demonstrated that 'catching up' is still feasible. Asia—excluding—Japan was the region with the lowest per capita GDP in the mid-twentieth century, but rapid growth in much of the region since the second half of the twentieth century has slightly reduced most measures of world inequality. Maddison (2001) shows that while 57 African countries were worse off in per capita GDP terms in 1998 compared to 1950, 40 per cent of private African wealth was held abroad and the average African was no better off than the average Western European nearly two centuries ago!

There is little disagreement that the world distribution of income has become considerably more unequal during the twentieth century, especially during the first half, and that current inequality is much greater than historical inequality in the nineteenth century (Williamson 1997, O'Rourke 2001), mainly due to growing inter-country disparities (for example see Lindert and Williamson 2001). All estimates suggest that income distribution amongst the world's population is more unequal than for any individual country, even the most unequal. The period since the mid-nineteenth century has seen generally increased international economic integration, though this has not been a smooth or continuous process. There is general agreement that inequality among countries became considerably greater between the Industrial Revolution and the Second World War, though the record since the end of the post-war boom or 'Golden Age' in the early 1970s is subject to greater debate.

Bourguignon and Morrisson (2001) show that average incomes have converged among European countries and European settler colonies in North America and Australia from the end of the nineteenth century through the first half of the twentieth century. They suggest that reduced inequality or slower increases in post-war inequality have been due to sustained rapid growth in East Asia and, more recently, India. This period was associated with the post-war Golden Age of the 1950s and 1960s. Also, decolonization in much of Asia and Africa, and higher growth in the South more generally continued up to the 1970s, although growth in the North slowed down tremendously in that decade.

But while inequality undoubtedly increased over the twentieth century as a whole, and declined after World War II, there has been a debate over the claims that it has continued to fall after 1980 (Sutcliffe 2003: Table 7), that is, the period associated with recent globalization. There is considerable and increasing evidence of growing global inequality (UNDP, *Human Development Report 1999*). However, there is no unambiguously strong evidence that inequality has sharply and consistently increased or declined in the last two decades of the twentieth century. Milanovic's (2002a) finding of a sharp increase in global inequality between 1988 and 1993 seems to contradict the findings of others for the 1980s and 1990s, but, of course, involves different data, methodologies and, most importantly, time periods. Meanwhile, Sutcliffe (2003) suggests that inequality has been growing at the extremes for both rich and poor, as intermediate income groups in the world's population move closer together (Melchior 2001). But actual trends here are moot as others suggest that the world's 'middle class' has remained relatively stable (Maddison 2001), shrunk (Milanovic 2000b) or grown (Sala-i-Martin 2002a, 2002b).

Maddison's later (2001) historical income estimates do not suggest the considerable decline in inequality since the 1980s indicated by his earlier estimates (Maddison 1995). It also seems likely that while internal inequality has grown rapidly in China and has probably also worsened in India, the rapid growth of these populous economies in recent decades has served to reduce world inequality, as most global inequality measures are mainly influenced by international disparities. The overall impression that inter-country inequality in the last two decades of the twentieth century either fell or levelled off (Firebaugh 1999) or 'was roughly stable' (Bourguignon and Morrison 2001) thus actually obscures the varied and contradictory trends underlying the data, measures and methodologies (Sutcliffe 2003).

Milanovic (2002a) has since suggested that the sharp increase in world inequality during 1988–93 was slightly reversed in the five years that followed, mainly due to sustained and rapid growth in China, East Asia, and India. Although there is little evidence of stability in world income distribution, there is no consensus on what happened. Milanovic (2002b) as well as Bourguignon and Morrisson (2001) emphasize that there is little evidence of income convergence on a world scale, while others (Quah 1996, Milanovic 2003) suggest a bipolar distribution (that is, convergence around 'twin peaks'), directly contradicting claims of convergence (that is Sala-i-Martin 2002a, 2002b).

Nonetheless, despite weak evidence for their case, advocates of globalization continue to claim that it has helped to promote economic growth throughout the world, and to bring about global convergence in terms of economic development and incomes. On the contrary, there has been a significant slowing of growth since the 1980s, a period normally associated with contemporary globalization. For example, Weisbrot, Naiman, and Kim (2000) show that economic growth has slowed dramatically in the last two decades (1980–2000) in most less developed countries except for China, East Asia, and India, as compared with the previous two decades (1960–80):

- During 1960–80, output per person averaged across countries grew by 83 per cent, while the same was 33 per cent during 1980–2000.
- Eighty-nine countries (that is, 77 per cent or more than three-quarters) saw their per capita growth rates fall by at least five percentage points between 1960–80 and 1980–2000. Only 14 countries (that is, 13 per cent) saw their per capita growth rate rise by as much between the two periods.
- In sub-Saharan Africa, soon after decolonization, average growth was 36 per cent during 1960–80, to contract by 15 per cent during 1980–98.
- In Latin America, GDP per capita grew by 75 per cent during 1960–80, but only by 6 per cent during 1980–98. Latin America's per capita GDP was 29.1 per cent of the US average in 1980, but fell to 21.8 per cent in 1990 and stayed at 21.2 per cent in 1998 (Moreno-Brid, Caldentey, Napoles 2004). With the reduction in Latin American per capita GDP growth during 1998–2003, pointed out by Jose Antonio Ocampo in Chapter 3 of this volume, the ratio is likely to have fallen further.
- Even in Southeast Asia, where high growth rates were achieved until the sharp contraction of 1998, growth was better in the earlier period with the slowdown during the early and mid-1980s, and the regional collapse in 1998.
- The only regional exceptions to this trend were East Asia and India, which grew faster from 1980 to 1998 than in the previous period. This

was mainly due to the quadrupling, over the last two decades, of the GDP of China, which has 83 per cent of the population of East Asia.

Some other recent work suggests significant increases in inequality with accelerating globalization, but the trends are not clear, and correlation does not mean causation. For example, the *Human Development Report 1999* (UNDP 1999) offered considerable evidence of growing global inequality in recent decades. Milanovic (1999) found that inequality in the distribution of individual incomes and spending more acute in 1993 as compared to 1988. Gini coefficient for incomes in 1993 was 66 adjusted for purchasing power parity (PPP), and almost 80 using current USD incomes. Milanovic found that income inequality rose during 1988–93 from the Gini for PPP-adjusted incomes in 1988 of 62.5. Depending on the measure used (Gini or Theil), inter-country inequality accounted for 75 to 88 per cent of total inequality. Inter- as well as intra-country inequality rose between 1988 and 1993, with the former rising much more when economic globalization was accelerating. Milanovic offers other dramatic evidence of global inequality:

- The bottom 5 per cent grew poorer while the richest quintile gained 12 per cent in real terms, that is, more than twice as much as mean world income (5.7 per cent)
- The richest one per cent people in the world received as much as the bottom 57 per cent, that is, less than 50 million received as much as the poorest 2.7 billion, that is more than 54 times as many people.
- An American with the average income of the poorest US decile is better off than two-thirds of the world's population.
- The top decile of the US population had the aggregate income of the poorest 43 per cent of the world's people, that is, the total income of 25 million Americans was equal to that of almost two billion people, or almost 40 times as many people.
- The ratio of the average income of the world's top 5 per cent to the bottom 5 per cent rose from 78 in 1988 to 114 in 1993.
- Seventy-five per cent of the world population received 25 per cent of the world's PPP-adjusted income, and vice versa.
- Eighty-four per cent of the world population received 16 per cent of the world's unadjusted USD income, and vice versa.

The last two decades have also seen changing government roles, with more regressive impacts, with tax systems becoming less progressive, or even more regressive. In many countries, income tax rates have become less progressive, causing direct taxes to become less progressive, if not regressive, in impact. Meanwhile, the share of direct taxes has declined compared to the generally more regressive indirect taxes. This has been accompanied by various efforts to reduce overall tax rates, in line with supply-side economic philosophy, which became especially influential during the 1980s under President Reagan, despite being dismissed as 'voodoo economics' by his 1980 Republican Party primaries' presidential rival, George Bush.

Lower tax revenues and increasing insistence on balanced budgets or fiscal surpluses have constrained government spending, especially what is deemed social expenditure, with some deflationary consequences. Privatization in many countries has temporarily increased government revenues, enabling governments to temporarily balance budgets or have surpluses on the basis of one-off sales incomes. Such budgetary balances are clearly unsustainable, but privatization has succeeded in temporarily obscuring the imminent fiscal crises such policies may lead to.

No region has accelerated growth by adopting policies imposed as conditionalities on borrowing countries. Understandably, globalization proponents are reluctant to claim credit for China, which maintains a non-convertible currency, state control over its banking system, and other major violations of IMF/Bank prescriptions, or even for India, which remains far less open than most other developing or transitional economies after two decades of pro-business—rather than liberal market—reforms. If globalization and other policies promoted by the IMF and the World Bank have not led to increased growth, it becomes extremely difficult to defend these policies. The 'costs' of these changes—the destruction of industries, unemployment, the harsh 'austerity' medicine often demanded by these institutions and by international financial markets have become burdens to society without any clear compensating benefits.

Stiglitz (2002) as well as Weisbrot, Naiman, and Kim (2000) also note that the IMF has made policy prescriptions in recent years that have undoubtedly reduced cumulative economic growth and the economic welfare of hundreds of millions of people. IMF policies in the economies of the former Soviet Union contributed to one of the worst economic disasters in the history of the world in the 1990s, with Russia losing more than half its national income. In Russia and Brazil in 1998, Fund-supported policies ultimately collapsed, causing serious economic damage.

According to William Easterly (2000), then a senior World Bank researcher, the poor did not gain as much from economic growth in countries to which the IMF lent money as they did in places with no programmes. 'The poor in developing countries are often better off when their governments ignore the policy advice of the International Monetary

Fund and World Bank.' IMF and World Bank policy-makers claim that their reforms often require necessary short-term pain for the sake of long-term gain, though there is little evidence to that effect either. Meanwhile, China, India, and other countries that have not scrupulously pursued IMF and World Bank economic programmes have seen more of their people lifted out of poverty by economic growth than nations taking advice from the Washington-based Bretton Woods international financial institutions.

To be sure, justifications for international inequality and dominance have been around for a long time, especially since the successful 'counter-revolution' against development economics during the 1980s with the ascendance of Margaret Thatcher and Ronald Reagan in the Anglophone West (Toye 1986). The revival of such imperial discourse has become more pronounced in recent years, with blatant discussion of the reconstitution of empire, for example with the revival of interest in 'social darwinism', 'failed states', 'vampire states', 'rogue states', etc. As is now well known, the initially triumphalist 'end of history' a la Fukuyama soon gave way to the Bernard Lewis–Samuel Huntington warnings about a 'clash of civilizations' between the Judaeo-Christian North Atlantic West (a recent invention after the Second World War) and the rest. The rest, of course, principally referred to the then economically ascendant and ostensibly Confucian East Asia, led by Japan and now China, and more recently, mainly Islam, previously embraced by this same West during the Cold War against the 'godless', 'evil [Soviet] empire'.

But rather than dwell in the realm of the political and cultural (Said 1993), this project has focused on the economic, to consider how economic globalization—earlier and more recent—has changed international economic relations in ways which either undermine or strengthen international dominance and exploitation. And while there is no automatic and simple relationship between the economic and the political, especially when 'security' considerations in the 'war against terrorism' seemed to have overwhelmed economic ones, there is good reason to believe that economic imperialism is alive and well, albeit considerably transformed.

The end of colonialism, the post-war Golden Age, significant changes in international economic specialization, serious efforts at multilateral institution building, initiatives to reduce international inequalities and promote economic development as well as the multifarious developments associated with globalization more generally have all transformed international economic and political relations. While the detailed record of what is simplistically aggregated together as globalization is actually quite complex, if not contradictory, much of what is referred to as economic globalization and liberalization at the international level has served to deepen, rather than reduce, international inequalities, though not necessarily in straightforwardly obvious ways.

THIS VOLUME: GLOBALIZATION, UNEVEN DEVELOPMENT, AND REGIONS

This is one of the two companion volumes that have come out of the Sephis-sponsored research project on 'The Long Twentieth Century', referring to the era of what some others have termed the 'new imperialism'. The term 'The Long Twentieth Century' has been most famously used by Arrighi (1994), in the course of a long treatise discussing four stages in the evolution of the 'world system' over the course of the last six or seven centuries. The 'long century' then refers to each of these stages, with the latest stage dating back to the last third of the nineteenth century, coinciding with the new imperialism of Hobson and Lenin.

The project on 'The Long Twentieth Century' was originally conceived in response to recent developments. A few days before 11 September 2001 the United Nations Commissioner for Human Rights, former Irish President Mary Robinson hosted the UN Conference against Racism and Other Forms of Discrimination in Durban, South Africa. She was later to lose her position, apparently after pressure from the US government. At the conference, a strong African–American contingent raised the question of reparations for slavery, which in turn encouraged others who argued for reparations for colonialism. Needless to say, such claims have underscored the need for more careful, comprehensive and rigorous attempts to account for colonial experiences. Instead, Ferguson's (2002, 2004) influential recent apologia for the British empire and plea for an American empire remind us that the modern imperial project remains not only alive and well, but actually re-ascendant in the early twenty-first century.

The contributions to this project are presented in two related, but distinct self-contained volumes. This volume is primarily concerned with the uneven consequences of integration into the global economy in the context of what has been termed modern or capitalist imperialism. This involved colonialism in Africa and much of Asia, but not in much of Latin America after the national independence movements of the nineteenth century. The next chapter suggests the need to reconsider the analysis of imperialism, while the chapters that follow review the uneven transformations of various regions—Latin America, Africa, the Middle East, India, and Southeast Asia. The variety of experiences despite some similarity in the global processes at work underscores the variegated nature of local transformations over time and helps explain their uneven consequences and outcomes. The final chapter examines the contemporary relevance of Lenin's theory of imperialism.

In Chapter 2 of this volume 'The Concept Of The Mode Of Production And The Theory Of Imperialism', Prabhat Patnaik poses a problem raised at the interface of two related, but apparently contradictory theories in the Marxist tradition—mode of production and imperialism, more usually associated with V.I. Lenin. Etienne Balibar (1970) sought to resolve the problem of the transition from one mode of production to another by introducing the notion of a 'transitional mode of production', which begs the question of transitions to and from the transitional mode (Jomo 1986). Instead, Samir Amin (1976) suggested that the mode of production is an abstract analytical concept—comparable to the structural functionalist notion of an 'ideal type'—unlike the related, but different abstraction of actual social relations known as the 'social formation'. Thus, actual societies, and therefore social formations, usually consist of elements from different modes of production 'articulated' in ways which define the specific nature of a social formation, including its dominant mode of production. For Amin and Patnaik then, imperialism implies the subordination of pre-capitalist modes of production by the capitalist mode. In light of the historical contribution of imperialism to the development of capitalism, Patnaik suggests that simply regarding this contribution as 'primitive [capital] accumulation' evades the serious analytical challenge posed by 'non-capitalist' capital accumulation for an adequate understanding of the dynamics of capitalism.

The Patnaik chapter raises fundamental issues in the analysis of hegemonic international economic integration between North and South, and the transformation of both in the context of the new unequal relations between the two. It also hints at how the relations and the respective transformations would have been profoundly influenced by their respective economic interests and socio-economic relations as well as their nature and circumstances of their connections. The remaining chapters of this volume survey the transformation of several major regions of the South during the long twentieth century. These chapters highlight not only the uneven development in the South, but also the unequal relations between North and South which characterized this period, often associated with Hobson's 'new imperialism'.

In 'Latin America And The World Economy In The Long Twentieth Century', José Antonio Ocampo offers a detailed and nuanced survey of the economic history of his continent. He identifies broad trends of economic development in Latin America and relates them to the world economy, especially the rest of the Atlantic rim, from the late nineteenth century. His survey is divided into three broad phases, which are then further dissected to reflect further variation by sub-region, economic organization, and output as well as external impacts. The era from the 1870s to the 1920s is characterized by Ocampo as the 'export age'. The following period from the 1930s to the 1970s is seen as dominated by 'state-led industrialization', while the subsequent period is portrayed as that of the 'neo-liberal order'. The poor growth record since the 1980s contrasts greatly with the economic gains during this earlier period, now reluctantly acknowledged as a 'golden age' by advocates of neo-liberal economic reforms. Ocampo's rich and nuanced historical analysis suggests that recent neo-liberal reforms have exacerbated Latin America's highly unequal distribution of income and wealth, arguably due to the continent's earlier integration into the world economy and the nature of that integration.

The consequences of sub-Saharan Africa's integration into the world economy under foreign domination are surveyed in the next two chapters. In 'Africa: The Long Twentieth Century', Bill Freund considers modern African history from the Berlin Congress of 1884, through the period of European colonial occupation, but also including the latest 'post-colonial' phase. He considers significant events and trends before the onset of colonial rule in Africa in the 1880s, including the gradual decline of the slave trade, which had dominated African commerce with other continents around the Atlantic. During the subsequent period of 'legitimate trade', European commercial exploration also sought to exploit the economic potential of hitherto unknown parts of Africa. Pursuing this potential, especially in southern, central, and eastern Africa, often required colonial rule to begin, protect, and extend such interests much more than required by trade promotion and facilitation. Freund also mentions 'African precursors of colonialism', arguing that if European colonial rule had not advanced so quickly at the end of the nineteenth century, much of Africa would have been partitioned by such emerging powers.

In a companion chapter on 'Imperialism In Africa', Lance van Sittert argues that its nature and consequences have been the product of the interaction between imperial and indigenous agents. He periodizes the long twentieth century, distinguishing the earlier period of 'Pacification' (1884–1914) from the subsequent 'Grand Colonialism' (1918–39). He dates the end of 'End of Empire' from the Second World War (1939–60), before distinguishing the honeymoon after Independence (1965–80) from the subsequent neo-liberal period. During the first half of the twentieth century, African resources and populations were annexed as captive raw material suppliers and markets for European industrial economies, resulting in classic one-crop or mineral 'open economies'. The second half of the twentieth century saw waves of indigenous populisms, nationalisms, and socialisms attempt, but fail, to break these historical bonds, typically by pursuing state-led import substitution industrialization, as elsewhere in the South, but for shorter periods and generally less success. The Western recession from the mid-1970s soon saw demand for African raw materials as well as state legitimacy collapse. In the post-Cold War period since then, most African governments have slowly, but surely, embraced the neoliberal orthodoxy of the Washington Consensus.

In 'The Middle East In The Long Twentieth Century', Faruk Tabak suggests a widening income gap between the Middle East and the North due to three processes. First, rapid changes in the region during the two periods of Western hegemony contrast with slow transformations associated with epochs of imperial rivalry. Second, the transition from the British to the American order, from formal to informal empire, over the twentieth century has deepened existing trends. The region's import-substitution industrialization has had mixed success, with growth highest during the post-war 'golden age'. Third, 'structural reasons', including the nature of the rural economy, explain the region's less than satisfactory economic performance.

In 'Southeast Asia: Imperial Possession and Dispossession in the Long Twentieth Century', Maria Serena Diokno tries to capture the very diverse nature of the region, deepened by its variegated colonial and post-colonial experiences from the late nineteenth century. Southeast Asia has often been defined negatively as a region for not being part of either 'Indian' South Asia or Sinic East Asia. Almost every major colonial power had a presence in the region including Portugal (Melaka, East Timor), Spain (Philippines), Holland (Indonesia), Britain (Malaysia, Burma, Brunei), France (Vietnam, Kampuchea, Laos) and the USA (Philippines), with only Siam (later Thailand) retaining at least nominal independence throughout. The different and changing interests and nature of these many imperialisms and the changing conditions in various parts of the region have resulted in distinct, if sometimes linked trajectories.

In 'India In The Long Twentieth Century', Sumit Sarkar notes that the transport and communications revolution from the mid-nineteenth century pulled together various levels of British Indian administration into a thinly disguised autocratic system. Thus, the late nineteenth century saw the unprecedented integration of the sub-continent and the centralization of imperial authority. A new colonial 'modernity' emerged with new 'inventions of tradition' as the British consolidated alliances with indigenous elites. India provided foodstuff and other raw materials, military manpower as well as a captive market for British manufactured exports which faced increasing competition and protection elsewhere. But export of capital to India was less significant compared to the US and other settler colonies, while India's consistent export surplus coexisted with massive, possibly growing, poverty. Highly exploitative methods, including indentured labour, were widely used to work plantations within India as well as elsewhere in the empire. Thus, while colonialism brought significant gains for some Indians, it enhanced suffering for many more.

In his concluding chapter 'Lenin's Theory of Imperialism Today', Prabhat Patnaik stresses the political significance of Lenin's original contribution before suggesting an economic programme drawing on a contemporary analysis of imperialism. He argues that Lenin's analysis was central to his break with European social–democratic 'revisionism' by broadening revolutionary struggles to involve nations oppressed by imperialism. This meant supporting the 'bourgeois–democratic liberation' movements and peasant movements in such countries. Patnaik notes that Lenin's imperialism is much misunderstood, most typically in terms of under-consumption, or over-production, but also as under-investment.

Karl Kautsky had proposed the notion of 'ultra-imperialism', where 'internationally united finance capital' engaged in the joint and relatively peaceful exploitation of the rest of the world. Instead, Lenin suggested that the peace was temporary, with agreement among imperialist powers dictated by the 'super-imperialist' power. For him, this did not mean the disappearance of nation-states as 'super-imperialism' would be exercised through the system of nation-states, rather than by a 'surrogate world state'.

While acknowledging that post-Second World War developments had changed capitalism—with de-colonization, Keynesian demand management and welfare measures—Patnaik insists that subsequent developments suggest that the Golden Age was clearly exceptional. While the globalization of capital in the present period is hardly new, he argues that contemporary capital flows are quite unconnected to the current account of the balance of payments. Although foreign direct investment usually involves concomitant commodity movements, short-term financial flows do not involve concomitant commodity movements. Hence, the contemporary fluidity of capital involves capital-as-finance, not capital-in-production—quite different from Hilferding's and Lenin's times.

Patnaik argues that the far-reaching consequences of the contemporary centralization-cum-globalization of finance capital have seen the living standards of most workers and peasants in the Third World drastically squeezed, the economic and political sovereignty of such countries circumscribed, their economic assets, especially in the public sector, transferred to private, often foreign hands, popular political power reduced, attenuating democracy, while identity conflicts have been promoted among the people, weakening their capacity to challenge the new imperium. In response, he prioritizes the tasks of strengthening independent nation-states on alternative class bases, developing alternative economic programmes to check and even reverse globalization, and pressuring states to pursue broad-based egalitarian development while protecting popular democratic rights.

REFERENCES

Amin, Samir, (1976), *Unequal Development: An Essay on the Social Formations of Peripheral Capitalism, translated by Brian Pearce*, Monthly Review Press, New York.

Arrighi, Giovanni, (1994), *The Long Twentieth Century: Power and the Origins of Our Times*, Verso, London.

Bagchi, Amiya, (2006), 'The Developmental State Under Imperialism', in Jomo K.S. (ed.), *The Long Twentieth Century: Globalization Under Hegemony: The Changing World Economy*, Oxford University Press, New Delhi, 227–77.

Balibar, Etienne, (1970), 'From Periodization to the Modes of Production', in Louis Althusser and Etienne Balibar (eds), *Reading Capital*, Pt 2, New Left Books, London, 209–24.

Barber, Benjamin R., (2003), *Fear's Empire: War, Terrorism, and Democracy*, Norton, New York.

Bourguignon, François, and Christian Morrisson, (2002), 'Inequality among world citizens: 1820–1992'. *The American Economic Review*, 92 (4), September, 727–44.

Dapice, David, (2003), 'Does the "Hyper-Power" Have Feet of Clay?', *Yale Global*, 3 March.

Easterly, William, (2000), 'The Lost Decades: Developing Countries Stagnation Inspite of Policy Reform, 1980–1998', processed, December, Development Research Group, World Bank, Washington DC.

Ferguson, Niall, (2002), *Empire: How Britain Made the Modern World*, Penguin, London. Published in the US as (2003) *Empire: The Rise and Demise of the British World Order and the Lessons for Global Power*, Basic Books, New York (2003).

—— (2004), *Colossus: The Rise and Fall of the American Empire*, Penguin Press, London. Published in the US as *Colossus: The Price of America's Empire*, Penguin Press, New York.

Firebaugh, Glenn, (1999), 'Empirics of World Income Inequality', *American Journal of Sociology*, 104 (May), 1597–1630.

Go, Julian, (2004), 'Waves of American Empire, 1787–2003: US Hegemony and Imperialist Activity from the Shores of Tripoli to Iraq'. Processed, Sociology Department, Boston University, Boston.

Hardt, Michael, and Antonio Negri, (2000), *Empire*. Harvard University Press, Cambridge, MA.

Ikenberry, G. John, (2004), 'Illusions of Empire: Defining the New American Order', *Foreign Affairs* 83 (2), March/April, 144–54.

—— (2001), 'American Power and the Empire of Capitalist Democracy', *Review of International Studies*, 27, 191–212.

Johnson, Chalmers, (2004), *The Sorrows of Empire: Militarism, Secrecy, and the End of the Republic*, Metropolitan Books, New York.

Jomo K.S., (1986), *A Question Of Class: Capital, the State, and Uneven Development in Malaya*, Oxford University Press, Singapore.

Lindert, Peter, and Jeffrey G. Williamson, (2001), 'Does Globalization Make The World More Unequal?'. NBER Working Paper 8228, National Bureau of Economic Research, Cambridge, MA.

Louis, William Roger, and Ronald Robinson, (1994), 'The Imperialism of Decolonization', *Journal of Imperial and Commonwealth History*, 22 (3): 462–511.

Maddison, Angus, (1995), *Monitoring the World Economy, 1820–1992*, Organisation for Economic Cooperation and Development (OECD), Paris.

—— (2001), *The World Economy: A Millennial Perspective*, Organisation for Economic Cooperation and Development (OECD), Paris.

Mann, Michael, (2003), *Incoherent Empire*, Verso, London.

Melchior, Arne, (2001), 'Global Income Inequality: Beliefs, Facts and Unresolved Issues', *World Economics*, 2 (3), July-September.

Milanovic, Branko (1999), 'True World Income Distribution, 1988 and 1993: First Calculation Based on Household Surveys Alone', Policy Research Working Paper 2244, Poverty and Human Resources, Development Economics Research Group, World Bank, Washington, DC.

—— (2002a), 'True World Income Distribution, 1988 and 1993: First Calculation Based on Household Surveys Alone', *Economic Journal*, 112 (476), January: 51–92.

—— (2002b), 'Worlds Apart: Inter-National and World Inequality, 1950–2000', processed, Research Department, World Bank, Washington, DC.

—— (2003), 'Income Convergence during the Disintegration of the World Economy, 1919–39', processed, World Bank, Washington DC.

Moreno-Brid, J. C., E. P. Caldentey, and P. R. Napoles, (2004), 'The Washington

Consensus: A Latin American Perspective Fifteen Years After', *Journal of Post-Keynesian Economics*, Vol. 27, No. 2 Winter 2004-5, 345-65.

O'Rourke, Kevin, (2001), 'Globalization and Inequality: Historical Trends', NBER Working Paper Series No. 8339, National Bureau of Economic Research, Cambridge, MA. (*http://www.nber.org/papers/w8339*)

Quah, Danny, (1996), 'Twin Peaks: Growth and Convergence in Models of Distribution Dynamics', *Economic Journal*, 106 (437), July, 1045-55.

Said, Edward (1979), *Orientalism*, Vintage Books, New York.

—— (1993), *Culture and Imperialism*, Alfred P. Knopf, New York.

Sala-i-Martin, Xavier, (2002a), 'The Disturbing 'Rise' of Global Income Inequality', NBER Working Paper 8904, National Bureau of Economic Research, Cambridge, MA. (*http://www.nber.org/papers/w8904*)

—— (2002b), 'The World Distribution of Income (estimated from individual country distributions)', NBER Working Paper 8933, National Bureau of Economic Research, Cambridge, MA. (*http://www.nber.org/papers/ w8933*)

Sharpe, Andrew, (2003), 'Angus Maddison Rewrites Economic History Again'. *Challenge*, 45 (4), July/August, 20-40.

Spiro, P. J., (2000), 'The New Sovereigntists: American Exceptionalism and Its False Prophets', *Foreign Affairs*, November/December.

Stiglitz, J. E., (2002), *Globalization and its Discontents*, Norton, New York.

Sutcliffe, Bob, (2003), 'A more or less equal world? World income distribution in the twentieth century', PERI Working Paper No. 54, Political Economy Research Institute, University of Massachusetts, Amherst. Also *Indicators, a journal of social health*, 2 (3), Summer.

Todd, Emmanuel, (2003), *After the Empire: The Breakdown of the American Order*, Columbia University Press, New York.

Toye, John, (1986), *Dilemmas of Development*. Blackwell, Oxford.

UNDP, (1999), *Human Development Report 1999*, Oxford University Press, New York.

Weisbrot, Mark, (2004), 'The Unbearable Costs of Empire', processed, Center for Economic Policy Research, Washington, DC.

Weisbrot, Mark, Robert Naiman, and Joyce Kim, (2000), 'The Emperor Has No Growth: Declining Economic Growth Rates in the Era of Globalization', processed, Center for Economic and Policy Research, Washington, DC.

Williams, William Appleman (ed.), (1973), *The Contours of American History*, New Viewpoints, New York.

Williamson, Jeffrey G., (1997), 'Globalization and Inequality: Past and Present', *World Bank Research Observer*, 12 (2), August, 117-35.

2

The Concept of Mode of Production and Theory of Imperialism

Prabhat Patnaik

There is an impression that what *The Communist Manifesto* called 'comprehending theoretically the historical movement as a whole' refers to a once-for-all act; once it has been achieved, it provides an understanding of every moment of history thenceforth, and creates an indissoluble unity of theory and praxis which from then on can consciously take mankind forward. This impression, however, is wrong. It reduces Marxism to the status of a 'revelation', a closed, complete system that sprang up one day like Minerva from the head of Zeus. Marxist theory by contrast is a phenomenon that is in a continuous process of reconstitution.[1] Even this process of reconstitution does not make the theory supposedly complete at every moment. Significant elements of incompleteness remain, and may do so for long stretches of time. It is only occasionally that the theory acquires that degree of completeness where, to use Lukacs' words, it 'bursts into praxis'. And with the passage of time, even that element of relative completeness slips away, necessitating yet newer efforts to reconstitute theory.

Non-incriminating thanks are due to C. P. Chandrashekhar, K. S. Jomo, Jayati Ghosh, Utsa Patnaik, and Rajendra Prasad for comments on an earlier draft of this chapter.
[1] This point is discussed in greater detail in Patnaik (1999).

These efforts, to be sure, do not start from scratch. The continuous attempt to reconstitute Marxist theory, without which it would have been dead long ago, occurs within a conceptual framework provided by Marxism itself. There is, in other words, a core of Marxist theory on the basis of which it is being continuously reconstituted. To say this is not to introduce a duality into Marxism, between a 'core' and a 'non-core'. The 'core' itself does not have a fixed boundary; nonetheless it exists.

This continuous attempt at reconstitution of Marxist theory is necessitated by a number of factors. First, the unfolding of the historical process itself takes novel directions that are not anticipated by the development of theory until then; second, even when the historical process unfolds in a manner that is in broad conformity with theory, the task of explicating this unfolding remains to be done; and third, the theoretical comprehension provided by existing Marxist analysis is never complete even with regard to the past, let alone the present and the future. This is precisely because of the non-duality referred to above. The specific concepts used by Marx, and their specific manner of use, are not separable from his own attempt to constitute a theory appropriate for praxis in his time. A reconstitution of Marxist theory must also encompass therefore a reexamination of certain concepts and conceptual universes. This *per se* is not being unfaithful to the Marxist tradition; on the contrary, it is essential for carrying the tradition forward. It is within this perspective that the present essay is devoted to an examination of the concept of the mode of production, as traditionally understood, from the point of view of the need to develop a theory of imperialism.

CAPITALISM AND IMPERIALISM

There is a paradox at the centre of Marxist theory. Nobody wrote as perceptively on the working of colonialism as Karl Marx did, not just on its overall historical implications, but on the mechanics of its economic functioning. Indeed, many have noted a remarkable resemblance between Marx's writings on the economics of colonialism in India and those of Dadabhai Naoroji, the 'Grand Old Man' of Indian nationalism who provided the basic theoretical foundation for India's anti-colonial struggle through his celebrated 'Drain Theory' on the appropriation of surplus from India by Britain.[2] And yet in the entire corpus of Marx's *theoretical*

---

[2] The parallel between Marx's and Naoroji's writings is drawn in Ganguli (1965). Naoroji's book, originally published in 1901, was republished in 1962. For a discussion of Indian nationalist writings on the economics of colonialism, see Bipan Chandra (1966).

writings on the 'Law of Motion of Modern Society' there is no role for colonialism.

This is not just an omission that can be explained in terms of the usual 'had-Marx-lived-he-would-have-taken-care-of-it' kind of argument; its roots lie deeper. Indeed it is instructive that in the entire Marxist tradition, with the notable exception of the Rosa Luxemburg stream (on which more later), there is no theory of colonialism, or more generally, a theory of imperialism that actually locates the phenomenon of imperialism (in the inclusive sense of covering both the quintessentially colonial and the subsequent periods) in the Law of Motion of the Capitalist Mode of Production. In Marx himself colonialism figures only in the discussion of the 'primitive accumulation of capital', but once capitalism has gone beyond this stage colonialism is assigned no further role.[3] The classic writings of Lenin, and Bukharin, even though they keep imperialism as their central focus, are concerned solely with the monopoly phase of capitalism and hence make no attempt to provide a theory of imperialism in the inclusive sense just referred to.

The question of course may be asked: why should imperialism, in this inclusive sense, at all be incorporated into the law of motion of capitalism? What is wrong with the position where Marxist theory currently stands and has always stood, namely that, *theoretically*, the role of colonialism was to aid the primitive accumulation of capital, and that imperialism was the natural outgrowth of the monopoly phase of capitalism?[4] The problem with this position, however, is that it makes the entire phenomenon of colonialism, once the capitalist mode of production has come into being, a mere happenstance, something that just happened to happen.

This is extremely unsatisfactory, since it puts an overwhelming real-life historical phenomenon outside the bounds of theoretical explanation. Colonialism happened to be there and benefited capitalism, but was in no way theoretically essential for its *modus operandi*; capitalism could well

---

[3] True, there are a number of concrete remarks made about colonialism throughout *Capital*; moreover, a certain role is assigned to colonial trade in the discussion of the 'counteracting tendencies' to the 'tendency of the rate of profit to fall'. Later Marxist writers have taken a cue from this, and developed theories of imperialism where imperialism is seen as bringing about one or the other 'counteracting tendency'. But since the 'falling tendency of the rate of profit' itself requires rather strong assumptions for its validity (see Patnaik 1997), and has a rather ambiguous status within the corpus of Marx's theory (Lenin scarcely made any use of it other than referring to it in his *Encyclopaedia* article on Marx), the theories of imperialism built on it can scarcely be seen to be incorporating imperialism into the 'Law of Motion' of the capitalist mode of production.

[4] For a discussion of Lenin's theory of imperialism, see Patnaik (1986 and 2000). A brief post-Lenin restatement of the link between monopoly and imperialism is Lange (1964).

have continued even without it. Since history is unique and leaves no scope for experimentation, one cannot rule out such a counterfactual on purely logical grounds; for the same reason however the claim that capitalism could not have continued without colonialism cannot be logically ruled out. While neither of the counterfactuals can be logically ruled out, we have to look at the question of plausibility (Patnaik 1997).

The fact remains that capitalism, from its very inception, has always had colonial possessions; the argument that it has fought for and retained colonial possessions over centuries, even though it could well have done without them, carries little conviction. A phenomenon as large as imperialism cannot be brushed aside as mere happenstance. Locating the phenomenon of imperialism within the Law of Motion of capitalism therefore remains a Marxist task.

Rosa Luxemburg (1963) stands out as the only one among the outstanding Marxist writers to provide a theory of imperialism, which covers both colonialism and 'imperialism' (in Lenin's sense) and which locates imperialism in this inclusive sense in the law of motion of capitalism itself. In doing so however, she gets embroiled, as we shall see, in a conceptual problem that makes her argument logically problematic in a way that the arguments of other classical Marxist writers are not. Her breaking fresh ground, even while remaining within the Marxist conceptual framework, creates logical problems; and this, I argue below, is because the classical Marxist conceptual framework as traditionally interpreted is incapable of accommodating a theory of imperialism as a part of the law of motion of capitalism. What I have called above a Marxist task cannot be accomplished within the Marxist conceptual framework as traditionally perceived.

CAPITALIZATION OF SURPLUS VALUE

When I talk of the conceptual problem with Luxemburg's argument, I am not referring to the usual quota of so-called logical problems that are invariably attributed to her theory ever since it made its appearance. After the labours of Kalecki (1971) and Joan Robinson (1963), and the widespread perception in the aftermath of the Keynesian Revolution that 'endogenous stimuli' alone might not explain sustained growth under capitalism, no one can possibly share Bukharin's (1972) view that 'Comrade Luxemburg's theory' is 'a simple reproduction of a simple logical error'.[5]

There are of course serious logical flaws in her argument of which I shall cite only three examples. First, she does not consider exogenous

---

[5] For a more elaborate discussion of this point, see Patnaik (1997).

stimuli other than pre-capitalist markets, such as innovations, which can also account for sustained growth under capitalism. Whether or not one agrees with this line of reasoning which attributes a significant stimulating role to innovations, and I personally do not (Patnaik 1972), it must be confronted by any one who argues that a sustained trend is not possible in a closed capitalist economy. Second, she argues as if, for the capitalization of surplus value, it is essential that its *entire* amount has to be sold to the pre-capitalist segment. The possibility that some sale to the pre-capitalist segment can generate domestic second-order effects, that would then enable the local capitalization of the remainder of the surplus value, is not reckoned by her. Third, she almost takes it for granted that the capitalization of the surplus value generated in the capitalist sector through sale to the pre-capitalist sector would mean an absorption or assimilation of the latter by the former, resulting in the eventual universal domination of capitalism, an acme that is followed by a collapse. The fact that capitalism may continue to grow through its interaction with the pre-capitalist sector, while the latter lingers on—as a pauperised and degraded permanent entity—is also not considered by her (though there are some stray references to such a possibility).

These flaws however neither invalidate her central theoretical argument that endogenous stimuli are insufficient to explain sustained dynamics under capitalism, and that incursions into pre-capitalist markets provide a basis for accumulation; nor do they constitute the conceptual problem referred to above. The latter consists in the fact that if capitalism exploits its domestic workers to extract a surplus value and then realizes this by selling to pre-capitalist markets and dispossessing the producers there, then there are *two different types of exploitation occurring simultaneously.* The theoretical relationship between these two different types of exploitation is not clear, and their simultaneous occurrence goes against the basic Marxist proposition that capitalism is fundamentally a system of exploitation of workers in the sphere of production.[6] In other words, one cannot retain every other aspect of the classical Marxist analysis of capitalism, and simply 'add on' a proposition about capitalization of surplus value requiring exchange with the pre-capitalist sector; the acceptance of this latter proposition must necessarily be accompanied, for logical consistency, with a reconstruction of the overall analysis of capitalism that Luxemburg did not do.

The issue has to do with the very concept of the mode of production. Let us look at it a little more closely.

6 This issue was raised, for the first time to my knowledge, by Irfan Habib (1995).

SELF-CONTAINED CAPITALISM?

Almost at the beginning of *The Communist Manifesto* we come across a set of binary opposites: 'freeman and slave, patrician and plebeian, lord and serf, guild-master and journeyman, in a word, oppressor and oppressed...'. The *Manifesto*, as is well-known, belongs to a phase of Marx's work when several of his key theoretical concepts had not yet been developed; nevertheless the concept of a mode of production characterized by the antagonism between the producers on the one hand and the appropriators of surplus on the other is a continuation of this perception of binary opposition. A mode of production is an integrated complex of social relations of production corresponding to a certain level of development of the social productive forces. The key to these relations of production lies in the property relations which in turn can be understood by looking at the mechanism of appropriation of surplus from the direct producers: property relations refer to the pattern of juridical claims on social product, their essence being the claim on surplus.

Embedded in this entire set of well-known arguments emphasizing the primacy of the sphere of production, however, is an implicit perception of a closed system, a system ideally seen as an isolated, self-contained entity, within which the drama of class-struggle is played out in accordance with its inner law of motion based on its own specific contradictions. The interaction of this essentially self-contained entity with the outside world can act at best as a catalyst, *through* its effect eventually on the basic contradiction and the central class-struggle between the class of direct producers and the class of appropriators of surplus; but it is not *per se* essential for understanding the inner law of motion of the mode of production.

In the famous Dobb–Sweezy debate (Hilton 1976) on the transition from feudalism to capitalism, Sweezy, who has often been accused of down-playing the primacy of the sphere of production, began by defining feudalism as a wholly self-contained entity, characterized by production-for-use, and saw the *dissolving* influence of trade as leading to its replacement by another entity, the petty mode of production dominated by merchant capital, which too, though not geographically, was analytically self-contained, and was a precursor to capitalism. Even Dobb who defined feudalism in terms of its class character gave, in accordance with a well-known remark of Marx, a secondary role to the dissolving influence of commerce. Neither of them gave any importance to the specific pattern of external commerce (for example, the modes of production across whom commerce was occurring). This is not surprising, since the concept of the mode of production, because it focuses on production and gives primacy to the sphere of production, is necessarily associated with the analytical exploration of a self-contained entity.

This of course is the strength of Marxism, its point of departure that makes it so powerful a tool of analysis. A theory that would attempt to look at everything at the same time in the name of comprehensiveness would end up being a mere description and no theory. A theory that would start at some other end, for example, from the sphere of exchange, would have at best a set of disjointed insights but would miss the historical process. A theory to be meaningful at all must have structured determinations; for it to have insights into the historical process, these structured determinations must give primacy to the sphere of production, which is what Marxism does. The problem, however, is that, when it comes to capitalism, this perception precludes any analytical role for imperialism.

CAPITALISM, NOT SELF-CONTAINED

This treatment of capitalism as a self-contained entity, which some have attributed to Marx's Ricardian lineage (Utsa Patnaik 1999), but which, in my view, is embedded in the traditional concept of the mode of production, constitutes an important weakness of Marxian theory. Let me cite an example both to illustrate this weakness and also to underscore my point that Marxian analysis *did* treat capitalism as a closed, self-contained system.

Nobody was more scathing in his criticism of the so-called Say's Law that denies the possibility of generalized over-production than Marx. The section on Ricardo's theory of accumulation (Ricardo, as is well-known, was a votary of Say's Law and did not accept the possibility of generalized over-production) in *The Theories of Surplus Value*, provides a lucid critique of Say's Law which in its essentials anticipates the subsequent Keynesian critique of it. And yet, having cleared the ground for an incorporation of aggregate demand into his analysis, Marx never did incorporate it.

This is not to suggest that he should have incorporated it in the manner in which Keynes did later. The point is not to ask: why didn't Marx write Keynes' *General Theory* before Keynes did? The Keynesian manner of incorporating aggregate demand, which was to say that a capitalist economy could settle at any level of economic activity, would have been both theoretically incompatible with the other part of Marx's theory, namely his theory of value, surplus value, and prices of production (in which the Ricardian lineage was most visible), and empirically inapt as a description of capitalism, which, certainly during Marx's time, and even later, barring episodes like the Great Depression, performed on the whole without too large a burden of unutilized capacity. Marx's theory of value and price is rooted in the conditions of production, as summed up for instance by certain material and labour input coefficients per unit of output. These coefficients would move around arbitrarily if output was determined by demand, that is, if demand bore no relationship to the benchmark level of capacity utilization with respect to which these coefficients were calculated. For example, if capacity utilization of fixed capital was half the benchmark level then *ipso facto* the fixed capital per unit of output would have doubled; hence the labour values, consisting of the amount of direct and indirect labour embodied per unit output would be affected not just by the conditions of production, but also by the conditions of demand, and therefore become meaningless.

My point therefore is not to critique Marx from a Keynesian perspective, but to see the internal unfolding of his own ideas. Both theoretically (from the perspective of his own value theory) and empirically Marx would have been persuaded that generalized over-production was not in general a serious problem. And he simply assumed so without giving any justification for the assumption. The mode of his assuming this was to say that the generalized over-production problem was only a cyclical one, and that the rest of his theory, including value theory, applied to the average state of the capitalist economy that is established through these cycles. But Marx nowhere gave a convincing explanation of why generalized over-production could not be a persistent phenomenon. The fact that empirically it had not been one did not warrant closing the issue theoretically. Doing so meant that the theory remained incomplete. And doing so was necessitated by the assumption of a closed self-contained system.

Marxist economists have traditionally fallen back on two propositions to explain why a crisis must be self-limiting, that is, why a state of generalized over-production must be necessarily and spontaneously transitory. One is the general proposition that under capitalism competition between capitals coerces each capitalist into accumulating. It is a Darwinian struggle where survival depends on the ability to introduce new technology that, in turn, requires at any time a minimum size of capital (this minimum increases over time); only those survive therefore which are of this minimum size, and to ensure survival each capital is forced to accumulate. Accumulation is an objective compulsion for the capitalist, not a mere voluntary decision. 'Accumulate! Accumulate! That's Moses and the Prophets', as Marx put it. The problem with this answer (which Bukharin had used against Luxemburg) however is that capitalists' desire to accumulate need not mean the undertaking of actual investment expenditure immediately. Accumulation may take the form of money capital, and indeed is likely to take this form in the midst of a crisis and shrinking aggregate demand, so that the pressure to accumulate need have no positive effect on aggregate demand.[7]

The second proposition states that the crisis has the effect of destroying some capital through scrapping; it thereby creates conditions anew for those who survive to undertake fresh investment that, in turn, stimulates a recovery. This argument assumes however that in a situation where some firms are going under, others would feel emboldened enough to enlarge investment expenditure. The consequence of scrapping on investment could as well be of the opposite kind, at least until the surviving firms feel that 'things have stabilized', in which case the crisis would go on and on, that is, things would never actually get stabilized.

The argument that crises are self-limiting, and that over-production is therefore necessarily transitory, a mere cyclical phenomenon, is thus a tenuous one. But this argument is theoretically absolutely essential if the perceived stability under capitalism is to be explained through an analysis of it as a closed system. The fact that Marx resorted to it only underscores my contention that Marx's analysis of capitalism was essentially that of a closed system.

Of course, generalized over-production is *not* a permanent phenomenon under capitalism. But the reason it is not has nothing to do with any spontaneous tendency of capitalism to overcome generalized over-production (to postulate which would amount to a *de facto* acceptance of Say's Law); it has to do with the availability of colonial, or more generally pre-capitalist, markets. In other words it is not that the problem of aggregate demand is a short-run problem that somehow spontaneously disappears in the long run; it is an ex-ante problem (which would manifest itself in a hypothetical closed capitalist economy and not necessarily as a mere temporary phenomenon) that does not reveal itself ex-post because of the availability of pre-capitalist markets. The short-run versus long-run distinction on the question of aggregate demand constitutes a mistaken identity for the ex-ante versus ex-post distinction. Marx's value theory discussion can be perfectly well reconciled with his categorical rejection of Say's Law if we bring in the fact of capitalism's access to pre-capitalist markets. But doing so would entail breaking out of the assumption that capitalism constitutes a closed system.

The fact that a person like Marx, so well-informed about colonialism, could still carry out his analysis of capitalism as if it was a closed system can be attributed to the theoretical compulsion enjoined by the concept of the mode of production, as suggested above.

[7] This issue is discussed at greater length in Patnaik (1997).

A consequence of this closed system analysis, other than the theoretical damage done to the cause of the oppressed in the colonial countries, is the unwarranted hostility towards Keynesianism among Marxist economists. The reference here is neither to the social philosophy and political outlook of Keynes which Marxists would naturally reject, nor to the precise conceptual building blocks of Keynesian economics, such as propensity to consume, which are methodologically unacceptable to Marxian economics, but to the Keynesian conclusion about the role of effective demand. Given Marx's trenchant critique of Say's Law, the Keynesian emphasis on effective demand should have been easily acceptable to the Marxian tradition; but it was not. The Keynesian Revolution, despite the fact that one of its co-authors was a Marxist economist Michael Kalecki, an engineer by training whose only introduction to economics was Marx's *Capital*, was for a long time rejected (or at best considered inconsequential) because of its focus on the 'sphere of circulation'. Much of Marxian economics operated as if Say's Law held, despite Marx's demolition of it.

This was hardly surprising: by arguing the possibility of generalized over-production, and yet relegating it to the status of a transitory phenomenon which capitalism spontaneously overcomes in the course of the cycle, Marx had effectively downgraded this possibility. He had demolished Say's Law, but Say's Law crept into his own analysis through the back door. The reason, as suggested above, was the dilemma he faced, namely to reconcile within the conceptual universe of a closed capitalist system the observed fact of its being reasonably stable with his own theoretical demonstration of the intrinsic possibility of its instability. He could have overcome this dilemma by jettisoning the conceptual universe of a closed capitalist system, as Rosa Luxemburg did;[8] but that would have gone against his concept of a mode of production where the focus was on the relationship between classes, especially the two binary opposites, that is anchored in the production process which is specific and internal to the system.

I am not arguing that this concept is faulty and should be abandoned; my point, which I discuss below, is that in the context of capitalism at any

---

[8] There is a hint in Volume II of *Capital* that Marx sees the precise problem that was later to occupy Rosa Luxemburg, but he resolves the matter by bringing in exports to the 'gold-producing sector' within capitalism. This however is patently unsatisfactory. Marx himself saw paper money under certain circumstances as being a substitute for gold (that is, a universe of commodity money, such as was assumed by him, did not have to have only the money commodity functioning physically as money); and if this money is issued by the government then in effect an export surplus to a destination outside of the mode of production proper, namely to the government, is being talked about. See Dobb (1973).

rate, the perception of the system as a whole cannot be co-terminus with this basic concept alone. The capitalist system is much more than the capitalist mode of production analysed by Marx.

CAPITALIST SYSTEM MORE THAN MODE OF PRODUCTION

Within Marx's analysis itself, even as it exists, there is at least one element of ambiguity. This relates to the concept of the 'reserve army of labour'. The capitalists exploit the workers in the process of production. By definition, the unemployed, belonging to the reserve army of labour, are not exploited (which prompted Joan Robinson's remark that for a worker the one thing worse than being exploited by capital was not being exploited). But surely, while the reserve army is not exploited in the same manner as the active army, it is exploited by the system nonetheless in a different way. What is more, the reserve army does not consist simply of the openly unemployed. It consists of different elements some of which are even employed, but 'outside the system'.[9] In other words, even Marx, while analysing the closed capitalist system, recognizes the existence of a universe outside the system but obviously linked to it, in the sense that the workers employed outside constitute a reserve army that can always be drawn into the active army inside.

Moreover, Marx's notion of the reserve army, as it stands, is somewhat restricted in scope, in the sense that capitalism actually requires a far larger reserve army for its functioning than even Marx recognized. To see this we have to make a brief excursus into Marx's theory of money, since his theory of the reserve army and his theory of money are closely linked.

Marx's analysis of money refers to a commodity money world where money is a produced commodity like any other, and its relative value vis a vis the world of commodities is determined by their respective conditions of production (which incidentally is different from Ricardo's theory of commodity money where the relative exchange ratio between money and the world of commodities changes with the change in the wage rate as well). For any given conditions of production, a rise in money wages, it follows, results *ipso facto* in a rise in real wages (a conclusion common between Ricardo and Marx, notwithstanding their other differences). We can therefore use the terms money and real wages almost interchangeably, and the reserve army's role *inter alia* is to keep down the rate of growth of the wage rate relative to productivity, so that (a) the rate of profit is always positive, and (b) any tendency for the rate of profit to decline in the

---

[9] This is true of what Marx calls the 'latent' form of relative surplus population.

accumulation process is spontaneously arrested through an appropriate expansion in the reserve army caused by a decline in the pace of accumulation as a result of the decline in the rate of profit (Goodwin 1967). In short, the role of the reserve army is to keep down wages relative to productivity, not necessarily to ensure that the level of wages does not increase, but rather to ensure that the share of wages does not. (Many writers postulate the wage-share as being a monotonic *function* of the ratio of the reserve to the active army, but the precise nature of this relationship is not germane to the current discussion.)

In a fiat money world however there is no question of conditions of production determining the relative value of money vis a vis commodities, since money is not a produced commodity. The relative value of money vis a vis commodities in such a universe is determined by the fact that the value of one commodity, labour power, in terms of money is fixed in the short-run and changes slowly in the long-run (which was Keynes' argument). And since labour power enters into the production of every commodity, this *ipso facto* fixes the relative value of money vis a vis all commodities.[10] In other words, the level of money wage rate determines the relative value of money vis-à-vis commodities; the stickiness of the money wage rate prevents any violent fluctuations in this relative value.

This stickiness means in effect that the workers, taken as a whole or a significant section of them, act as price-takers. For workers to act as *price-takers* it must be the case that they are not organized. Keynes (1946: Chapter 17), who correctly postulated the stickiness of money wages as a condition for the stability of the capitalist system, attributed this stickiness not to the fact of workers, or a substantial section among them, being unorganized, but to the existence of 'money illusion' among organized workers, that is, among the trade unions themselves, who supposedly do not notice a decline in real wages since their attention is focussed exclusively on the money wages. But this was a weak and patently untenable argument, which monetarism was quick to seize upon for staging a successful revival from the position to which it had been reduced as a consequence of the Keynesian onslaught: it introduced the concept of a 'natural rate of unemployment' which denied any scope for successful State intervention in demand management of the sort that Keynesianism had argued for. The rigidity of money wages, at least of a certain section of

---

[10] Of course, it does not have to be labour power; the relative value of any commodity that enters into the production of other commodities, and which cannot become a 'free good' vis a vis other commodities, being fixed in terms of money, would do. But this latter fixity must *ipso facto* entail a fixity of the money wage rate of the workers engaged in the production of this commodity.

workers (which is quite enough for the stability of the system), arises because they are unorganized. Workers act as price-takers because they are unorganized. And they remain unorganized because they live amidst a reserve army of labour.

The notion of a reserve army that restrains the bargaining strength of trade unions and ensures that the share of wages does not increase, and the notion of a reserve army that ensures that a substantial section of workers remains unorganized, are two very different entities. Workers remain unorganized only when they constitute part of a vast pauperized mass, in whose context it is not even clear that the term 'reserve army of labour', which suggests at least periodic or potential active duty, is at all applicable. If we do use the term, then we must recognize that keeping workers unorganized, and hence trapped as price-takers, requires a much larger reserve army of labour than what would be necessary merely for ensuring that real wages do not rise faster than labour productivity secularly. Since Marx, who first proposed the notion of the reserve army of labour, confined himself only to its latter role, and not its role in stabilizing the 'wage-unit' (to borrow a Keynesian term), his concept is somewhat restricted.

Capitalism requires that even if there are autonomous reasons for a fall in real wages, resulting in a fall in wage share, even then the stickiness of money wages is not disrupted. The reserve army therefore must be large enough to ensure that a significant section of the workers cannot enforce any particular ex-ante wage share.[11] They should not be able to defend some particular level of real wages relative to productivity by jacking up money wages whenever there is a fall below that level (so that hyper inflation is prevented). They must be part of a vast pauperized mass.

This mass, or, putting it differently, the enormous amount of reserve army required for this *denouement*, cannot be geographically located within the metropolitan capitalist economies without giving rise to major social upheavals; it has to be located geographically outside. What is more, it must also be located sociologically outside the capitalist system, within modes of production other than the capitalist one, strictly defined, but which are linked to the capitalist mode of production (just as Marx had visualized in the case of his concept of the reserve army). It follows then, on the basis of this argument, that the simultaneous existence of other modes of production surrounding it is a condition for the existence of the capitalist mode of production itself.

Of course, this simultaneous existence is necessary not for this or that

[11] A detailed discussion of the matter is contained in Patnaik (1997).

particular reason. Its necessity arises not merely for the sake of finding an external market to stimulate accumulation, so that the system operates close to capacity; nor does it arise merely for the sake of stabilizing the system by preventing accelerating inflation when the system does work close to capacity. (Such accelerating inflation would occur if *all* workers whose products were used by capitalism could enforce ex-ante wage-shares.) It is not just one reason, but a whole range of them. And for this whole range of reasons, the overall functioning of capitalism requires that it be linked to other modes of production; it thrives by sponging on them, by making them subservient to its own will.

SUBORDINATING OTHER MODES OF PRODUCTION

The vision of capitalism as a 'closed system', it follows, is completely off the mark. The concept of a mode of production, defined in terms of its internal appropriation mechanisms, and hence as an epistemologically self-contained entity, which may be relevant for earlier modes of production, is not relevant for capitalism, since it tends to detract from its linkages with other modes of production with which it must simultaneously co-exist. This is not to critique the concept of the mode of production, or to belittle Marx's gigantic labours in unravelling the law of motion of capitalism, starting from an analysis of the origin of surplus value within it, but merely to underscore the insufficiency of even that Herculean effort.

This is necessary for one very important reason. Marx and Engels had written in the *Manifesto*: 'The bourgeoisie, by the rapid improvement of all instruments of production, by the immensely facilitated means of communication, draws all, even the most barbarian, nations into civilization. The cheap prices of its commodities are the heavy artillery with which it batters down all Chinese walls, with which it forces the barbarians' intensely obstinate hatred of foreigners to capitulate. It compels all nations, on pain of extinction, to adopt the bourgeois mode of production; it compels them to introduce what it calls civilization into their midst, that is, to become bourgeois themselves. In one word, it creates a world after its own image.'

The clear suggestion here is that the revolutionary nature of the bourgeois mode of production necessarily results in its universal diffusion, a suggestion that reappears in Rosa Luxemburg as well, who developed a whole theory of the breakdown of capitalism on the argument that when capitalism had become the universally prevalent mode of production, expanded reproduction would become an impossibility. Even though the

Sixth Congress of the Communist International had rejected this suggestion and recognized the fact that in Third World countries integration into the orbit of world capitalism did not lead to a replication internally of the capitalist mode of production (it had adopted the thesis that 'pauperization of the peasantry' in the Third World did not lead to its 'proletarianization'), this 'diffusionism' has been a persistently recurring theme within the Marxist tradition. The argument of this chapter not only rejects 'diffusionism', but amounts to saying that the capitalist mode, contrary to common belief, can exist only within an environment of pre-capitalism, not in the pristine form of course, but moulded, shaped and dominated by capitalism and made to cater to its needs.

The capitalist mode, it follows, is both revolutionary and yet not quite revolutionary enough. It does break down the insulation of existing pre-capitalist societies, it does ruthlessly draw them into the vortex of its own accumulation process, but not necessarily by creating within them, in a dominant form, the structures of the bourgeois mode of production itself. They are transformed by, and hegemonized by, metropolitan capitalism, but they themselves never get transformed into bourgeois societies.

While this fact may be accepted by many, the question may be asked: why should we not be content with encapsulating it within some other concept, for example, 'the capitalist world system'? Why should we insist on retaining the concept of the mode of production at all? The answer to this question is as follows: concepts, and the theories using them, are of value essentially as aids to praxis. The preference for one concept over another must ultimately be determined by the degree to which it aids praxis, more specifically the degree to which it helps in carrying forward revolutionary class-struggle by making possible the concrete analysis of the concrete conditions. Nothing that has been said earlier questions the validity of Marx's basic insights into the dynamics of the capitalist mode of production; it merely wishes to locate that dynamics within a larger totality. To understand that dynamics, to identify the plethora of classes located within this larger totality, and to see the changes in the interrelationship between these classes the concept of the mode of production is absolutely necessary. Without it, one would be in the realm of mere description, albeit 'rich description', but not in the realm of analysis.

While retaining the concept of the mode of production however we must recognize that the capitalist mode of production is always located within a 'cluster', surrounded by pre-capitalist modes of production, which are 'hegemonized', but nonetheless very clearly extant and by no means obliterated. The tendencies immanent to capitalism, unravelled by Marx, operate surely, but in a manner refracted by its interactions with this surrounding universe. Exploitation within this totality is of diverse forms: there is above all the exploitation of workers directly employed by capital through the appropriation of surplus value; there is the exploitation of the metropolitan reserve army which is kept in depressed living conditions, and has the role of keeping down the bargaining strength of the trade unions in the metropolis; then there are the unorganized workers in the periphery who are exploited through unequal exchange and made to act as price-takers so as to sustain the stability of the value of money; finally, there is the vast pauperized mass amidst whom these unorganized workers are placed which is also exploited, through even more depressed living conditions than the metropolitan reserve army, and upon whom the system rests ultimately for its stability. In addition to these, there are, of course, the different forms of exploitation by the pre-capitalist hegemonic classes.

Recognizing this complex totality seems to me to be a much better way of proceeding than treating capitalism as a self-contained mode of production like the earlier ones, and hence missing out on the phenomenon of imperialism (in the inclusive sense). We should therefore not change in any basic sense the concept of mode of production; we have to remove from it the connotation of a self-contained entity by recognizing that the capitalist mode, unlike the previous ones, exists necessarily by hegemonizing, but not eliminating these previous ones. No mode of production that is so dependent on the world market, that comes into existence by constituting a world trading system, could be meaningfully cognized as a self-contained entity.

IMPERIALISM: CONSTANT FEATURE OF CAPITALISM

Let us now pull together the different strands of the argument of this chapter. The basic concept of Marxian analysis is the mode of production. Since it takes as its point of departure the production process in any society and the manner of extraction of surplus from those engaged in direct production, the mode of production is seen essentially as a self-contained entity, and the 'law of motion' governing it is worked out within this perspective. This procedure, applied universally by Marxist analysts across all modes, is particularly evident in the analysis of capitalism, which has been seen as a mode of production epistemologically on a par with any other, and one on which Marxian analysis has been particularly focussed. The result of this has been that imperialism, not just in Lenin's sense but in the more inclusive sense that incorporates the colonial phase as well, which has been a constant feature of capitalism, has not figured centrally in the Marxian analysis of it: (leaving aside the monopoly phase) it figures only in discussions of primitive accumulation, and in concrete analyses of capitalism, but not in its law of motion, in the basic theory of its functioning.

There are, however, overwhelming reasons to believe that it must figure there, that capitalism cannot be analysed as a self-contained system on a par with earlier modes. Once we recognize, as Marx did, the possibility of a demand constraint leading to generalized over-production, then, as Rosa Luxemburg had pointed out, we have to look for 'exogenous stimuli' to explain accumulation as a sustained process; and the main exogenous stimulus is export to pre-capitalist markets (even when trade is balanced with these markets). The fact that protracted generalized over-production has not been generally observed, should not be taken as proof of its ex ante impossibility. And pointing out the weakness of Narodnik-style arguments about the impossibility of capitalism in a particular country, arguments which constitute distorted (because they are epistemologically erroneous) conclusions from this proposition about exogenous stimuli, cannot be used to obfuscate the validity of this proposition.

In addition however, there is a further fact. Already in Marx, the concept of the reserve army as it appears points implicitly to the existence of other modes of production alongside and dominated by capitalism. The scope of this concept as it appears in Marx is itself however somewhat restricted. Its role there is confined to one of keeping down the bargaining strength of workers, so that the rise in real wages relative to productivity is kept in check. In a fiat money world however, the stability of the system requires that the money wages of at least a substantial section of workers should be sticky in the short-run and change slowly over time, which would happen if these workers act essentially as 'price-takers'. When workers act as 'price-takers', they themselves are usually underemployed, that is, can be said to belong to some sort of a semi-reserve army; what is more, they do so only when they are surrounded by vast unutilized labour reserves, which is usually the case in Third World economies from whom capitalism draws much of its raw materials and primary commodities. The reserve army that capitalism typically operates with therefore is much larger than what Marx had visualized, and typically this reserve army is split into two parts, a smaller one that exists in the metropolis, and a much larger one that exists in the periphery ensconced within modes of production that are different from capitalism, but, nonetheless subjugated by it, and hence different too from their own pristine forms.

Capitalism therefore necessarily exists within a complex environment, within a cluster of pre-capitalist forms. While this fact is recognized by many, the theoretical devices they advance for cognizing it, such as 'the capitalist world system' tend to do away with the Marxian concept of the mode of production. This in my view is unwise since it amounts to throwing the baby out with the bathwater. A much better way out is to retain the concept of the mode of production, to retain and build on all the insights that Marx derived from this concept, but to recognize that capitalism, contrary to the ruthlessly single-minded revolutionary nature usually attributed to it, functions throughout its life within an environment constituted by a cluster of pre-capitalist modes of production, whom it alters, transforms, dominates, and exploits. The notion of exploitation it follows must also be broadened to take account of the different types of exploitation prevalent under capitalism, apart from the basic extraction of surplus value. The solution to the apparent contradiction between the concept of the mode of production and the theory of imperialism is not to abandon the centrality of either but to recognize theoretically a phenomenon that has been on view for long, namely that the capitalist mode has some very specific characteristics attached to it.

REFERENCES

Bukharin, N. I., (1972), *Imperialism and the Accumulation of Capital*, reprinted in Kenneth Tarbuck (ed.), *Imperialism and the Accumulation of Capital*, Allen Lane, The Penguin Press, London.

Chandra, Bipan, (1966), *The Rise and Growth of Economic Nationalism in India*, People's Publishing House, Delhi.

Dobb, M. H., (1973), *Theories of Value and Distribution since Adam Smith*, Cambridge University Press, Cambridge.

Feinstein, C. H. (ed.), (1967), *Socialism, Capitalism and Economic Growth*, Cambridge University Press, Cambridge.

Ganguli, B. N., (1965), *Dadabhai Naoroji and the Drain Theory*, Asia Publishing House, New Delhi.

Goodwin, R.M., (1967), 'The Growth Cycle', in C. H. Feinstein (ed.), *Socialism, Capitalism and Economic Growth*, Cambridge University Press, Cambridge.

Habib, Irfan, (1995), 'Problems of Marxist Historiography', in *Essays in Indian History*, Tulika, Delhi.

Hilton, Rodney (ed.), (1976), *The Transition from Feudalism to Capitalism*, New Left Books, London.

Kalecki, Michal, (1971), 'The Problem of Effective Demand with Rosa Luxemburg and Tugan Baranovsky', in *Selected Essays on the Dynamics of the Capitalist Economy 1933–1970*, Cambridge University Press, Cambridge.

Keynes, J. M., (1946), *The General Theory of Employment, Interest and Money*, Macmillan, London.

Lange, Oskar, (1964), 'The Role of the State in Monopoly Capitalism', in *Papers on Economics and Sociology*. Pergamon, Oxford.

Luxemburg, Rosa, (1963), *The Accumulation of Capital*, Routledge, London.

Naoroji, Dadabhai, (1962), *Poverty and Un-British Rule in India*, Government of India, Delhi.

Patnaik, Prabhat, (1972), 'External Markets and Capitalist Development', *Economic Journal*, 82 (328), 1316–23.

—— (1986), 'Introduction', in Prabhat Patnaik (ed.). *Lenin and Imperialism*, Orient Longman, Delhi.

Patnaik, Prabhat, (1997), *Accumulation and Stability Under Capitalism*, Clarendon Press, Oxford.

Patnaik, Prabhat, (1999), '*The Communist Manifesto* After 150 Years', in Prakash Karat (ed.), *A World to Win*, Leftword Books, New Delhi.

Patnaik, Prabhat, (2000), 'Introduction', to V. I. Lenin, *Imperialism the Highest Stage of Capitalism*, Leftword Books, New Delhi.

Patnaik, Utsa, (1999), 'The Costs of Free Trade: The WTO Regime and the Indian Economy', *Social Scientist*, 27 (1–2), November/December: 3–26.

Robinson, Joan, (1963), 'Introduction' to Rosa Luxemburg, *The Accumulation of Capital*, Routledge, London.

Tarbuck, Kenneth (ed.), (1972), *Imperialism and the Accumulation of Capital*. Allen Lane, The Penguin Press, London.

3

✠

Latin America and the World Economy in the Long Twentieth Century

José Antonio Ocampo

A distinctive feature of Latin America (and the Caribbean) vis-à-vis Africa and Asia was its earlier, deeper integration into currents of European-led mercantilist expansion. When industrial capitalist development accelerated in the centre of the world economy in the second half of the nineteenth century, Latin America had already undergone more than three centuries of deep transformation of its economic and social structures.

Furthermore, as a result of the turmoil generated in Europe by the French Revolution, most of Latin America became independent in the early nineteenth century. The construction of nationhood was, in any case, traumatic and incomplete in most countries, in at least two different senses. First, it meant recurrent civil strife in many countries throughout the nineteenth century, a fact that contributed to the generation of political systems in which oligarchic rule was closely intertwined with military power. This meant, in turn, that the victory of economic liberalism in the nineteenth century was not accompanied in most countries by the development of liberal political institutions. Second, in economic terms, the lack of modern communications meant that countries were

This chapter draws from the contributions of the author to the project on Latin American Economic History led by Rosemary Thorp, and published in Thorp (1998a) and Cárdenas, Ocampo, and Thorp (2000a, 2000b).

really a set of localities, economic archipelagos, in which different parts of nations were often better integrated to the ports of Europe or the USA than amongst themselves. The development of a true internal market was thus a relatively late process in most countries.

However, early integration into the world economy and political independence did not represent economic autonomy for Latin America when a deeper phase of global economic integration took off in the last decades of the nineteenth century. With very few exceptions, the insertion of Latin America into the world economy continued to rely, as in the colonial past, on its natural resources. Unstable capital flows and, in some countries, international labour migration also helped to shape the central features of the 'export age' of Latin American economic development.

The gradual growth of an internal market and a more diversified modern economic structure facilitated the adjustment of the region when the world economy came under increasing strains in the inter-War period and, particularly, in 1930s. Although the commitment to a raw material-based export economy did not disappear suddenly, industrialization based on the internal market increasingly became the major source of economic growth. This transition, which involved the gradual development of new forms of state intervention in the economy, was successful, as reflected in the fact that Latin America became the region of the world that experienced the fastest growth in the inter-War period.

Economic reconstruction of the world economy after the Second World War thus found a region that had become self-confident due to its successful inter-War experience. State-led industrialization deepened but never entirely replaced raw material dependence, particularly in the smaller countries. It also allowed the larger countries to share in the growth of world trade in manufactures, a process that was reinforced by regional integration. The return of private capital flows since the 1960s helped, in turn, to manage the balance of payments constraints that had been recurrent since the 1930s and tended to deepen in the last phases of state-led industrialization. External capital helped to sustain growth after 1973, but the boom–bust cycle of international finance proved fatal, and led to the worst economic crisis, the 'lost decade' of 1980s.

The attempt to lift the economy through economic liberalization had some dividends in terms of economic growth, facilitated, in turn, by renewed external financing. However, productive restructuring proved more traumatic than envisaged by neo-liberal reformers, and led to slow rates of economic growth, even during the period of better performance between 1990 and 1997. Furthermore, heavy dependence on external financing proved fatal again in the face of a new boom–bust cycle of international finance, leading the region into a new 'lost half decade' in 1998–2002.

This chapter presents the broad trends of economic development in Latin America and its relations to the world economy during the long twentieth century. The analysis is divided into three broad phases. We will refer to the period from 1870s–80s to 1920s as the 'export age', that between the 1930s and the 1970s as the phase of 'state-led industrialization', and the most recent period as the 'neo-liberal order'.

THE EXPORT AGE

Deeper Integration into the World Economy

Most economic expansions in Latin America up to 1920s were export led, in the sense that export growth was not only faster than but also determined the cyclical patterns of GDP growth. The dominant role played by exports did not mean, however, that export sectors absorbed the major share of the labour force or, indeed, that they represented large shares of GDP. Indeed, in most countries, the export economies left large contingents of labour under the sway of traditional rural structures. Export expansions were primarily based on the exploitation of previously under-utilized natural resources. However, in Latin America, they varied considerably in magnitude, timing, stability, product composition, and the degree of diversification of economic activity that accompanied export development.

Overall, the export expansion of Latin America was similar to that of world trade in the last decades of the nineteenth century but more dynamic than the latter in the first three decades of the twentieth century. By late 1920s, Latin America's share in world trade had reached 9 per cent, an increase over the 7 per cent typical of the last decades of the nineteenth century (Table 3.1). Growth was accompanied by major variations in the commodity composition. Temperate zone agricultural products and meat, industrial minerals and oil absorbed an increasing share at the cost of precious metals and more traditional agricultural and forest staples, with the major exception of coffee, which maintained slightly under a fifth of regional exports.

By far, the most spectacular export expansion was experienced by Argentina from 1870s to the First World War (Gerchunoff and Llach 1998). However, as time passed, all countries benefited from increasing integration into the world economy. Dependence on European versus US markets became a crucial determinant of relative export performance after 1914. Indeed, exports to the dynamic US economy was one of the reasons

TABLE 3.1
Latin American Exports, 1860–1929

	1859/61	1899/1901	1911/13	1927/29
Value of exports (USD million)				
Latin America[a]	292	664	1493	2954
Argentina	13	163	437	964
Excluding Argentina	279	501	1055	198
Share of world trade (%)		7.1	8.6	9.2
Share of Third World exports (%)	41.8	37.4	38.4	36.4
Commodity composition[b]				
Traditional products				
Agricultural and forest	41.2	28.5	24.5	16.9
Minerals	18.8	14.2	13	6.6
Coffee	18.2	18.5	18.6	18.0
Dynamic products				
Agricultural	3.9	22.2	24.4	27.7
Minerals and oil	0.2	1.2	4.7	14.2

Notes: Traditional agricultural and forest products: sugar, tobacco, leather, and rubber; Traditional minerals: precious metals, guano, and nitrates; Dynamic agricultural products: cereals, wool, and meat; Dynamic minerals: copper and tin.

[a] Data refers to developing countries of America excluding the British Antilles.

[b] Percentage shares of total exports, excluding unclassified. Includes the British Antilles.

Sources: Latin American and Third World Exports: Bairoch and Etemad (1985: Table 5.1); Value of World Trade: Madisson (1995: Table 1–3); Commodity composition: Bairoch and Etemad (1985: Table 5.3).

why Latin America as a whole was able to avoid following the European slowdown after the First World War, but its effects were more fully felt in the northern part of Latin America. Dependence on this market was sometimes a mixed blessing, if the commodities exported to it became the target of entrenched US protectionism.

The nineteenth century was a period of improving commodity in terms of trade, particularly if the fast reduction in transport costs since 1870s is taken into account (Bértola and Williamson 2003). Although the decade of the 1890s was a turning point for some commodities, particularly coffee, the general trend of commodity prices was still positive in the early twentieth century. From the First World War onwards, commodity prices became extremely unstable and experienced a strong negative shock in 1920s, which was reinforced in 1930s (Ocampo and Parra 2003). Domestic and international regulations of commodity markets thus became an attractive option since the First World War as a way of managing overproduction and depressed prices, and became a widespread practice in 1930s (Rowe 1965: Part IV).

Export growth was accompanied by movements of both capital and labour. After the financing boom of 1820s, associated with the independence war debts and pioneering mining and colonization projects, generalized moratoria restricted access to foreign lending for several decades. Indeed, for some countries, the nineteenth century story was one of renegotiations of the external debt, short periods of access to capital markets and renewed default. Those which gained stable access in the last decades of the nineteenth century were, in any case, subject to the boom–bust cycles that characterized external financing: the loan frenzy of the 1880s, followed by 1890. Barings crash, the early twentieth century boom, sharply interrupted by the First World War, and the Wall Street bond boom of 1920s, followed by 1929 crash (Marichal 1989).

Up to the First World War, the major source of financing was Britain, but it was supplemented by France, Germany and, increasingly, the USA. European capital was mainly invested in railroads, other infrastructure projects and government bonds, that were used, in turn, for infrastructure investments and war (mainly civil, but also border conflicts). The US already had a fifth of foreign capital invested in Latin America in 1914, with a relatively larger share of direct investment. In fact, Latin America was an early outlet of US capital, accounting for close to half of all capital exported by the US prior to the First World War. Unlike European investments, which stagnated after the First World War, US funds continued to flow during the war and the 1920s in the form of direct investments in oil, mining, agriculture and, to a lesser extent, public utilities. However, it was portfolio financing that took the lead in 1920s, when the Wall Street became the major source of bond financing for Latin American governments and private firms, some of them US investment ventures (United Nations 1955).

On the other hand, Latin America absorbed close to a fifth of the 62 million people who emigrated from Europe and Asia between 1820 and 1930, most of them in the half-century prior to the First World War (Hatton and Williamson 1994). Argentina and Brazil became the major recipients of European labour, followed by Chile and Uruguay, who received large contingents relative to their smaller populations. Foreign migrant entrepreneurs and technicians, particularly from Europe, were also important, even in countries that were not recipients of massive immigration. Plantation agriculture throughout the Caribbean, the Caribbean coasts of Latin America, and Peru generated additional flows of labour, some of it from Asia (primarily China and India) under various types of indenture, but also intraregional flows, such as the movements of black labour from the Antilles to banana plantations of Central America, the Cuban sugar industry, and construction of the Panama Canal.

In aggregate terms, export growth and its accompanying capital and labour flows led to economic growth from 1870s onwards. The stagnation of per capita GDP, which broadly characterized the region since independence was followed by growth at rates similar to the average for industrial countries and faster than the world average (Table 3.2). This pattern of early expansion allowed Latin America to place itself as a 'middle income' region of the world, with an average per capita GDP slightly above one-fourth of that of the US, estimated on the basis of purchasing power parities. Given fast population growth, it also meant an increasing share of world output.

As Triffin (1968) and the contributors to Aceña and Reis (2000) have pointed out, the gold standard operated in an asymmetric manner to the detriment of countries in the periphery, which saw during crises a simultaneous fall of commodity prices and a pro-cyclical reduction of external financing. In turn, externally generated cycles were transmitted domestically through strong dependence of public sector finances on customs revenues and links between the balance of payments and the money supply. The major victim was public and private investment, which was subject to a particularly sharp cyclical pattern. Although some countries learned to live with such strong cycles while maintaining the 'rules of the game' of the gold (and silver) standard, it generated long episodes of currency inconvertibility. Among the larger countries, Argentina, Brazil, Chile, and Colombia experienced long episodes of inconvertibility.

These episodes, as well as the late abandonment of the silver standard in some countries, generated an inflationary propensity relative to world levels. It also meant that nominal depreciation could be partly counted upon as both a protectionist and an export-promoting device during crises. In turn, this implied that establishing or re-establishing the gold standard after episodes of inconvertibility had high costs, both in terms of the scarce fiscal resources that had to be used to guarantee the required reserves, and the associated relative price adjustments, which had adverse effects on export and import-competing activities.

Apart from the monetary institutions, governments played a central role in the development of domestic banking in most countries as also in

TABLE 3.2

Latin America and the World Economy

	1820	1870	1913	1929	1950	1965	1973	1980	1990	2000
Per capita GDP by region										
Western Europe	1232	1974	3473	4111	4579	8441	11,416	13,197	15,966	19,002
USA, Australia, NZ, Canada	1202	2419	5233	6673	9268	12,967	16,179	18,060	22,345	27,065
Japan	669	737	1387	2026	1921	5934	11,434	13,428	18,789	21,069
Asia (excldg Japan)	577	550	658		634	936	1226	1494	2117	3189
Latin America (LA)	692	681	1481	2034	2506	3439	4504	5412	5053	5838
Eastern Europe and ex-USSR	686	941	1558	1570	2602	4333	5731	6231	6455	4778
Africa	420	500	637		894	1164	1410	1536	1444	1464
World	667	875	1525		2111	3233	4091	4520	5157	6012
Interregional disparities (%)										
LA/USA	55.1	27.9	27.9	29.5	26.2	25.6	27.0	29.1	21.8	20.8
LA/World	103.7	77.8	97.1		118.7	106.4	110.1	119.7	98.0	97.1
LA/Africa	164.8	136.2	232.5		280.3	295.4	319.4	352.3	349.9	398.8
LA/Asia (excldg Japan)	119.9	123.9	225.2		395.5	367.2	367.4	362.2	238.7	183.1
LA share of world output (%)	2.2	2.5	4.4		7.8	8.0	8.7	9.8	8.3	8.4

Source: Author's calculations based on Maddison (2001) and author's database.

the determination of labour institutions, how rents from natural resources were to be distributed and used, and what links were to be developed between export and other domestic economic activities. Although it was certainly not the type of interventionist state built up from 1930s in Latin America (as in the rest of the world), it also did not fit the laissez faire image constructed by some nostalgic analysts of the export era.

Diverging Structural Patterns

The nature of the commodities sold abroad and their domestic linkages, as also their domestic institutional underpinnings, determined the effects that they had on economic and social structures.[1] The basic institutional issues revolved around how labour was mobilized, how natural resources were made available to the export sectors and how the rents from the latter were shared. Wage and, more generally, mobile labour was very scarce, an issue reflected in the universal complaints of labour shortages by contemporary analysts (Bulmer-Thomas 2003: chapter 4). This reflected the fact that pre-capitalist economic structures tended to restrict labour mobility, and that a mobile labour force is the most important 'institution' of modern capitalism, including the particular form it adopts in most developing countries as an unlimited supply of labour—a feature that only became entrenched in Latin America during the phase of state-led industrialization (see section 'State-led Industrialization' in this chapter).

Given restrictions to labour mobility, access to the most developed free labour market of the world at the time, that is, that of Europe, was crucial to guarantee a dynamic response to the opportunities that the international economy provided. This was the pattern observed in the settler economies of the southern Cone. This process facilitated rapid economic growth based on massive immigration, a free labour market and higher standards of living than in the rest of region, but also the early rise of social conflicts associated with modern labour movements. The use of other pools of internationally mobile labour had more limited scope. The abolishment of slavery in the Caribbean provided a labour supply from which the banana plantations of Central America and some Cuban sugar

---

[1] Traditional typologies (Furtado 1976, Sunkel and Paz 1976, Cardoso and Faletto 1979) have emphasized the contrast between mineral and agricultural-exporting economies and, in the latter case, between settler economies producing temperate zone agricultural products and more traditional societies producing tropical agricultural commodities. The distinction between temperate and tropical agriculture is also important to the extent that it was closely interlinked to different flows of international migration, as temperate zone agriculture depended on flows of European labour, whereas the production of tropical commodities used indentured Asian labour (Lewis 1969).

plantations benefited. Chinese indentured labour was also used in Cuba and Peru.

Countries that did not have access to international migration had to rely entirely on domestic developments to generate a mobile labour force. This form of labour mobilization was generally sub-optimal, leading to a growth process in which the supply of mobile labour was the crucial scarce factor—a significant contrast to the unlimited supply of labour that characterized all the Latin American economies once capitalist development was in full swing. Smallholders provided another possible source of domestic labour, which played an important role in the development of export sectors in some countries (coffee in Colombia and Costa Rica, tobacco in Cuba), and in the supply of food for the cities and export centres. However, given the limits posed by land concentration, this form of labour mobilization was limited in scope.

Pockets of surplus population in peasant economies and, more generally, population pressures had started to build up in several countries prior to the export age, and its development was enhanced by the liberal reforms of the nineteenth century. These 'free' workers were mobilized as temporary or permanent wage labourers or, more frequently, as tenants, subject to variable mixes of labour obligations, sharecropping and rights to use a land plot to produce subsistence foodstuffs. Non-economic restrictions on labour mobility, such as debt peonage, were frequently involved. In cases where such a mobile labour force did not develop, labour mobilization sometimes used, as in the colonial past, outright coercion, now mixed with cash incentives. This was generally the rule in those localities where the indigenous population continued to be important.

An associated issue to that of labour mobilization was how to eliminate traditional inflexibilities in the land market, most of them associated with the role of the Catholic Church, as well as with Indian reserves and other forms of communal property. The liberal reforms of the nineteenth century, focused precisely on eliminating restrictions to land mobility and direct land taxation (a major mechanism of Church financing), as well as on the abolishment of slavery and the elimination of some of the state monopolies. State land grants served, on the other hand, to reproduce an agrarian system based on land concentration.

The nature of production, processing, and transportation determined the industrial structure of the export sectors. Large-scale capital penetrated those activities where fixed capital and economies of scale were important. This was the case of mineral and oil exploitation as well as sugar and banana plantations. Foreign capital played a dominant role in all of them. In other cases, foreign capital tended to control marketing and processing, but not raw material production. The nature of industrial concentration was not always dictated by technological imperatives, however. The contrast between the large-scale coffee plantation that developed in most Latin American countries, despite the lack of any economies of scale in production, and the small and medium size farms characteristic of a few countries, is a remarkable example. It indicates that the determinants of the industrial structure were, in this case, institutional, that is, land concentration to guarantee control of the labour force, rather than commodity-determined.

Diversification

Links between the export sector and other domestic economic activities involved two major issues. The first was the control of the rents generated by the exploitation of natural resources. The second was the extent of diversification of economic structures that resulted from the forward and backward linkages generated by export activities. In those cases where foreign investors were major players, the issue of rents was closely linked to the 'returned value' of exports, that is, the share of gross output that remained within national boundaries. This percentage depended on the capacity of the state to effectively extract part of the rent through direct or indirect (export) taxes. Taxation of mineral sectors was important in some cases, but much less developed in others. In all mineral economies, this issue was at the forefront of the domestic political debate.

In agricultural export economies, there was a broad-based opposition by landlords to direct land taxation. In these as well as in the mineral economies that did not tax export sectors, domestic protection was thus the major way of indirectly taxing export activities. It was actively used by most governments. Indeed, despite its commitment to export growth and liberal economics, Latin America had already in the 1860s the highest import tariffs of the world, a feature that continued to be valid in the protectionist wave that characterized the world economy—or rather, that part of the world economy that enjoyed tariff autonomy—since the 1870s (Coatsworth and Williamson 2003).

Closely associated with taxation was how government revenues were allocated. In this regard, a major indicator of modernization was the moment in which the more traditional areas of spending (general administration, defence, and debt service) gave way to the increasing allocation of resources to transportation and education.[2] Although private foreign capital was closely involved in the development of the domestic

---

[2] In this regard, see the different country studies included in Cárdenas, Ocampo, and Thorp (2000a).

transportation network, particularly railways, and in urban infrastructure, state investments were crucial in most countries. Thus, an active 'tax and invest' policy was crucial to guarantee rapid overall growth in export economies, as Palma (2000) has argued for Chile. Towards the end of our period of analysis, with the rise of motor vehicle transportation, state investments played an even greater role.

The second type of interaction involved both direct and more indirect linkages between the export sector and other domestic activities. Different products had different processing and transportation requirements. Mineral ores must be processed close to the point of production to minimize transportation costs. This led to the development of smelting and sometimes refining facilities, which lay behind the early industrialization efforts of mining economies. Like mining ores, sugar also needs to be processed close to where the raw material is produced. With refrigerated transportation, meat exports required the development of packing-houses. Other commodities, such as oil and bananas, required special capital-intensive transportation networks but no significant processing. In these cases, large capital investments in raw material export sectors had limited direct effects in terms of industrialization.

The indirect links were associated, foremost, with consumer demand generated by rising incomes. Stronger demand effects were present when either European wage labour or peasant farming was involved, rather than other forms of labour mobilization. A particularly important issue, in this regard, is whether the rising demand for foodstuffs was met by domestic supply. Experiences varied considerably in this regard. Some agricultural economies were exporters of food. In others, however, food imports became sizeable and import substitution of those foodstuffs became an important issue at a larger stage of development.

The increasing domestic demand for manufactures led not only to rising imports, but also to domestic industrialization. Indeed, as extensive research in recent decades has shown, manufacturing development clearly predated the 1930s. Manufacturing growth was induced in several countries through different channels. The first were, as we have seen, the processing requirements of export commodities, a forward linkage. The second was the combination of backward demand linkages and high transport costs, which generated a 'natural import substitution' of some manufactures—beer, printing and, later, cement. Indeed, the term import substitution may be inappropriate in these cases, as domestic production directly accompanied demand growth without significant imports ever developing.

Additional links were associated with tariff policy. Although high tariffs had a fiscal origin, they also had protectionist effects. In fact, contrary to modern intellectual trends, export growth and protectionism were not viewed as opposite, but rather as complementary strategies, as elements of one single modernization drive. Some Latin American countries (Brazil, Chile, Colombia, and Mexico) practised very active protectionism long before inward-looking development. In those cases, early industrialization since the late nineteenth century was closely associated with protection.

The tariff schedules of the time were generally based on specific tariffs, including a variant: ad valorem tariffs paid according to an official price list. Specific weight tariffs gave high protection to the production of industrial goods with low value per weight, for instance, higher protection for simple, rather than sophisticated textiles. Also, under both systems, inflation eroded protection, but deflation increased it. This generated a peculiar counter-cyclical pattern of protection, which was compounded with that of exchange rates in those countries that did not follow gold standard rules. Thus, during external booms, manufacturing was discouraged by falling ad valorem tariffs (due to inflation) and real appreciation, but promoted by rising demand. In turn, during crises, deflation increased ad valorem tariffs; this effect plus that of devaluation, when used, encouraged import substitution. In addition, during the First World War, the physical scarcity of some manufacturing goods imported from Europe generated additional incentives to domestic production.

Manufacturing development also depended on other factors, particularly size and domestic market integration—a joint effect, in turn of export growth, urbanization, and the development of modern infrastructure. The positive effects of infrastructure development could be maximized when there was a strategy of national integration. In other cases, however, the development of modern transportation initially tended to disintegrate the domestic market, by improving the communication of different localities with the rest of the world while internal communications continued to rely on traditional means of transportation. However, in the long run, modern transportation always helped to integrate the domestic market. The shift from railways to road transportation also played a role in this regard, but it came in a period of transition to state-led industrialization.

The export sector was also a major node of technological transmission and diffusion, the major building block of a modern entrepreneurial class and the source of a skilled labour force. At an institutional level, the development of mining and trade codes, and improved banking and currency regulations, made significant strides during this stage of development. Overall, export growth was the crucial factor behind overall economic development. National differences in export performance were a crucial determinant of the large divergence in levels of development that characterized the region prior to the First World War (Bulmer-Thomas 2003: chapter 5; Cárdenas, Ocampo, and Thorp 2000a: chapter 1).

TABLE 3.3
Latin America: National Disparities, 1929–2000

(per capita)

	1929		1950		1973		1980		2000	
	GDP	HSLI	GDP	HSLI	GDP	HSLI	GDP	HSLI	GDP	HSLI
Argentina	727	51	827	61	1329	69	1333	71	1460	74
Bolivia			235	24	310	39	337	45	329	56
Brazil	177	21	235	31	612	53	801	58	874	64
Chile	540	40	577	49	859	63	958	68	1602	75
Colombia	276	28	383	41	615	57	770	62	925	68
Costa Rica	570		371	51	754	65	887	69	998	73
Ecuador			244	30	407	51	522	56	507	62
Dominican Rep.			234	36	473	52	549	58	685	64
Guatemala	267		342	24	495	41	588	46	583	55
El Salvador	186		273	11	429	23	426	28	475	31
Haiti			118	26	133	41	159	46	91	54
Honduras	264	24	227	42	283	59	316	64	317	71
Mexico	324		507	25	950	44	1138	45	1284	50
Nicaragua	213		219	45	451	63	299	66	186	72
Panama			462	41	963	56	1053	62	1255	66
Paraguay			297	32	386	52	575	56	560	64
Peru	253		331	30	582	47	622	48	560	60
Uruguay	781		865	63	939	68	1148	70	1457	75
Venezuela	372	23	695	42	1251	63	1230	66	1015	70
Average										
LA6	332	31	432	44	819	60	970	65	1077	71
LA19	–	–	392	37	727	53	859	57	939	63
Standard deviation										
LA6	21.7	11.8	19.6	9.9	14.5	5.6	9.9	4.5	10.9	4.0
LA19	–	–	22.4	13.3	24.7	11.8	24.9	11.5	32.7	10.9

Notes: GDP: Per capita gross domestic product in 1970 PPP (purchasing power parity) dollars.
HSLI: Historical standard of living index.
LA6: Argentina, Brazil, Chile, Colombia, Mexico, and Venezuela.
LA19: All countries listed above.

Source: Author's calculations based on Oxford Latin American Economic History Database (OXLAD) and Astorga, Bergés, and FitzGerald (2003).

Conditions were changing towards the end of the export age, however, leading to some narrowing of regional disparities in levels of development (Table 3.3). The miracle of the export age, Argentina, slowed down considerably since the First World War (Cortés-Conde 1997), as other success stories (Chile, Cuba, and Uruguay) also experienced difficulties. At the same time, some medium-size laggards (Colombia, Peru, and Venezuela) were experiencing a late export boom. Also, after a dismal record in the nineteenth century, Brazilian economic growth accelerated (Haddad 1980). Moreover, this was the first case in which GDP growth significantly exceeded export growth. This was the first sign of a new era to come.

STATE-LED INDUSTRIALIZATION

A New Era Slowly Comes of Age

The Great Depression of the 1930s represented a fatal blow to export-led growth in Latin America.[3] It threw world trade into disarray, leading to a collapse of multilateralism, a deepening of the protectionist trends that had been in place for several decades, and a severe recession in the US, the industrial centre on which Latin America had depended once Western Europe had entered into a long-term slowdown after 1914. Commodity prices fell, confirming the long-term adverse shift they had experienced in the 1920s. This was accompanied by a reduction of export volumes in some countries even prior to the Wall Street crash of October 1929.

In addition to that, the external financing boom of the 1920s, which had benefited most countries of the region, was followed by a sharp interruption in capital flows, generating the most severe and broad-based boom–bust cycle of external finance ever experienced by Latin America up to then. Furthermore, the final collapse of the gold standard and the US financial system threw the world financial system itself into disarray. It would take three decades for a new international system to emerge and even longer for private capital flows to return to Latin America.

The collapse of exports and the sharp swing in external financing generated tensions in the balance of payments and fiscal accounts that Latin American countries were used to, but this time, the scale of the events led to a broad-based abandonment of the gold standard. Some countries left it early in the crisis, but even those that tried hard to keep within the rules of the game had few arguments to do so once the mother of the gold standard, the UK, abandoned it in September 1931.

---

[3] For a detailed treatment of the effects of the Great Depression in Latin America, see the volume edited by Thorp (2000) and Bulmer-Thomas (2003: chapter 7).

The large-scale use of exchange controls, bilateral trade, and payments agreements in the industrial world also generated a demonstration effect that was easy to follow. Import rationing had been widely used by industrial countries during the First World War and, again, during the Second World War), and also became part of the Latin American arsenal. Other instruments were more specifically Latin American, particularly the use (and later abuse) of multiple exchange rates. The few countries that avoided either active exchange rate management and/or exchange controls were small countries under strong US influence or using dollar as a means of payments.

On top of that, tensions generated by the boom–bust financial cycle led to broad-based default on the external debt. This happened prior to the crisis (in 1928) in Mexico, and since 1931 in the rest of Latin America. Only Venezuela and Argentina avoided moratoria, the latter as part of a trade deal with the UK that is still a matter of heated debate (O'Connell 2000). By 1935, 97.7 per cent of foreign dollar bonds issued by Latin America were in default, excluding those issued by Argentina; as late as 1945, 62.8 per cent remained in that status (United Nations 1955).

The lack of external financing made strong balance of payments adjustments unavoidable. It involved various mixes of devaluation, protectionism, exchange controls and multiple exchange rates, with default on the foreign debt as the major factor easing adjustments. Import controls would join the package later in the decade. Relative price changes, induced by the joint effect of this pattern of adjustment and the collapse of the terms of trade, generated a strong incentive to substitute imports. Industrialization thus received an additional push, which primarily benefited those (generally large) countries that had already undergone industrial sector expansion during the export age. Small, but also some medium-sized countries also benefited from import substitution of agricultural goods.

In turn, the abandonment of monetary orthodoxy, together with the fiscal ease generated by external debt moratoria facilitated the adoption of loose monetary and fiscal policies, which enabled the recovery of domestic demand. This was supported by direct interventions in the credit market, which included creation of several state banks. The early and generally successful recovery of Latin America during the Great Depression was thus facilitated by various mixes of import substitution of manufacturing and agricultural goods, and the recovery of domestic demand based on expansionary macroeconomic policies.

The death of the gold standard thus gave birth to counter-cyclical macroeconomic policies, but the nature of such policies was very different in the centre and in the periphery of the world economy. Keynesian demand management was, of course, the form it took at the centre but the external origin of economic cycles in the periphery made interventions in the balance of payments central to such policies. Indeed, a focus on expansionary demand management during the downswing was not viable in economies subject to externally generated cycles, as it would exacerbate the balance of payments crisis. Thus, demand management was possible only to the extent that alternative mechanisms were adopted to guarantee balance of payments adjustment, including, in the 1930s, a peculiar form of 'adjustment', debt moratoria.

This framed the macroeconomic debate in the following decades, with Latin American authorities focusing on how to rationalize foreign exchange earnings during crises—but also, increasingly, how to generate new export earnings—in order to avoid the pro-cyclical demand management required to reduce pressure on the balance of payments. On the opposite side, the IMF, created in 1944, would press for such pro-cyclical demand management, following patterns that were not unlike the rules of the game of the gold standard, now eased by the additional multilateral financing made available during crises.

The nature of macroeconomic adjustment generated new forms of state intervention and effects on economic structures that would have long-term implications, but such repercussions would only become evident with the passing of time. Indeed, contrary to the view that the Great Depression generated a sharp change in the development patterns in Latin America, the recent economic history literature has emphasized a gradual transition from export-led growth to state-led industrialization. As we have seen, industrialization and protectionism were already in place during the export age.

In turn, based on the expectation, supported by historical experience, that exports would recover after the cyclical downswing, the commitment to export growth remained. So, the dominant view continued to be that industrialization and export development were complementary. Obviously, to the extent that industrialization and domestic agriculture became the effective sources of growth, it was only natural that they would receive increasing attention from the authorities. This led in the late 1930s to the design of special state institutions to promote new manufacturing activities, particularly industrial development banks and direct state ownership of strategic sectors, with the 1938 nationalization of the oil industry in Mexico as a landmark.

The Second World War provided another major industrialization push, mixed with more interventionism in foreign trade. The interruption of import supplies generated the rationale for promoting a whole new array of manufacturing activities in those countries where industrialization had taken root. In turn, the search for war allies led the US not only to reach agreements with many Latin American countries to build up strategic raw material inventories (the Japanese also did so in the early part of the war), but also to promote the Inter-American Coffee Agreement and to finance, through the Export-Import Bank, several initiatives of Latin American governments, many of them in import-substitution sectors. In this way, and somewhat paradoxically, the US helped to build the interventionist Latin American state (Thorp 1998b).

The accumulation of international reserves during the Second World War, a large part of them inconvertible sterling balances, led to inflation, but also to some novel experiences. One of them was monetary sterilization. This was an additional step in developing active central banking, a familiar institution in the post-Second World War period. The second was the supply of funds that would serve to finance a major investment drive in the early post-War period, as well as the purchase of foreign investments in infrastructure and public utilities in some countries, notably Argentina.

EVENTS, IDEAS, AND INSTITUTIONS INFLUENCING STATE-LED INDUSTRIALIZATION

The events of the 1930s and the Second World War served as the womb in which the new era came into life, but the gestation period was long and lacked clear direction for some time. The maturing of this process was closely linked to the privileged position that Latin America had occupied in the early post-War period. It stood as a region that had avoided the war, accumulated significant international reserves and experienced the fastest expansion in the inter-War period, increasing its share of world production by more than three percentage points, to 7.8 per cent in 1950 (see Table 3.2). It is no surprise that it chose to deepen its pattern of transformation. This meant, on the one hand, a more conscious industrialization drive and, on the other, an explicit choice for a less interventionist state than in other parts of the world. The second statement may seem paradoxical. However, the options in the post-War period were not between state intervention and a return to a liberal past, but rather between central planning and mixed economies with more moderate forms of state intervention. Latin America chose the latter that is, less rather than more state intervention.

The term 'import-substitution industrialization' has been widely used to characterize the period from the end of the Second World War to the 1970s. However, this is not a very helpful label, as the new policies were much more about an expanded role of the state than about import substitution. Second, protectionism and industrialization already had a long past in Latin America. Third, exports continued to play a fundamental role, not only as a source of the foreign exchange and, in mineral economies, government financing, but also of economic growth, particularly in the smaller economies. Also, in some medium and large countries, export promotion was introduced as an essential component of development strategy since the mid-1960s, generating a 'mixed model' that combined import substitution with export promotion. The model was also mixed in the sense that it actively promoted agricultural modernization with similar instruments to those used to encourage industrialization. On top of that, there was often no net import substitution during the process and import substitution was not always the leading source of growth, even in new industries, whereas domestic demand played a more consistent role.

Therefore, state-led industrialization is a more useful label for the new development strategy (Thorp 1998a; Cárdenas et al. 2000b). The state assumed, indeed, a broad set of responsibilities. In the economic area, apart from intervention in trade and foreign exchange markets, they included an enlarged (even a monopolistic) role in the development of infrastructure; the creation of commercial and development banks, and the design of mechanisms to force private financial institutions to channel funds to priority sectors; and the encouragement of domestic private enterprise through protection and government contracts. In the social area, it included a larger role in the provision of education, health, housing and, to a lesser extent, social security.

The process also included major social and political transformations. Falling mortality rates and a lagged transition in fertility generated strong population pressures, with population growth peaking at 2.8 per cent a year from the mid-1950s to the mid-1960s, combined with rapid urbanization, the fastest in the developing world. Power structures were redefined in the context of a more urban society and new state-business relations. Old and new adverse trends in wealth and income distribution were reflected in the explosion of both old rural tensions and the development of new urban-based conflicts.

A theory of state-led industrialization was articulated in the late 1940s and early 1950s by the United Nations Economic Commission for Latin America (or CEPAL, its Spanish acronym),[4] under the leadership of Raúl Prebisch. This theory had major repercussions throughout the developing world, and on international theoretical and policy debates, particularly

---

[4] Throughout, we will use the Spanish acronym rather than the English one, ECLA, later ECLAC, when the Caribbean joined the organization.

through its influence (and that of Prebisch) on the United Nations Conference on Trade and Development (UNCTAD). However, many patterns, ideas, and practices predated the creation of CEPAL. As a historian of economic thought has put it, 'Industrialization in Latin America was fact before it was policy, and policy before it was theory' (Love 1994: 395). In any case, CEPAL brought about a theoretical defence of the new strategy, together with a sense of regional identity. Its defence of industrialization was more a theory of capital accumulation than of economic efficiency.[5] In particular, industrialization was seen as the mechanism to transfer technical progress from the centre to the periphery of the world economy, in the face of the slow growth and adverse terms of trade of primary commodity markets.

However, from the late 1950s, CEPAL became an early critic of the excesses of substitution and state intervention, and an advocate of rationalizing import substitution through active export strategies and regional integration. As such, it played a central role in the design of the Latin American Free Trade Association (ALALC, its Spanish acronym, later the Latin American Integration Association), the Central American Common Market and the Andean Group. CEPAL also helped to press for reforms in the social area, many of which were adopted later by the US Alliance for Progress.

Furthermore, CEPAL's views on industrialization and state intervention agreed, to a large extent, with contemporary wisdom, which identified development with industrialization (Love 1994). Moreover, during the Second World War, the US backed the push for industrialization in Latin America, and US private interests were not entirely against the new trend after the war, as they saw the opportunities for selling capital goods to Latin America and investing in protected markets. Furthermore, the World Bank supported state interventionism, invested in many import substitution projects and continued to defend, up to the late 1970s, the idea that industrialization was essential to economic development (Webb 2000).

The strategy also responded to the circumstances surrounding the early post-Second World War years. The marginalization of Latin America from the early post-Second World War priorities (Thorp 1998b) was compounded by the fact that, despite favourable short-term trends, continued reliance on primary exports did not seem a good alternative in light of past trends. Since the mid-1950s, the renewed downward trend of

---

[5] In his semi-autobiographical book, Furtado (1989) provides a fascinating early history of CEPAL. Evaluations of CEPAL's contributions have been done by Fishlow (1985), Love (1994), Bielschowsky (1998) and Rosenthal (2004).

commodity prices generated a new wave of balance of payments crises. In the face of repressed demand, the foreign exchange reserves accumulated during the Second World War soon vanished, generating a sense that the balance of payments constraint—the dollar shortage—was as much a Latin American as a European reality. Inconvertibility in European countries was an additional restriction in the early post-Second World War years for those countries for which Europe was the main export market.

On the other hand, high levels of protection were still the rule in the industrialized countries and it was clearly necessary to undergo a long period of continuous growth in international trade to convince countries and authorities that had lived through its collapse to regard it as a reliable alternative. Although the General Agreement on Tariffs and Trade (GATT) was signed in 1947, the failure of the US Congress to ratify the creation of the International Trade Organization (ITO) killed the idea of a stronger world trade institution for several decades. Furthermore, it soon became clear that the areas in which developing countries had more export potential—agriculture and textiles—would be exceptions to trade liberalization within GATT. All of these helped to frame the export pessimism that characterized the post-War years and the sense that import substitution efforts were essential to overcome the persistent balance of payments constraints.

Although largely self-centred, particularly in its early stages, the golden age of growth in the industrial centre trickled down to the developing countries, opening, in particular, opportunities for manufacturing exports from the periphery. Mechanisms were also designed to enhance the diffusion of progress to the periphery, particularly the Generalized System of Preferences (GSP) and commodity agreements. Additionally, although the growth of the international financial system concentrated largely on financial transactions among developed countries, since the mid-1960s, it began to offer alternatives to multilateral banks and bilateral agencies, the major source of financing since the 1940s.

After the Cuban Revolution, Latin America became more central to US foreign policy. The creation of the Inter-American Development Bank (IDB) was the most immediate manifestation, soon followed by the Alliance for Progress, launched in Punta del Este, Uruguay in 1961. As was pointed out, this initiative largely adopted the agenda that CEPAL had been pushing since the 1950s, including mixed economy planning, regional integration, agrarian reform, tax reform, and greater investment in social sectors. But the flow of funds was less than promised, and the tied character of US aid soon became a source of friction.

Phases and Diversity of Industrialization Experiences

Latin American industrialization went through four different stages. The first was as a natural by-product of export expansion and, as we saw, depended on the linkages generated by the export sectors, on market size and integration, and on domestic protection. The second was an empiricist phase of state-led industrialization, largely induced by pragmatic responses of policy-makers to the external shocks of the 1930s. Import shortages during the Second World War also generated several plans to promote new industries and reduce import dependence, particularly in sectors considered essential or strategic.

Despite abundant foreign exchange reserves, balance of payment crises soon became a recurrent issue in the post-Second World War years. The evaporation of dollar exchange reserves in the face of repressed import demand was followed by the new commodity price shock of the mid-1950s. Following the experience of the 'empiricist phase', external adjustment requirements followed a pattern by which each crisis increased the level of protection. Now, however, a more conscious industrialization strategy came into existence, based on a variable mix of instruments that had been tried before: tariff and non-tariff protection; multiple exchange rates and rationing of foreign exchange; development banks and regulations on the allocation of private lending and interest rates; tax incentives and public sector investment in infrastructure and in strategic sectors, including energy. New instruments were also designed, including 'laws of similars' that essentially prohibited imports of competitive goods, and requirements for established industries to purchase domestic raw materials and intermediate goods that is, trade-related investment measures (TRIMs) in WTO terminology. This classic stage of state-led industrialization lasted from the late 1940s to the early 1960s in most medium-sized and larger economies.

An essential characteristic of the model was that, instead of changing the structure of protection to promote new industries, new layers of protection for new sectors were superimposed on older layers, generating a geological pattern of protection that would become an essential characteristic of state-led industrialization in Latin America. This was obviously due to the political economy that characterized the process, in which protection for a specific sector was viewed as a permanent conquest by the sector that benefited from it. The cumbersome system of protection that developed was not exempt from criticism, including that of CEPAL.

The major rationalization of the structure of protection during this period was regional and sub-regional trade integration. According to

CEPAL's original view, regional integration would reduce the costs of import substitution by increasing the size of the market, a critical element for the more advanced sectors of import substitution in the larger economies, but also to generate industrialization at all in the smaller economies. Additionally, it was expected that integration would impose some market discipline on protected sectors, which easily became subject to high levels of industrial concentration (even monopolies) at the national level, and as would serve as a platform to develop new export activities, particularly in manufacturing.[6]

However, the Central American Common Market aside, regional integration soon manifested in the same political economy questions that rationalization of protection generally faced. After a few successful multilateral rounds in the early 1960s, the Latin American Free Trade Area faced strong national opposition to the liberalization of competitive imports. Thus in its later stages, it concentrated on bilateral agreements among member countries to facilitate complementary imports. The Andean Group faced similar pressures after its creation in 1969 and thus concentrated on intraregional trade liberalization of competitive imports.

Export pessimism was also a feature of this classical period, but there were significant regional differences. A few countries aside, the 1945–55 export record was dismal. However, the picture improved significantly from the mid-1950s, particularly for small economies, which experienced rapid export growth since then (Table 3.4). Indeed, for many economies, particularly the Central American economies, import substitution was basically superimposed on what essentially remained a primary export model. Thus, the strong downward trend in the share of exports in GDP, that characterized the first decade after the end of the Second World War, was reversed from the mid-1950s in the small economies, and stabilized in many medium-sized ones after that.

The mixed views on the opportunities that exports provided were not extended to foreign direct investment (FDI), where a policy of promoting investment by multinationals in new import substitution activities became a central ingredient of state-led industrialization in Latin America. FDI was also seen as a reliable source of private external financing in a world economy that offered few opportunities of that sort. However, many countries in the region simultaneously took an increasingly hard line stand against traditional forms of foreign investment in natural

---

[6] During the Second World War, the interruption of supplies from industrial countries had generated an active intraregional trade in manufactures, as well as some manufacturing exports from Mexico to the US. However, this experience languished soon in post-War period (Thorp 1998b).

TABLE 3.4
Latin America: Exports and GDP Growth (simple averages)

	1945–55	1956–65	1966–73	1974–80
Export Growth (%)				
Large and medium countries excluding Venezuela	1.8	4.6	4.7	6.3
Small countries	1.5	7.0	7.4	2.6
Total excluding Venezuela	1.7	5.8	6.1	4.4
Venezuela	4.2	7.8	–2.2	6.4
Total	1.8	5.8	5.5	4.7
GDP Growth (%)				
Large and medium countries excluding Venezuela	5.2	4.3	5.5	4.7
Small countries	4.6	4.5	5.3	4.1
Total excluding Venezuela	4.9	4.4	5.4	4.4
Venezuela	9.9	6.9	3.7	1.7
Total	5.2	4.5	5.3	4.3

Source: CEPAL.

resources and infrastructure. The control of natural resources would be a recurrent issue in the region. Thus, Latin America did not reject FDI, but directed it according to perceived national interests, and indeed the region attracted the largest flows of FDI to the developing world.

The fourth phase can be characterized as the mature stage of state-led industrialization. However, the dominant characteristic of this period was the increasing diversity of regional trends. Three major strategies can be differentiated, which were sometimes adopted sequentially in individual countries, with the first oil shock as the turning point. A fourth strategy was central planning, but Cuba was an isolated case in this regard. We will thus concentrate on the other strategies.

The first and dominant trend, particularly from the mid-1960s to the first oil shock—and the closest to the views of CEPAL—gave increasing emphasis to export promotion, generating what we have called a mixed model. In a sense, this made the strategy of the medium and larger economies closer to that which the smaller countries had followed even during the classical period. This strategy built on existing integration agreements, but particularly on the new opportunities provided by the growing imports of light manufactures by industrialized countries.

Following established patterns, the new strategy imposed a new layer of export incentives on the old layers of protection, which included a mix of tax incentives (particularly tariff drawbacks and rebates), free trade zones, credit facilities and export requirements on firms. Generally, this was accompanied by some rationalization of the pre-existing structure of protection and foreign exchange management (particularly, the unification or simplification of the multiple exchange rate system) and by a more active exchange rate policy, including a more flexible exchange rate system, the crawling peg, to manage recurrent overvaluation in inflation-prone economies.

Interestingly, the revalorization of the role of exports was now accompanied by a more mixed view of FDI. The idea that domestic investors should play a central role in new manufacturing sectors had been present since the Second World War, particularly in countries where there was a militarist view of strategic sectors (Argentina and Brazil). In many cases, this role was actually assumed by state firms. However, the defence of national, vis-à-vis foreign, investors got increasing attention in the 1960s and 1970s, and was linked with placing limits on royalties and profit remittances, widely associated with the view that multinationals were getting excessive benefits from their investments in the region. The nationalizations of the copper industry in Chile and of the oil industry in Venezuela in the early 1970s were part of a pattern that had older roots. It should be emphasized, nonetheless, that Latin America continued to receive close to 70 per cent of all FDI flows to the developing world in 1973–81 (Ocampo and Martin 2004: Table 3.2).

The second strategy was to further deepen import substitution. Peru is the best example of a country that opted for a more inward-oriented policy in the late 1960s, against regional trends. We should add the ambitious industrial investment plans in intermediate and capital goods of Brazil, Mexico, and Venezuela after the first oil shock, which was accompanied, in any case, by a major export drive in Brazil and in the latter two countries by booming oil revenues.

The third strategy was a frontal attack on the role of the state in economic development. Indeed, since the mid-1960s, there has been a gradual shift in intellectual debates towards a more liberal view of economic policies. As in the nineteenth century, liberal economics was not always married with liberal politics. This was reflected in the Southern Cone countries (Argentina, Chile, and Uruguay), where major market-based reforms in the second half of the 1970s were accompanied by military dictatorships.

Economic and Social Performance Under State-led Industrialization

Latin American economic performance during the three and a half decades that followed the Second World War was remarkable. GDP grew by 5.5 per cent per year in 1950–80, or 2.7 per cent per capita (Table 3.5). As a result of fast growth, the Latin American share of world production continued to increase, reaching close to 10 per cent in 1980, two percentage points more than three decades earlier (see Table 3.2). Per capita income growth lagged behind the world average up to the mid-1960s, but exceeded it after that. The manufacturing sector was the engine of growth, reaching a peak share of 26 per cent of GDP in 1973, seven percentage points more than in 1945, a feature shared by all countries.

TABLE 3.5
Latin America: Growth and Productivity, 1950–2002

	1950–80	1980–90	1990–2002
GDP Growth			
Weighted average	5.5	1.1	2.6
Simple average	4.8	1.0	2.9
GDP Per Capita			
Weighted average	2.7	−0.9	1.0
Simple average	2.1	−1.2	0.9
GDP Per Worker			
Weighted average	2.7	−1.7	0.1
Simple average	2.4	−1.9	0.0
Total Factor Productivity[a]			
Weighted average	2.0	−1.4	0.2
Simple average	1.9	−1.4	0.6

Note: [a] Argentina, Bolivia, Brazil, Chile, Colombia, Costa Rica, Ecuador, Mexico, Peru, and Venezuela.

Sources: CEPAL. Total factor productivity (TFP) according to Hofman (2000) and author's database.

The temporal pattern of GDP growth was a very rapid recovery in the early post-War period, interrupted by a series of balance of payments crises. Then, growth stabilized for the region as a whole somewhat above 5 per cent. In the late 1960s and early 1970s, there were clear signs of acceleration, reaching a peak in 1968–74 (7.2 per cent yearly, or 4.2 per cent per capita annually). Furthermore, although growth slowed down after the first oil shock, it continued to be very fast (5.0 and 2.5 per cent, respectively), particularly if the reference is worldwide slowdown then in place. However, as we will see, its foundations were becoming increasingly shaky. Growth was not uniform among countries. Slow growth in the success stories of the export age (Argentina, Chile, Cuba, and Uruguay) led to some convergence in per capita income among the largest countries. However, this tendency aside, there was actually a divergence in per capita GDPs between 1950 and 1980 (Table 3.3).

Along with growth came labour productivity gains. Labour productivity increased at an annual rate of 2.7 per cent in 1950–80 (Table 3.5). This reflected both capital accumulation and technical change. Total factor productivity increased rapidly up to 1973, but slowed down after that. Productivity performance was comparable or superior to that of the US, but below the most dynamic developed market economies and the East Asian newly industrialized countries (NICs) (Hofman 2000: Chapter 6). Productivity growth was part of a larger process of development of technological capabilities, which involved technological transfer, but also the adaptation and induced generation of technologies (Katz and Kosacoff 2000). Manufacturing exports since the 1960s can hardly be understood without taking into account this accumulation of technological capabilities.

Institutional development underwent a similar, dynamic process (Thorp 1998a: Chapter 5). With a few exceptions, modern Latin American economic institutions are the product of this stage of development. In the social area, although there were precedents in the export age, the extension of universal basic education, development of modern health, labour training and, to a lesser extent, social security systems received a significant push during state-led industrialization. While labour unions and entrepreneurial organizations had been born during the export age, they expanded during this period, together with the extension of modern business–labour relations.

Agriculture was not absent from this story of productivity growth and institutional development. Despite its lower growth record, agricultural production grew at an annual rate of 3.5 per cent in 1950–75, faster than the world average, but with significant differences in the performance of different countries (CEPAL 1978). Although macroeconomic and pricing policies generated biases against agriculture, the development of new state institutions to support agriculture was remarkable and its positive effects tended to predominate. Such institutions included technological, credit and marketing services, sometimes more developed than those designed to support industrial development. This was particularly the case for technological services, which were quite effective in introducing new crops and improving cultural practices. Tax policy, including lower tariffs on agricultural inputs and machinery, was generally supportive of agriculture. An open agrarian frontier and large state-financed infrastructure also played a role in many countries.

On the other hand, the major drawback of state-led industrialization was its inability to fully exploit the benefits from dynamic world trade in the post-War period. Latin America's share of world trade approximately halved between 1950 and 1980.[7] Failure to share in the benefits from the expansion of trade in primary commodities was the main explanation of this decline (Table 3.6 and Ffrench-Davis, Muñoz, and Palma 1998). Since export growth in many small countries was dynamic (see Table 3.4), this overall trend was mainly determined by the large countries. Argentina, the leader in the export age, had dismal export performance up to the mid-1960s. Brazil's record was no better, but this was part of a longer-term trend, going back to the early twentieth century. Mexico also had very poor export performance from the mid-1950s to the mid-1970s. Venezuela, a major Latin American exporter by the 1960s, reduced its exports of oil in the 1970s as the result of its entry into the Organization of Petroleum Exporting Countries (OPEC).

The policy shifts of the 1960s in several medium and large-sized countries towards a mixed model had positive effects in terms of export dynamism. Rising manufacturing exports to industrial countries and intra-regional trade was the major result of this shift, leading to an increase in the share of manufacturing in total exports (see Table 3.6 and CEPAL 1992). In the largest countries, this included exports of machinery and equipment to other Latin American countries, as well as of technology, in the form of licences and engineering services. New agricultural products were also added to the export basket in many countries.

The inability to rationalize the complex pattern of import protection had important costs. For established industries, import protection ceased to play a positive role as an incentive to capital accumulation, and increasingly became a source of rent and/or defence against cyclical or permanent exchange rate overvaluation—and of high industrial concentration. Moreover, it distorted the relative price shifts necessary to induce import substitution and export diversification, and forced it to rely

---

[7] There are significant differences in available statistics, but all of them show a strong downward trend from the end of the Second World War to the 1970s. The IMF series indicate that the share of Latin America in world trade increased from 7.9 per cent in 1938 to 12.2 per cent in 1948, 11.7 per cent in 1950 and back to 7.8 per cent in 1960. UNCTAD's series, which has a larger coverage, indicates that it was 10.9 per cent in 1950, 6.7 per cent in 1960 and an average of 4.3 per cent in the 1970s. Maddison's (2001) estimates indicate, on the other hand, that the share of Latin America in world trade increased from 7.9 per cent in 1929 to 9.3 per cent in 1950 and then fell to 3.9 per cent in 1973.

TABLE 3.6
Latin American Exports, 1953–2000

	SITC	1953	1958	1963	1968	1973	1980	1990	2000
Latin American Export Composition									
Total	0–9	100.0	100.0	100.0	100.0	100.0	100.0	100.0	100.0
Food	0+1	52.7	46.0	37.8	38.0	38.6	26.9	21.7	13.3
Raw materials excldg fuels	2+4	19.4	17.3	18.4	16.2	15.4	11.9	11.9	6.9
Fuels	3	19.6	28.1	31.4	27.0	21.2	37.5	26.1	17.0
Chemicals	5	1.2	1.0	1.4	1.9	2.6	2.9	5.1	4.7
Machinery	7	0.1	0.2	0.6	1.3	4.6	6.0	11.7	35.8
Other manufactures	6+8	6.8	6.9	10.2	15.4	17.0	14.3	23.0	21.8
Latin America/Developing Countries									
Total	0–9	35.9	32.8	30.5	23.2	19.2	14.9	15.0	18.1
Food	0+1			43.2	42.1	41.1	36.9	30.9	37.5
Raw materials excldg fuels	2+4			25.1	23.8	22.5	24.4	29.6	30.3
Fuels	3			45.1	25.8	16.5	12.1	18.3	14.6
Chemicals	5			20.5	13.6	12.2	12.2	11.0	15.8
Machinery	7			4.0	3.2	7.7	9.1	8.5	20.1
Other manufactures	6+8			14.0	13.8	11.7	11.9	10.4	13.4
Latin America/World									
Total	0–9	10.1	8.3	6.8	5.5	4.7	4.8	3.7	5.7
Food	0+1	23.9	19.4	15.1	15.2	13.1	12.5	9.3	12.0
Raw materials excldg fuels	2+4	11.0	9.3	9.2	8.3	7.4	8.5	9.0	11.8
Fuels	3	19.5	20.4	27.0	18.0	11.4	9.3	11.5	9.7
Chemicals	5	2.7	1.5	1.4	1.4	1.6	1.8	2.0	2.8
Machinery	7	0.0	0.1	0.2	0.2	0.7	1.1	1.2	4.9
Other manufactures	6+8	2.6	2.2	2.5	2.9	2.7	2.7	2.9	4.7

Note: SITC = Standard international trade classification codes.
Sources: United Nations. *Yearbook of International Trade Statistics, 1958*; and author's
    calculations from UN-COMTRADE.

excessively on non-price instruments, including TRIMs. The system of
protection was also partially self-defeating in terms of its explicit objective
of reducing dependence on imported inputs and technology, and may have

actually increased it. The system lacked the concept of protection as a time-bound instrument and the related idea of the need to tie incentives to performance.

Regional integration facilitated the dynamic growth of intraregional trade in manufactures in the 1960s and 1970s. The major benefits were associated to the creation of larger markets for complementary goods, but the liberalization of competitive goods was limited by domestic protectionism, with the Central American Common Market as a major exception. Moreover, the attempts to plan the production of new complementary investments aimed at the regional or sub-regional markets were, almost invariably, outstanding failures.

The rise of multiple exchange rate systems in the early post-Second World War period made the exchange rate system a fairly close substitute for trade policy. The ability to implicitly tax competitive imports and traditional exports, and to subsidize complementary imports, using exchange rates as an instrument, was attractive in terms of administrative convenience. Export taxation was a particularly difficult issue and, indeed, in most countries, discriminatory exchange rates were the only means available to tax exports. In this area, however, there were significant improvements since the mid-1950s (under strong IMF pressure) and, particularly, in the mature stage, when most multiple exchange rate regimes were simplified or eliminated.

Contrary to the view of overvaluation as a central feature of state-led industrialization, Jørgensen and Paldam (1987) have shown that there was *not* a tendency towards long-term appreciation of the real official exchange rate in any of the eight largest Latin American countries during 1946–85.[8] A more worrisome feature was the very sharp fluctuations around long-term trends in the real exchange rate, particularly in the more inflation-prone economies (particularly Brazil and the Southern Cone countries), a pattern that the introduction of the crawling peg in the 1960s tried to change. Real exchange rate instability certainly had adverse effects in terms of generating stable incentives for new exports, and generated an additional demand by import-competing sectors for protection, as a defence against cyclical real exchange rate appreciation.

In social terms, the standard of living experienced the fastest rates of improvement ever experienced by Latin America during this period, as

[8] On the contrary, according to their results, there were real long-term devaluations in Brazil and Venezuela. Most importantly, there were discreet devaluations of the real exchange rates of several countries in the early post-War period that had permanent effects (Mexico in 1948, Peru in 1949–50, Brazil in 1953, Chile in 1956, Colombia in 1957, and Venezuela in 1961).

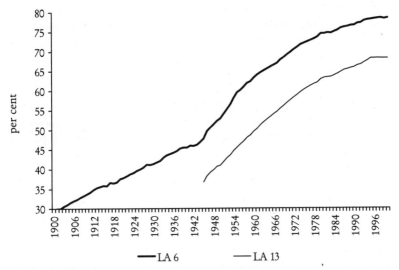

Figure 3.1   Latin America: Living Standard Index Relative to USA

Notes: LA6: Argentina, Brazil, Chile, Colombia, Mexico, and Venezuela; LA13: Bolivia,
Costa Rica, Ecuador, Dominican Republic, Guatemala, El Salvador, Haiti,
Honduras, Nicaragua, Panama, Paraguay, Peru, and Uruguay.
Source: Astorga, Bergés, and FitzGerald (2003).

estimated by GDP per capita, adult literacy and life expectancy indicators
(see Figure 3.1 and Astorga, Bergés, and Fitzgerald 2003). Furthermore,
despite the lack of convergence in per capita GDP levels, there was a
significant convergence in living standards across the region during 1950–
80 (see Table 3.3).

Contrary to the fears that were constantly expressed, employment
generation was reasonably dynamic. The non-agricultural labour force
grew at a very fast rate in 1950–80, 4 per cent per year, faster than that
experienced by the US between 1870 to 1910. Although this was reflected
in growing informality in the cities, the reduction of employment in
traditional agriculture was very rapid, generating a reduction in overall
(urban and rural) underemployment, from 46 per cent in 1950 to 38 per
cent in 1980 (García and Tokman 1984). In a sample of fourteen countries
analysed by these authors, nine experienced reductions in underemployment, generally associated with dynamic growth, some with more and
others with less intensity.

The benefits from rural modernization concentrated in the hands of
large landowners, thus reproducing a highly skewed distribution of income

and wealth in rural areas that had long historical roots. There were several agrarian reforms, the most ambitious being associated to major social and political change.[9] Other processes, many of them induced by the Alliance for Progress in the 1960s, were less ambitious. Small rural producers also benefited in many countries producing food for the cities, from interior colonization in countries with open spaces—promoted as part of, but really as a substitute for agrarian reform—and, most importantly, from migration to the cities. Indeed, the modernization of the rural sector, together with rapid population growth, produced the unlimited supply of labour—a feature that, as we have seen, was absent in most countries during the export age.

The generation of a labour surplus also had major implications for international migration. Although a few countries continued to attract Europeans, particularly Venezuela during its long oil boom, the old international migration flows lost dynamism after the First World War. The share of Latin American residents born outside the region experienced long-term decline since the 1960s as a result of the death of old immigrants and return migration. At the same time, intraregional migration increased, with Argentina and Venezuela becoming the major poles of attraction, particularly for populations in neighbouring countries. More importantly, emigration to industrialized countries took off. In the 1970s, the stock of migrants from Latin America and the Caribbean to the US increased from 1.7 to 4.4 million, with geographical proximity a major determinant of the relative significance of such flows.

The record in terms of poverty reduction and, particularly, income distribution was mixed but, unfortunately, there are significant data gaps in this area. Poverty probably declined in most countries through the period of state-led industrialization, although with significant lags in several cases. CEPAL's first overall estimate of poverty, available for 1970, indicates that 40 per cent of Latin America's households were poor; this proportion declined to 35 per cent in 1980 (around 40 per cent of the population, given the larger size of poor households), a level which has not been reached again in the following decades. In any case, income distribution remained highly skewed in most cases and experienced opposite patterns towards the end of the period in different countries. Social progress certainly trickled down to a 'middle class', which included the urban population employed by the state and by large and middle-sized private firms and some small entrepreneurs, with the extent of that

---

[9] Mexico in the 1930s, Bolivia in the 1950s, Cuba in the 1960s, Chile and Peru in the 1960s and early 1970s, and Nicaragua in the 1980s.

'middle class' varying considerably from country to country according to the level of development.

THE NEO-LIBERAL ORDER
A New Debt Crisis, A New Transition

The transition from state-led industrialization to the neo-liberal order was faster than that from the export age to state-led industrialization. It involved several interrelated factors. First, in sharp contrast to the previous transition, theory predated policies, and both experienced increasing radicalization for some time. Moreover, there was explicit institutional backing for the new policies at the global level, through the World Bank, which played the central role in pressing for structural reforms in the 1980s. There were also, as previously, demonstration effects from the industrial world, particularly by the Thatcher and Reagan Administrations.

The second factor was rising social conflict, but the links are less clear in this case, and involved a more limited number of countries. The Southern Cone countries were the epicentre of conflict in the early 1970s, and the earlier champions of reforms, but they had also been the worst performers during the period of state-led industrialization. In Central America, where conflicts exploded somewhat later, they were more rural in character and rooted in land concentration and, perhaps, in the primary export model, rather than in its peculiar marriage with weak state-led industrialization.

A third factor was associated with the constraints state-led industrialization faced in its mature stage, associated with both increasing foreign exchange and investment requirements, and an endemically low savings rate. Both trends are shown in Figure 3.2. In the 1970s, the region continued to grow at rates similar to those of the previous two decades, but only by running an aggregate trade deficit, compared to the small surplus characteristic of the 1950s and 1960s. Also, the same growth momentum was associated with a higher investment ratio.

Nonetheless, it is unlikely that without the debt crisis, any Latin American economy would have collapsed from the sheer weight of the inefficiencies of state-led industrialization. But, even more importantly, it is unclear why Latin America could not have embraced a more balanced strategy, as in the smaller countries from the mid-1950s and in most medium and large economies from the mid-1960s. Indeed, something closer to the equally protectionist and state-led, but outward-oriented models of the Asian tigers could have evolved, with success in building an export base. In any case, such an alternative was overtaken by other events.

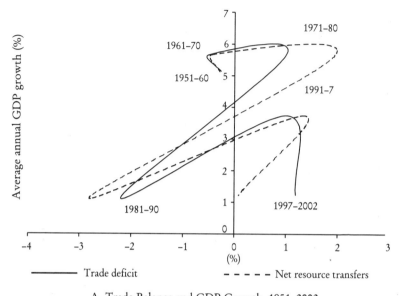

A. Trade Balance and GDP Growth, 1951–2002

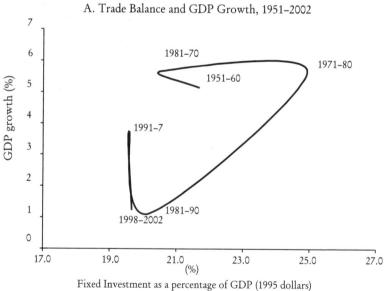

Fixed Investment as a percentage of GDP (1995 dollars)

B. Fixed Capital Investment Ratio and GDP Growth, 1951–2002

Figure 3.2 Latin America: Growth, Investment, and Trade Balance, 1951–2002

Source: CEPAL

Another constraint faced by state-led industrialization was the tendency to overburden the state with fiscal responsibilities without adequate resources. As Fitzgerald (1978) has argued, this was reflected in three outstanding trends:

(i) a rise in government expenditure as a proportion of GDP, but with a lower proportion for welfare compared to industrialized countries;

(ii) a shift in tax composition away from property and income taxes to indirect and wage taxation; and, as a consequence,

(iii) rising borrowing requirements to finance transfers to the private sector, rather than progressive redistributive policies.

Besides the aforementioned processes, a fourth factor, the sharp boom-bust cycles of the 1970s and 1980s, played a crucial role in the transition. A notable feature of the quarter-century after the Second World War was the absence of significant external financing. As Figure 3.3 indicates, net resource transfers were slightly negative throughout the 1950s and 1960s. In the context of recurrent external shocks, the lack of adequate means to finance balance of payments deficits, including very moderate IMF financing, obviously reinforced the temptation to use protectionist policies as a mechanism of adjustment. Those countries that had better access to external financing, Mexico, in particular, also developed foreign debt problems early on.

This period of scarce external financing was followed by the extremely sharp boom-bust cycle of the 1970s and 1980s, which had only one precedent, the external financing cycle of the 1920s and 1930s. The low, sometimes negative, real interest rates of the 1970s, and their coincidence with strong commodity prices through most of the decade—particularly, but not exclusively, for petroleum—generated strong incentives to use external financing on a large scale (Ffrench-Davis, Muñoz, and Palma 1998). In fact, Latin America absorbed more than half the private debt that flowed into the developing world during 1973-81, mostly as long-term syndicated loans from commercial banks and as short-term funds (Ocampo and Martin 2004: chapter 3). Meanwhile, it continued to be the region in the developing world attracting the largest FDI flows.

Internally, this high demand for external funds was associated, as we have seen, with rising trade deficits as well as saving-investment and fiscal gaps. The domestic financial institutions intermediating external funds were accumulating growing financial risks, but this new trend was due to domestic financial liberalization, rather than state-led industrialization, and thus became most troublesome in the Southern Cone countries. The extent of exchange controls and their capacity to cope with the incentives for capital flight that the crisis generated have also been important. Capital

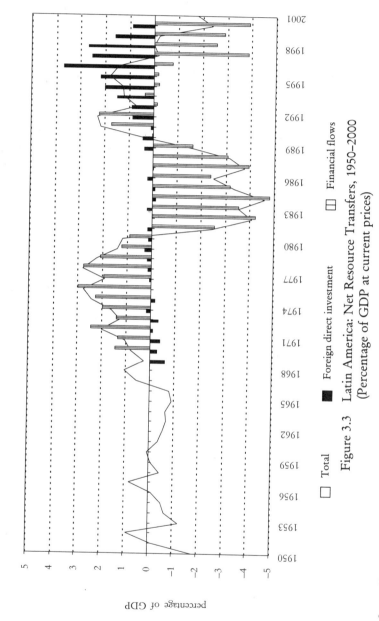

Figure 3.3 Latin America: Net Resource Transfers, 1950–2000 (Percentage of GDP at current prices)

□ Total   ■ Foreign direct investment   ▨ Financial flows

Source: ECLAC estimates, on the basis of IMF, *International Financial Statistics.*

flight became massive in Argentina, Mexico, and Venezuela, which lacked significant controls on capital movements.

The weight of these internal factors proved crucial in determining the relative impact of the debt crisis of the 1980s in different countries. This indicates, in turn, that it was macroeconomic dynamics, rather than distortions in the protection structure that proved critical. Furthermore, the fact that the export economies of Latin America had faced similar difficulties in managing a sharp external financial cycle in the 1920s and 1930s and that the liberalized economies would face a similar phenomenon in the 1990s, indicates that the propensity to boom and bust in the face of unstable external financing is a fairly general phenomenon, and certainly not a particular feature of state-led industrialization.

In any case, it was the external dynamics that proved critical in the end (CEPAL 1996: chapter 1). The turning point was the 1980 decision of the US Federal Reserve Board to sharply raise interest rates to cut inflation. This had a direct effect on the debt service and the current account deficits, as a large share of the debt had floating interest rates. In turn, it unleashed a strong recession in the industrial world and a new adverse structural downturn in real commodity prices (Ocampo and Parra 2003). The interest rate shock had no precedents. A strong recession in industrial countries and structural breaks in terms of trade did have precedents, but only in the somewhat distant past in the latter case. Therefore, the magnitude of the ex post risks that Latin America had to assume was not only unexpected, but also hard to foresee. Debt dynamics turned explosive after the interest rate shock: the debt ratios, which had been rising steadily through the 1970s, but remained bearable, experienced sharp upward shifts in the early 1980s (Figure 3.4).

The situation quickly became critical due to the persistence of the debt crises as well as the slow and weak international policy responses. The joint effect of the sudden stop in external financing, that lasted a decade, and rising debt service obligations was a massive external shock, which transformed previously positive net resource transfers, equivalent to 2 to 3 per cent of GDP, into net negative outward transfers of 4 to 5 per cent of GDP (Figure 3.3). Díaz-Alejandro (1984) summed up the developments as follows: 'What could have been a serious but manageable recession has turned into a major development crisis unprecedented since the early 1930s mainly because of the breakdown of international financial markets and an abrupt change in conditions and rules for international lending. The non-linear interactions between this unusual and persistent external shock and risky or faulty domestic policies led to a crisis of severe depth and length, one that neither shocks nor bad policy alone could have

Figure 3.4 Latin American External Debt Dynamics, 1970–2000
(External Debt as a Proportion of GDP and Exports)

Source: Author's calculations based on IMF *International Financial Statistics* and CEPAL.

generated'. Thus, an enduring feature of international financing, its severe instability, served to kill both the export age and state-led industrialization!

A comparison with the 1930s indicates that the negative resource transfer was the critical factor then too. As Figure 3.5a indicates, the opportunities to increase real export income were greater in the 1980s than in the 1930s. Thus, the major difference with the Great Depression was that the massive capital account shock saw no solution in sight. IMF financing and, more broadly, official financing came to the rescue, in larger magnitudes than in the past, but they were modest relative to the effects of the sharp reversals of private resource transfers. Furthermore, the emergency official resource infusions came with unprecedented structural conditionalities. In 1930s, debt moratoria had been the solution for all countries except Argentina. In 1980s, Latin American countries considered the possibility of forming a debtors' cartel, but never took the necessary decisive steps. Debt write-offs eventually came, but in moderate magnitudes, and often too late, after the debt crisis had done major damage. As a result, whereas the trade surpluses that the Latin American economies were forced to generate in the 1930s were small and temporary, in 1980s, they were forced to generate large trade surpluses for close to a decade (Figure 3.5b).

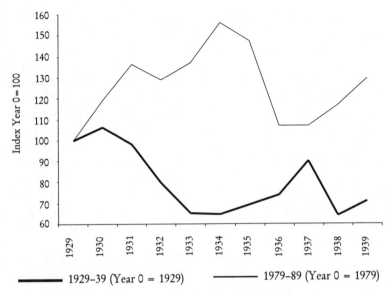

A. Trade balance FOB as a percentage of exports
(minus average of previous decade)

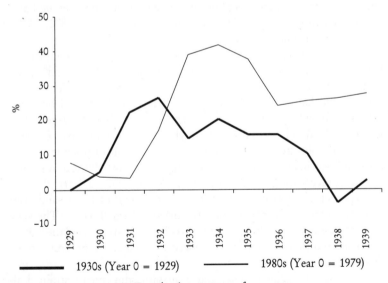

B. Purchasing power of exports
(exports deflated by manufactured prices index, MUV)

Figure 3.5   A Comparison of Two Crises: The 1980s and the 1930s

Four stages can be distinguished in the evolution of the debt crisis. Up to September 1985, there were massive adjustments, initially based on the assumption that the crisis was only temporary in nature. There was also an effective creditors' cartel, backed by the industrialized countries, which saw serious risk of contagion due to the high exposure of their banks in Latin America (180 per cent of the capital of the nine largest US banks). Due to the asymmetrical nature of the debt negotiations, Latin American countries ended up nationalizing large parts of the private external debt. In September 1985, the first Baker plan was announced, including structural adjustment led by the World Bank, better financial conditions and modest additional resources. The insufficiency of the package led, two years later, to a second Baker plan, which added debt buybacks, exit bonds with low interest rates, and debt swaps. The final stage only came in March 1989 with the Brady plan, which included a (modest) debt reduction (Ffrench-Davis, Muñoz, and Palma 1998).

Although the last two initiatives finally led to reductions in the debt ratios (Figure 3.4), the earlier trend of rising debt had already been reversed by large trade and current account surpluses, at the cost of a lost decade in terms of economic growth (Table 3.5). The share of Latin America in world GDP, which had been increasing for more than a century, fell by 1.6 percentage points, as per capita incomes in Latin America, which had remained stable relative to the US since 1870, fell by seven percentage points (Table 3.2).

The recession was initially strong. A moderate recovery took place in 1984–7, but it was followed by renewed difficulties at the end of the decade. Only a few countries were able to renew growth on a stable basis in the second half of the 1980s, generally those with small debt ratios (Colombia) or where external official lending was relatively large (Chile and Costa Rica). The social effects of the crisis were massive. Poverty increased sharply, from 40.5 per cent to 48.3 per cent of the population. This trend was made worse by worsening income distribution in several countries, exacerbating an already poor distribution record. Formal sector real wages fell in most countries—sharply in several of them—and even more employment was pushed into the urban informal sector. The very rapid progress in relative living standards that had characterized the period of state-led industrialization was replaced by a far more modest rate of progress (Figure 3.1).

Massive fiscal, exchange rate, and monetary adjustments strained already vulnerable structures. The real exchange rate depreciation necessary to support external adjustment was invariably accompanied by rising inflation, of magnitudes that Latin America had not known before. Five countries ended up experiencing one or two episodes of hyperinflation from the mid-1980s to the early 1990s (Argentina, Bolivia, Brazil, Nicaragua, and Peru). Financial sector restructuring was also massive, particularly in the Southern Cone countries, generating fiscal and quasi-fiscal costs equivalent to 40 to 50 per cent of GDP. Internal distribution issues were closely tied to the need to transfer resources to the government to service the external debt and to clean up the domestic financial meltdown. This transfer was easier in countries with direct access to export earnings (basically through state firms that exported oil and minerals), where governments benefited directly from devaluation. In other countries, there was an internal transfer problem (transferring enough fiscal resources for government debt service) that was particularly difficult to manage (CEPAL 1996).

Increasing Integration into the World Economy[10]

As we have seen, the Southern Cone countries had taken the first steps towards neo-liberal reforms, and there has been a broader trend towards rationalization of existing state interventions in the 1970s. The debt crisis led to some backtracking, particularly towards renewed use of protection as a mechanism for adjustment. Thus, it was only in the mid-1980s that liberalization took off in the region as a whole and gained speed over time. A decade later, the policy scenario had totally changed. Although the launching of the Baker Plan, and the structural reforms agenda of the World Bank on which it was based, played a central role, a sense of ownership by governments of the reform agenda was clearly present. Indeed, the democratic wave in Latin America from the mid-1980s adopted the neo-liberal agenda as its own. Unlike nineteenth century patterns and the experience of the 1970s, liberal economics was now matched with liberal politics.

There were divergences between the nature of the reforms and the new forms of state regulation emerging in various countries. Significant liberalization was evident in all countries in trade, external capital flows and the domestic financial sector. In the tax area and, particularly, with privatization and labour markets, reforms were less ambitious and more diverse, with social security reforms somewhere in between. Reforms led to deeper integration of Latin America into the world economy. From 1990 to 2000, the region posted the fastest growth of export volumes in its history (close to 9 per cent per year), leading to an increased Latin American share in world markets for the first time since the export age, as well as significant

[10] For a more extensive analysis of the issues presented in this and the following section, see CEPAL (2003), Ocampo (2004), and Stallings and Peres (2000).

diversification towards manufacturing (Table 3.5). At the same time, the region became a magnet for FDI (Figure 3.3).

Dynamic participation in world trade was matched by active participation in international negotiations and promotion of new trade agreements, with regional integration leading the way. Existing agreements experienced a virtual collapse in the early 1980s, but this was followed by revitalization of existing agreements in the later part of that decade, and a wave of new agreements, particularly the constitution of the Southern Common Market (Mercosur) in 1991 and a myriad of free trade deals. Between 1990 and 1997, intraregional trade boomed, particularly in the two major South American integration processes, Mercosur and the Andean Community (by 26 and 23 per cent per year, respectively). The expansion of trade within the two South American trade integration blocs was abruptly interrupted after the East Asian crisis hit the region in 1997, giving way to strong fluctuations in intraregional trade and weakening commitments to regional integration.

An additional innovation was the rise of free trade agreements with industrial countries, led by Mexico and Chile. As the North American Free Trade Area (NAFTA) came into force in 1994, the US launched the initiative to create a Free Trade Area of the Americas (FTAA), involving all countries in the region except Cuba. However, negotiations have been slow and, by the early 2000, US-led regional integration remained effectively fragmented in a series of bilateral or multilateral agreements with the US.

Export expansion has involved two basic patterns of specialization, which approximately follow a regional North–South divide. The Northern pattern, shared by Mexico, and several Central American and some Caribbean countries, is characterized by manufacturing exports with high content of imported inputs (in its extreme form, *maquila* exports), mainly geared towards the US market. This pattern goes hand in hand with traditional agricultural exports and agricultural export diversification in Central America, as well as the growth of tourism in Mexico and the Caribbean.

The Southern pattern, typical of South American countries, is characterized by a combination of extraregional exports of commodities and natural-resource-intensive (and, in many cases, also capital-intensive) manufactures, and active intraregional trade, dominated by manufactures. In case of Brazil, this has been mixed with some technology-intensive manufactures and services. There is also a third pattern of specialization, in some Caribbean economies, in which service exports (financial, tourism, and transport services) predominate.

Trade specialization and FDI patterns have been closely linked. Thus, the Northern specialization pattern has attracted multinationals actively involved in internationally integrated production systems, whereas in South America, investment has concentrated in services and natural resources. FDI has included large shares of acquisitions of existing assets, first through privatization and then through private buyouts. A corollary of this process has been the rapid increase in participation of foreign firms in production and sales, at the expense of public sector firms in the first half of the 1990s, and of both public and private firms in the second half.[11]

Labour emigration to the industrial countries, particularly the US, is another salient feature of the new forms of integration into the world economy. Flows of Latin American labour to the US, which had picked up at the end of the period of state-led industrialization, now became a torrent, induced both by push (the debt crisis of the 1980s and civil wars in Central America, and also the new slowdown since the Asian crisis) as well as pull factors. Thus, the number of immigrants of Latin American and Caribbean origin in the US increased from 4.4 million in 1980 to 8.4 million in 1990 and 14.5 million in 2000; another 25 per cent or more can be added to this figure to account for illegal migrants. There have also been flows to more distant destinations, particularly Western Europe (with a former source country, Spain, becoming the most significant destination), Canada and Japan. The number of Latin American and Caribbean emigrants to more distant destinations has been estimated by CEPAL at 2.8 million in 2000. The 1990s also saw renewed moderate intraregional flows. A major result of these developments has been the rapid rise of remittances as a major source of foreign exchange for Latin America. They have increased from US$1.9 billion in 1980 to US$5.7 billion a decade later, US$19.2 billion in 2000 and around US$33 billion by 2003, that is, over 1 per cent of total GDP, but much higher in some, especially smaller economies.

Poor Macroeconomic Performance and Social Gains from the Reforms

Success in increasing its shares in world markets and in attracting FDI was accompanied by advances in some macroeconomic areas, particularly improvements in fiscal conditions and reductions in inflation rates.

---

[11] Thus, according to CEPAL estimates based on the sales of the largest thousand firms operating in the region, the share of foreign firms increased constantly, from 29.9 per cent in 1990–2 to 41.6 per cent in 1998–2000. The share of domestic private firms increased from 37.7 to 42.7 per cent during the first half of the decade, but then fell to 41.3 per cent. That of public sector firms fell continuously, from 32.5 to 17.1 per cent.

However, success in all these areas did not lead to rapid economic growth. Indeed, the average growth rate of 2.6 per cent a year during 1990–2002 is less than half of that for the period of state-led industrialization (Table 3.5). Against the background of the lost decade of the 1980s, this means that Latin American income levels have diverged from those of industrialized countries for almost a quarter of a century. It also means that the share of Latin America in world GDP has remained stagnant at the reduced levels reached after the lost decade of the 1980s (Table 3.2).

A major reason for the poor growth performance has been the weakening of the link between GDP growth and external resource transfers or, what is equivalent, between GDP growth and the trade balance. As we have indicated, this link had already weakened in the 1970s (dynamic growth continued only on the basis of a higher trade deficit and increasing resource transfers), but it further deteriorated in 1990–7 compared to the 1970s (much lower growth but with similar trade deficits and resource transfers) and, once again, in 1998–2002. This was determined by a series of adverse trends in the productive structure: (a) the decline in import substitution industries, which has not been counterbalanced by faster export growth; (b) the high demand, in dynamic sectors, for imported capital and intermediate goods, a trait of internationally integrated production systems, which, together with the previous factor, has reduced production linkages; and (c) the weakening of the national innovation systems inherited from the preceding stage of development, as engineering functions and research and development that used to be performed by local firms have been transferred out of the region; this factor predominated over positive technological trends, particularly the rapid growth of connectivity. As a result of these factors, the multiplier effect and the technological externalities generated by the high-growth activities associated with exports and FDI have been weak. In a sense, the new dynamic activities are enclaves of globalized production networks, which have so far proved incapable of inducing rapid overall economic growth.

Slow growth has been matched by poor productivity performance (see Table 3.5). Productivity did increase in dynamic firms and sectors, with contributions by external competition, FDI and privatization. However, contrary to the expectations of reformers, positive productivity shocks did not spread, but instead led to greater variation in productivity levels in the economies. The growing number of world-class firms, many of them subsidiaries of transnational corporations, was thus accompanied by the growth of low-productivity informal-sector activities, which accounted for seven out of every ten new jobs created in Latin American urban areas over the 1990s. This growing dualism in productive structures also reflects the fact that restructuring was not neutral in terms of its impact on different economic agents.

An additional adverse feature of macroeconomic performance has been greater sensitivity to the volatility of external financing. The renewal of capital flows in the early 1990s was interrupted briefly in 1995 and more permanently since the Asian crisis, leading to negative transfers through financial flows, similar in magnitude to those of the lost decade of the 1980s. FDI has served as a compensatory factor for some time, but its sharp fall in the early 2000s generated large negative overall net resource transfers in 2002–3 for the first time in more than a decade (Figure 3.3).

Volatile external financing was transmitted domestically through pro-cyclical fiscal and, particularly, monetary and credit policy, in a clear return to a pattern typical of the export age. This also resulted in a greater propensity towards domestic financial crises, reflected in their greater frequency, a phenomenon that hit half the Latin American countries during the 1990s (CEPAL 2003: chapter 3). Moreover, as domestic savings have remained depressed, investment has become highly dependent, at the margin, on external savings. Fixed investment rates experienced partial recovery in 1991–7, but nonetheless remained below the average for the 1970s, and fell again, in 1998–2002, to levels similar to those of the 1980s (Figure 3.2b).

Growth has followed these major swings in external financing. Thus, the period of fair economic growth in 1990–7, of 3.6 per cent a year, which was, in any case, significantly below the average for 1950–80, was followed by a broad-based slowdown in 1998–2002. Since 1998, per capita GDP has contracted for Latin America as a whole and for half the countries in the region. Furthermore, all patterns of rapid growth have been interrupted, including those of Chile and the Dominican Republic, the two most dynamic economies in Latin America in the 1990s. In social terms, the adverse effects of slow economic growth and structural transformation have tended to prevail over the positive effects of rising social spending, with living standards following the modest improvements that have characterized the 1980s, rather than the more rapid improvement of the period of state-led industrialization (Figure 3.1).[12]

The most problematic feature has been weak employment growth. In this regard, the Northern pattern of specialization in manufactures (and some services) has proved much more effective in generating employment, particularly wage-labour employment, in tradable sectors, than the Southern specialization in natural-resource-intensive goods. Open unemployment

[12] For a full evaluation of social trends, see CEPAL (1997 and 2001).

rose by almost three percentage points during the 1990s and shot up in some countries, particularly after major external shocks. Indicators of deterioration in job quality are even more widespread, as shown by the rising share of urban informal sector employment, which rose from 43.0 to 48.4 per cent in the 1990s. This deterioration is also evident in the relative increase in temporary employment, in reduced coverage of social security systems, particularly for workers in small enterprises, and even in the number of individuals working without written labour contracts. The poverty rates, which had shot up during the last decade, declined to 43.5 per cent in 1997, although the number of poor stagnated at roughly 200 million. These positive trends in poverty were sharply reversed in 1998–2002, when some 20 million more fell below the poverty line. Whereas per capita GDP has exceeded 1980 levels by some 6 per cent, poverty rates have remained three percentage points above pre-debt-crisis levels in recent years. This is a reflection of the adverse trends which income distribution has continued to face. Indeed, although comparing data on income distribution over long periods of time is a complex matter, there is no country in the region where inequalities have declined relative to what they were three decades ago; on the contrary, there are many countries where it has increased. There are, however, considerable dis-agreements as to why distribution has tended to deteriorate. Some studies emphasize the adverse distributive effects of the structural reforms, but others focus on more global trends associated with technological and other factors influencing wage/skill differentials.[13] In light of the previous analysis, rising dualism is certainly an important link between structural reforms and the deterioration in income distribution.

In any case, the messianic tone with which reforms were heralded (Balassa et al. 1985; Edwards 1995) and the early positive evaluations of the reforms, prompted by the recovery of economic growth in 1990-7 (IDB 1997; Burki and Perry 1997), have been followed by extensive revaluation of these earlier assessments (CEPAL 2003; Kuczynski and Williamson 2003). The mere comparison of the recent growth record with that achieved during state-led industrialization contradicts the expectations that neo-liberal reforms would accelerate economic growth. Indeed, it is symptomatic of the weakness of this association that even supporters of economic liberalization now regard the state-led industrialization period as a golden age, and the growth rates achieved during that period as a goal for future Latin American performance (Kuczynski and Williamson 2003: 29, 305). Beyond that, and despite the stronger democratic forces that

[13] See, for example, Altimir (1997), Berry (1998), Morley (2001), CEPAL (1997, 2001), and IDB (1999).

characterize the new order, the new paradigm has, if anything, ended up reinforcing the worst structural feature of Latin America, a feature that the two preceding forms of integration into the world economy had also exacerbated, that is, its very unequal distribution of income and wealth.

REFERENCES

Aceña, Martín Pablo and Jaime Reis (eds), (2000), *Monetary Standards in the Periphery: Paper. Silver and Gold, 1854–1933*, St. Martin's Press, New York.

Altimir, Oscar, (1997), 'Desigualdad, empleo y pobreza en América Latina: efectos del ajuste y del cambio en el estilo de desarrollo', *Desarrollo económico*, 37 (145), Buenos Aires, Institute of Economic and Social Development (IDES), April–June.

Astorga, Pablo, Ame R. Bergés, and Valpy FitzGerald, (2003), 'The Standard of Living in Latin America During the Twentieth Century', Working Paper Series No. 103, Latin American Centre, University of Oxford, March.

Bairoch, Paul and Bouda Etemad, (1985), *Structure par produits des exportations du Tiers-Monde*, Centre d'Histoire Economique Internationale, Université de Genève, Geneve.

Balassa, Bela, Gerardo M. Bueno, Pedro-Pablo Kuczynski, and Mario Henrique Simonsen, (1986), *Toward Renewed Economic Growth in Latin America*, Institute for International Economics, Washington, DC.

Berry, Albert, (1998), *Confronting the Income Distribution Threat in Latin America: Poverty, Economic Reforms, and Income Distribution in Latin America*, Lynne Rienner, Boulder.

Bértola, Luis and Jeffrey G. Williamson, (2003), 'Globalization in Latin America before 1940', NBER Working Paper No. 9687, National Bureau of Economic Research, Cambridge, MA.

Bielschowsky, Ricardo, (1998), 'Cincuenta años de pensamiento de la CEPAL', in *Cincuenta años de pensamiento de la CEPAL*. Fondo de Cultura Económica-CEPAL, Santiago.

Bulmer-Thomas, Victor, (2003), *The Economic History of Latin America since Independence*, second edition, Cambridge University Press, Cambridge.

Burki, Shahid Javed and Guillermo E. Perry (eds), (1997), *The Long March: A Reform Agenda for Latin America and the Caribbean in the Next Decade*, World Bank Latin American and Caribbean Studies Viewpoints, Washington, DC.

Cárdenas, Enrique, José Antonio Ocampo and Rosemary Thorp (eds), (2000a), *The Export Age: The Latin American Economies in the Late Nineteenth and*

Early Twentieth Centuries, An Economic History of Twentieth Century Latin America, Volume One, Palgrave Press for St. Antony's College, Basingstoke.

——, (2000b), *Industrialisation and the State in Latin America: the Post War Years. An Economic History of Twentieth Century Latin America*, Volume Three, Palgrave Press for St. Antony's College, Basingstoke.

Cardoso, Fernando Henrique, and Enzo Faletto, (1979), *Dependency and Development in Latin America*, University of California Press, Berkeley.

CEPAL, (1978), *25 años en la agricultura de América Latina: Rasgos principales 1950–1975*. Cuaderno No. 21, Economic Commission for Latin America and the Caribbean, Santiago.

—— (1992), *El comercio de manufacturas de América Latina: evolución y estructura 1962–1989*. Estudios e Informes de la CEPAL, No. 88, Economic Commission for Latin America and the Caribbean, Santiago.

—— (1996), *The Economic Experience of the Last Fifteen Years: Latin America and the Caribbean, 1980–1995*, Economic Commission for Latin America and the Caribbean, Santiago, July.

—— (1997), *The Equity Gap: Latin America, the Caribbean and the Social Summit*, Economic Commission for Latin America and the Caribbean, Santiago.

—— (2001), *Social Panorama of Latin America, 2000–2001*, Economic Commission for Latin America and the Caribbean, Santiago.

—— (2002), *Globalization and Development*, Economic Commission for Latin America and the Caribbean, Santiago, April.

—— (2003), *A Decade of Light and Shadow: Latin America and the Caribbean in the 90s*, Libros de la CEPAL, No. 76, Economic Commission for Latin America and the Caribbean, Santiago.

Coatsworth, John H. and Jeffrey G. Williamson, (2004), 'Always Protectionist? Latin American Tariffs from Independence to Great Depression', *Journal of Latin American Studies*, Vol. 36.

Cortés-Conde, Roberto, (1997), *La economía argentina en el largo plazo*, Editorial Sudamericana, Universidad de San Andrés, Buenos Aires.

Díaz-Alejandro, Carlos F., (1988), 'Latin American Debt: I Don't Think We are in Kansas Anymore', reprinted in Andrés Velasco (ed.), *Trade, Development and the World Economy: Selected Essays of Carlos F. Díaz-Alejandro*, chapter 15, Basil Blackwell, Oxford.

Edwards, Sebastián, (1995), *Crisis and Reform in Latin America: From Despair to Hope*, Oxford University Press for the World Bank, New York.

Ffrench-Davis, Ricardo, Oscar Muñoz, and Gabriel Palma, (1998), 'The Latin American Economies, 1959–1990', in Leslie Bethell (ed.), *Latin America: Economy and Society since 1930*, Cambridge University Press, Cambridge.

Fishlow, Albert, (1985), 'El estado de la ciencia económica en América Latina', in IDB, *Progreso Económico y Social en América Latina*, chapter 5, Inter-American Development Bank, Washington, DC.

FitzGerald, Edmund Valpy K., (1978), 'The Fiscal Crisis of the Latin American State', in John F. J. Toye (ed.), *Taxation and Economic Development*, Frank Cass, London.

Furtado, Celso, (1976), *Economic Development of Latin America: A Survey from Colonial Times to the Cuban Revolution*, Second Edition, Cambridge University Press, Cambridge.

—— (1989), *La fantasía organizada*, Tercer Mundo Editores, Bogotá.

García, Norberto, and Victor Tokman, (1984), 'Transformación ocupacional y crisis', *Revista de la CEPAL*, No. 24, December.

Gerchunoff, Pablo, and Lucas Llach, (1998), *El ciclo de la ilusión y el desencanto; un siglo de políticas económicas argentines*, Ariel Sociedad Económica, Buenos Aires.

Haddad, Claudio L.S., (1980), 'Crecimiento economico do Brasil, 1900–76', in P. Neuhaus (ed.), *Economia Brasileira: Uma Visao Histórica*, Editora Campus, Rio de Janeiro.

Hatton, Timothy J. and Jeffrey G. Williamson, (1994), 'International migration, 1850–1939: An economic survey', in T. J. Hatton and J. G. Williamson (eds), *Migration and the International Labour Market, 1850–1939*, Routledge, London.

Hofman, André, (2000), *The Economic Development of Latin America in the Twentieth Century*, Edward Elgar, Cheltenham, UK.

IDB, (1997), *Latin America After a Decade of Reforms, Economic and Social Progress in Latin America 1997*, Inter-American Development Bank, Washington, DC.

—— (1999), *Facing Up to Inequality in Latin America, Economic and Social Progress in Latin America 1998–1999*, Inter-American Development Bank, Washington, DC.

Jørgensen, S.L. and Martin Paldam, (1987), 'The Real Exchange Rates of Eight Latin American countries 1946–1985: An interpretation', *Geld und Wärung* (Monetary Affairs) 3(4), December.

Katz, Jorge and Bernardo Kosacoff, (2000), 'Technological Learning, Institution Building and the Microeconomics of Import Substitution', in Enrique,Cárdenas, José Antonio Ocampo, and Rosemary Thorp, (2000b), *Industrialisation and the State in Latin América: the Post War Years. An Economic History of Twentieth Century Latin America*, Volume Three, chapter 2, Palgrave Press for St. Antony's College, Basingstoke.

Kuczynski, Pedro-Pablo and John Williamson (eds), (2003), *After the*

Washington Consensus: Restarting Growth and Reform in Latin America, Institute for International Economics (IIE), Washington, DC, March.

Lewis, William Arthur, (1969), *Aspects of Tropical Trade, 1883–1965*, Wicksell Lectures, Almqvist & Wicksell, Stockholm.

Love, Joseph L., (1994), 'Economic Ideas and Ideologies in Latin America since 1930', in Leslie Bethel (ed.), *The Cambridge History of Latin America* 6(1), Cambridge University Press, Cambridge.

Maddison, Angus, (1995), *Monitoring the World Economy, 1820–1992*, OECD Development Centre, Paris.

—— (2001), *The World Economy: A Millennial Perspective*, OECD Development Centre, Paris.

Marichal, Carlos, (1989), *A Century of Debt Crisis in Latin America: From Independence to the Great Depression, 1820–1930*, Princeton University Press, Princeton.

Morley, Samuel, (2001), *The Income Distribution Problem in Latin America and the Caribbean*, Libros de la CEPAL, No. 65, Santiago.

Ocampo, José Antonio, (2004), 'Latin America's Growth and Equity Frustrations During Structural Reforms', *Journal of Economic Perspectives*, Vol. 18, No. 2, spring.

Ocampo, José Antonio, and Juan Martin (eds), (2004), *Globalization and Development: A Latin American and Caribbean Perspective*, Stanford University Press, Stanford.

Ocampo, José Antonio and María Angela Parra, (2003), 'The Terms of Trade for Commodities in the Twentieth Century', *CEPAL Review*, No. 79, April.

O'Connell, Arturo, (2000), 'Argentina into the Depression: Problems of an Open Economy', in Rosemary Thorp (ed.), *An Economic History of Twentieth Century Latin America, Volume 2, Latin America in the 1930s: The Role of the Periphery in World Crisis*, chapter 8, Palgrave Press for St. Antony's College, Oxford.

Palma, Gabriel, (2000), 'Trying to "tax and spend" oneself out of the "Dutch Disease". The Chilean Economy from the War of the Pacific to the Great Depression', in Enrique Cárdenas, José Antonio Ocampo and Rosemary Thorp (eds), *The Export Age: The Latin American Economies in the Late Nineteenth and Early Twentieth Centuries. An Economic History of Twentieth Century Latin America*, Volume One, chapter 8, Palgrave Press for St. Antony's College, Basingstoke.

Rosenthal, Gert, (2004), 'ECLAC: A Commitment to a Latin American Way Towards Development', in Yves Berthelot (ed.), *Unity and Diversity in Development Ideas: Perspectives from the UN Regional Commissions*, United

Nations Intellectual History Project Series, Indiana University Press, Bloomington.

Rowe, J. W. F., (1965), *Primary Commodities in International Trade*, Cambridge University Press, Cambridge.

Stallings, Barbara and Wilson Peres, (2000), *Growth, Employment and Equity: the Impact of the Economic Reforms in Latin America and the Caribbean*, The Brookings Institution, Washington, DC, and CEPAL/Fondo de Cultura Económica, Santiago.

Sunkel, Osvaldo and Pedro Paz, (1976), *Subdesarrollo latinoamericano y la teoría del desarrollo*. Ninth edition, Siglo Ventiuno, Mexico, DF.

Thorp, Rosemary, (1998a), *Progress, Poverty and Exclusion: An Economic History of Latin America in the 20th Century*, Johns Hopkins University Press for Inter-American Development Bank, Baltimore.

—— (1998b), 'The Latin American Economies, 1939–c.1950', in Leslie Bethell (ed.), *Latin America: Economy and Society since 1930*, Cambridge University Press, Cambridge.

—— (ed.), (2000) *An Economic History of Twentieth Century Latin America, Volume 2, Latin America in the 1930s: The Role of the Periphery in World Crisis*, Palgrave Press for St. Antony's College, Oxford.

Triffin, Robert, (1968), *Our International Monetary System: Yesterday, Today, and Tomorrow*, Random House, New York.

United Nations, (1955), *Foreign Capital in Latin America*, Department of Economic and Social Affairs, New York.

Webb, Richard, (2000), 'The Influence of International Financial Institutions on ISI', in Enrique Cárdenas, José Antonio Ocampo, and Rosemary Thorp (eds), *Industrialisation and the State in Latin America: the Post War Years. An Economic History of Twentieth Century Latin America*. Volume Three, chapter 4, Palgrave Press for St. Antony's College, Basingstoke.

4

Africa in the Long Twentieth Century

Bill Freund

If we consider modern African history from the perspective of a 'long century', panning developments from the Berlin Conference of 1884 and the occupation of Egypt in 1882 through the period of colonial occupation, to cover a generation and more of national independence, colonialism must loom very large as a dominant factor. Through this chronological intervention, the latest phase becomes 'post-colonial', rather than a fundamentally new era on its own. Whether this kind of perspective will hold up into the future is probably a question that must be answered in the manner of Chou En-Lai's famous riposte to the question about the influence of the French Revolution: it is too early to say.

Colonialism was, up to a point, a revolution that remade Africa, but many African specialists as well as commentators on Africa qualify this in stressing the continuities of culture and society that override modernist impulses affecting Africa from top down. One finds this perspective both in pejorative accounts of Africa and in the effusions of pan-African nationalists, both of whom equally insist on the essential identity of Africa as a whole (but typically with the Sahara, not the Mediterranean, as its real northern boundary). The persistence of beliefs about the body that pre-date the arrival of biomedicine, continuity in relationships between men and women, patterns of discourse about authority and power, the stuff of typical anthropological study, in fact, points to significant levels of continuity which can be legitimately stressed in some kinds of assessment.

Another point of view, one with which I would be identified (Freund 1984, 1994), stresses instead a modernist perspective, and sees a wave of transformation irrevocably affecting key parts of Africa. However, this must not be confused with a particularly rosy view of what modernism is. 'Development', in my view, inevitably involves loss as well as gain in human terms, and certainly is likely to impose new forms of differentiation and conflict in Africa, just as it has elsewhere. Nor has development imposed itself in Africa with anything like the success it has enjoyed in post-Second World War Asia. Conducted on lines that do represent significant continuity with the colonial period after national independence; it has been at best a very faltering process.

However, I continue to believe that the colonial period does represent, on the whole, a big historical break that changed material life progressively, and substantially caused the integration of Africa into the wider world. Indeed, until this point, it is strongly arguable that Africa was only a geographical expression. It did acquire a kind of unity and its articulate elites acquire some sense of commonality in the world, precisely through the colonial experience and what followed. Whether Africans are 'more or less' alike, is a question that is not raised as often as it should be, in part because consciously or subconsciously, the identity of Africa is linked to the notion of a coherent African biological race, even today. It is, for instance, acceptable in scholarly circles sympathetic to African nationalism, sometimes to consider people of visibly African descent as African regardless of their actual material or cultural life and activities or where they live.

In fact, it may be more helpful to break up Africa into (still geographically very extensive and varied) regions. North Africans and Egyptians are Africans, whatever their skin colour, and Muslim West Africans from the savannah feel relatively more at home with them than they would with South Africans of any colour. Malagasy and Mauritians, of whatever descent, must be considered as Africans, not as people who somehow don't belong. Highland Ethiopians speak languages structurally closer to Hebrew than Kikongo or Yoruba, but they are still very much Africans. Nor can Africa be understood if one excludes Kenyans of Asian origin or South Africans of European origin from one's reckoning, or simply insist on them as intruders.

The nature of this chapter perhaps does not allow scope for emphasizing the diversity of Africa and Africans as much as I would like to do. Instead, for the purposes of this limited discussion, I will try largely to emphasize time, rather than space, and to consider the long century in terms of what temporal subcategories emerge from the historical literature as the most significant.

However rapid and dramatic the onset of colonial rule in Africa after 1880 was, it needs to be stressed that it was preceded by significant events and trends that foreshadowed later changes. One of these, paradoxically, was the gradual decline of the slave trade, which had come to dominate African commerce with other continents. While the slave trade went very well together with the development of a limited number of commercial entrepôts, it did not require, indeed it repelled, the sort of systematic rule that colonialism entailed. In West Africa, the dominance of slaving resulted, generally, in a decline in European knowledge of and direct contact with the peoples of the interior and promoted the significance of intermediaries. At most, the slave trade era promoted certain trade routes and the development of what we might call social capital connected to its financial requirements, which would continue beyond the decline of slave trade per se.

By contrast, the subsequent period of so-called legitimate trade encouraged an era of European commercial exploration, which usually involved trying to learn more about the economic potential of hitherto unknown parts of Africa. If A.G. Hopkins' studies of West Africa (Hopkins 1973) are convincing in showing how the extension and then, crisis and breakdown in trade there led to aggressive fingers poking into the interior, we have to add the possibilities created by improved bio-health techniques for outsiders in the African environment and the emergence of paid bodies of African troops in the service of colonial power and equipped with the technology of an industrial age, for which local armies were rarely any match. In other parts of Africa, explorers discovered territory that contained potential for European settler agriculture and the availability of important raw materials, especially minerals, useful for European economic development. Exploiting these possibilities, more important in southern, central, and eastern Africa than trade interests, required eliminating local political power and creating colonial rule to introduce, protect and extend such activities.

Less obvious today, however, are the African precursors of colonialism. In fact, colonial rule was preceded by the dramatic expansion of some form of government by African conquerors themselves. In West Africa, this is linked in a way difficult to disentangle from pressures emanating from outside with a series of religious revolutions that created formidable states of unprecedented size and scope. The Sokoto Caliphate created in the first decade of the nineteenth century, if one accepts its federal structure as belonging to a single political entity, certainly ruled more Africans, millions of subjects, than any previous African state ever had. It administered a huge territory and sustained a very varied range of economic activities and substantial urban populations. Elsewhere, we must look at the predatory, but not uncreative growth, often quite spectacular, of the Egypt of Muhammad Ali and his successors, of Minilik's Ethiopia, of the unification of most of Madagascar under Radama I, of the activities conducted under the flag of the Sultans of Zanzibar and then the kingdoms that began to emerge in the zone of ivory production extending from the Great Lakes or the ephemeral empire of Samory in Mali and the Ivory Coast, as they are today constituted. In southern Africa, whites, preceded by groups of mixed race, emanated from the Cape Colony in the process known as the Great Trek. Their movements helped to bring about a process of state formation (Lesotho, Swaziland, Kwa Zulu) among various African people in the process of reforming. Almost all of these initiatives depended on the acquisition of new weaponry. In the making were large new states emerging through violence: a kind of African pre-partition. Had colonial rule not advanced so fast, much of Africa would have been partitioned by these emerging continental powers, swallowed up by the bigger fish.

THE LONG CENTURY AND COLONIALISM

By the start of the First World War, only one of these African powers survived as an independent entity: Ethiopia, cut off, to its discomfiture, from the sea. Everywhere else, the drawing of lines on the map in Europe was followed by colonial occupation and the triumph of imperialism, buoyed by cultural self-confidence and intellectual supremacy at home. In Africa, conquest was not immediately followed by the taking of immense profits. On the contrary, it was soon clear that without the institution of infrastructure, the seizure of land and water resources and the harnessing of significant amounts of labour, a capitalist system could not progress, and outside capitalism, what the French call the *economie de traite*, trade derived from existing forms of resource extraction, produced limited results.

Moreover, the pioneer phase of colonialism was in fact conducted in a context of hardship and disaster. Many parts of Africa (Kenya, mainland Tanzania, Namibia, Zimbabwe, most of the Portuguese colonies, the constituent parts of French Equatorial Africa) were at first administered by chartered companies, willing to impose their rule by force with few scruples, but unable and unwilling to make expenditures only yielding long-term results. This experiment with company rule was typically disastrous and led to violent encounters such as the Abushiri Rising along the Mrima coast of Tanzania in 1888–9. In most cases, direct colonial rule followed.

The most notorious extreme example was in the huge space of the Congo Basin (Ascherson 1963 Hochschild 1998). Here, the King of the Belgians, Leopold II, was able to create a supposed free trade zone under the auspices of the Congo Free State through deft diplomatic manoeuvring. The Free State expanded its rule through forests and savannas by force, paid for by the obligatory collection of wild rubber, 'red rubber'. The envy of other powers was a major reason why this regime finally ended in 1908 in scandal, following exposure of abuses. It was the Belgian state, in accordance with the king's wishes, which then took over the territory. By this time, moreover, a rail and boat system through Belgian territory had been created for evacuating the immense copper reserves of Katanga province in the extreme south of the territory to the advantage of big capital in Belgium.

In many regions, however, the onset of colonialism went together with hardship, disease and social disruption on a large scale, which represented the African component of a wave of historic disaster that went together with imperial aggression (Davis 2000). In particular, the establishment of roads and railways and towns required very substantial amounts of what the British called 'political labour'—forced labour that often operated, especially in the early phases, under very brutal conditions. Conquest itself, especially outside the confines of large well-organized states, was often very disruptive of African life in every sense of the word. Evidence suggests that in much of central and eastern Africa as well as parts of West Africa, a serious demographic decline characterized the last decades of the nineteenth and the early twentieth centuries.

However, there were some important exceptions to this. In West Africa, where conquest had to some extent reflected pressures from commercial interests and had the support of the comprador trading class of the coastal towns, the logic of colonial conquest was beneficial to new economic forces. Before the end of the nineteenth century, African cultivators had begun to plant substantial quantities of cocoa trees in the forest hinterland of the Gold Coast. Systematic growing of kola trees near the rail line beyond Lagos represented commercial expansion within the new Nigerian economy. There was a new prosperity, even if the lion's share of benefits accrued to a small number of concentrated imperial trading, shipping, and financial interests.

In South Africa, the dominant event of the period was the Second Anglo-Boer War. The interior republics, especially the South African Republic north of the river Vaal, may have been heading towards the establishment of more exclusivist and one-sided racial social orders than in the old Cape Colony, but they were an impediment, all the same, to British imperialism. The Republic potentially had a very substantial economic capacity once immense gold mines began to be discovered within its borders from 1885. The war, which followed a British ultimatum, was immensely destructive and violent, notorious for the extent to which Boer families were herded into concentration camps, where disease spread rapidly and lethally.

However, the Witwatersrand gold mines, with their immense requirements of men and money, pulled in an unprecedented amount of capital to one corner of the African continent. The Randlords and the professional strata around them began to situate themselves relatively permanently in the new economic centre of Johannesburg. Post-War reconstruction under imperial auspices furthered the development of a transport system, of capitalist agriculture and of the social and commercial infrastructure appropriate to an industrial society through swathes of southern Africa. The number of gold miners before the First World War reached 200,000 and the majority were recruited through a structured policy aimed at capturing migrant circulatory labour over a huge area (Crush, Jeeves, and Yudelman 1991). Skilled miners were at first largely immigrants, but were gradually replaced by local whites on a dramatically, if not always formalized, racist basis. These latter were in turn, incorporated into the political system in stages (Yudelman 1983). In 1910, the Union of South Africa was established; it gave all whites political rights within a context where international relations, military affairs, and the economic high ground fitted the Union's role within the British Commonwealth. The wealth of the Rand made possible a more rapid transition to capitalism in much of southern Africa than elsewhere. Disruption and displacement were part of this picture, but the social application of new forms of wealth was greatly heightened.

COLONIAL CAPITALISM AND ITS ANTITHESIS

As colonial rule in Africa stabilized, it did so in terms of a conservative quid pro quo (Phillips 1989). Given the absence of pots of gold at the end of most rainbows, colonial administrators came, to a very large extent, to rely on a manipulated form of traditional authority, as it was called, to maintain stability on a shoestring in most colonies. 'Chiefs', sometimes powerful men from pre-colonial polities, sometimes literally promoted gardeners and cooks, were placed in positions of considerable patrimonial power, while 'native law', shorn of elements seen as indecent by Europeans, became the basis of day-to-day administration. In general, native law excluded such possibilities as individual Africans acquiring property rights in land outright, especially outside towns; as such, it ironically became a means for holding capitalism at bay. Africans were expected to make some contribution to the economy measurable in cash, but colonialism did not wish to turn them into proletarians or to transform their societies beyond a point. The colonial ethos of indirect rule, promoted especially systematically by the British, took on the form of a political philosophy. Indirect rule covered up the worst abuses of the colonial system. For instance, the continued survival of slavery as an institution often permitted the continuance of forced labour systems through to the Second World War via African recruiters. However, it also provided a legitimate social structure where representation from new classes was scarce or absent. One model for indirect rule was Lord Lugard's federal Nigeria; another, slightly older, was Natal Colony and the so-called Shepstone system for administering 'the Zulu' there, but British experience in India was generally a potent historical model whereby European imperialism could rest on a minimum of European state expenditure and troops from home (cf. Mamdani 1996). Resting on this structure, the inter-War years were very much more peaceful in colonial Africa.

Probably the chief exception, largely to be found in eastern and central Africa, lay in those colonies where European settlers arrived and received privileged treatment, including large allotments of land, rising to a majority of the land in the country in the case of South-West Africa (Namibia) and half in the case of Southern Rhodesia (Zimbabwe, land settlement of 1930). Even in West Africa, old towns found themselves encircled and effectively dominated by new, largely or entirely racially exclusive zones reserved to official and non-official Europeans in many cases. Elsewhere, accommodating even relatively small numbers of whites meant large-scale commitments on the part of colonial administrations and provoked intense potential conflict. Nevertheless, settler societies, such as Southern Rhodesia and Kenya and, in a later period, the Belgian Congo and Angola, saw far more of a transition to capitalism and the provision of more industrial and other forms of sophisticated economic, institutional, and infrastructure development. The lodestar of settler Africa was, of course, South Africa, where between 1910 and the mid-1930s, there was substantial movement towards erecting a systematic process of what was called segregation between the races, in which the fruits of modern development were largely restricted to whites, while blacks continued to experience customary authority structures, much as under indirect rule, with regimes in restricted pieces of territory.

In this context, even apparently 'modern' initiatives of importance existed within settings that reflected adaptation to African social forms. The largest-scale mining operation in West Africa, the tin mines of the Jos

Plateau of Nigeria, depended primarily on massive amounts of short-term migrant labour coming from a vast range of territory and organized through Muslim, Hausa-speaking, labour recruiters (Freund 1981). Chiefs who commanded labour were key to the initial development of the government coal-mines near Enugu in eastern Nigeria (Brown 2003). Large numbers of migrants established relationships with local patrons to put in place successful cash cropping exercises in the cocoa farms of the Gold Coast and the peanut fields of the Gambia (Amin 1974). Adepts of the Muridiyya, a new Muslim religious order, systematically grew peanuts for the French oil market on marginal land in Senegal in order to provide tithes for their leaders. West Africans were prominent among the migrant workers who grew cotton in the Gezira region of the Sudan, while the Banyarwanda, virtually lacking a cash crop of their own, migrated to Uganda to grow coffee. The great mineral enterprises of central Africa, the copper mines of the Belgian Congo, and then, across the frontier, in the Copperbelt of Northern Rhodesia, were at first real killers of men (Perrings 1979). However, they worked out recruitment and housing systems that gradually reduced the worst conditions and stabilized very profitable export industries. Mine workers remained residents of compounds or 'centres extra-coutumiers', although they learnt how to organize effectively. In part, they turned themselves into the 'urban man'. The Northern Rhodesian Copperbelt only began to produce large-scale returns at the end of the 1920s. In general, by this time, the colonial political economy and form of rule had stabilized. Jacques Marseille, in his polemical account of the French colonial economy, suggests that the obviously profitable mechanisms that could be extracted from this system were largely known and set in place, perhaps even a decade earlier (Marseille 1984). There were very significant limits to the possibilities of accumulation within, however. He argues that hopes of vast profits gave way to the reign of special interests, above all certain trading companies, which held an interest in the kind of colonial ties that had already become prevalent.

The inter-War years witnessed cultural and social shifts that reflected changing and disturbing means of developing livelihoods and coping with a cash economy. Luise White (2000), has demonstrated how frequently Africans in this period imagined European rule in terms of bloodsuckers, or vampires. Compared to the nineteenth century, far greater numbers turned to new forms of religious belief that seemed to present consolation and relevance in the new era. Islam advanced, while nominal Muslims became more orthodox in their practice. Christian missionaries in some colonies enjoyed large-scale success. Moreover, as they came to accept Christianity, Africans started to change it; they needed a Christianity that empowered them and infused their spirit, reinforcing some older customs while legitimating social innovation. On the basis of Christianity and the education which missionaries were largely responsible for making available, a new elite was formed in the African population, an elite which could operate in between colonial authority and the masses, usually defined in terms of status acquired from formal education and residence in the growing towns. This elite organized itself into structures aimed at mutually benefiting Africans. Migrants to town went to relatives and friends from home; they usually gave new organizational life a strongly ethnic definition. Promoting an ethnicity, even one essentially formed only under colonialism, was a way of pushing for a better life through social networks that formed communities.

Marriages in earlier African society had involved exchanges between extended households aware of the blessings of labour as well as childbirths that a new wife could bring. The large patriarchal rural household was often early to begin to disintegrate as younger men found ways of establishing themselves independently. One result was that marriages started to become more fragile and the old form of marriage less appropriate. The colonial town was a place where women cast out by the old system could establish households and attract men of different and more favourable terms. In general, the long-established basis for African family life began to weaken. Yet, much of the discourse of marriage, of ageing, of health, of human inter-relationships, did not change; Africans tried to assimilate new phenomena into older contexts and concepts.

THE BREAKDOWN OF COLONIALISM

The 1930s represented a holding operation from the perspective of colonial political economy. The potential for new investment in Africa faded and the raw materials produced in African colonies fell dramatically in value. When revival took place, it was increasingly linked to war preparation. When war broke out, it became clearer to the colonial powers how impoverished Africa had become and how limited its contribution to the war effort could be.

In one sense, the war had a relatively limited impact in Africa. There was little fighting in sub-Saharan Africa, the major exception being the campaign for Italian East Africa that involved restoring independence to Ethiopia after six years of Italian rule. However, the social pressures which the demands of the war caused were considerably more significant, and the impact of these years far wider. During the war, demands for African labour on battlefields elsewhere, in the mines, in food production and in the transport and communications networks, accelerated very sharply. While wages increased, they were not able to buy the necessary goods for surviving in the rapidly growing colonial cities. There was forced labour in the mines in the Northern Rhodesian Copperbelt and the Nigerian tin mines, for example. Towards the end of the war, and especially in the years following, waves of resistance, showing unprecedented levels of organization, swept through many African colonies, spearheaded by workers in these sectors. Nigeria, for instance, experienced a general strike in 1945. Major regional railway strikes affected French West Africa and the two Rhodesias in the following two years, both involving large-scale community involvement. Nairobi, the Kenyan capital, became a hotbed of new forms of organization of the burgeoning African population. In some cases, militant politicians who had come to form territorially based parties and political associations capitalized on these types of unrest. Kwame Nkrumah, hired by conservative members of the Gold Coast elite to return from his American studies and head such an organization, shrewdly made use, in this way, of a virtual urban uprising in Accra in 1948 and a major strike movement in 1950 on his route to power (Aluko 1974).

Nor was agitation and struggle purely an urban affair. Social historians of the past thirty years have discovered that precisely as a new ideology of development was being pursued far more urgently than previously, officials in the countryside were insisting on onerous and often impractical or foolish labour-intensive practices which alienated significant rural populations. Strikes in the Gold Coast need to be seen alongside popular hostility to uprooting cocoa trees as a means of controlling swollen shoot disease.

Development as an idea can be seen to connect, of course, to the whole colonial project, but it was now pursued much more intensely as continued justification for this project, and as a means for finally extracting real wealth from the colonies. Low and Lonsdale (1976) have famously referred in this regard, with reference to East Africa, to a 'second colonial occupation'. Lines of rail were extended, air services greatly expanded and roads reached hitherto difficult to access sections of the continent. Ambitions in this regard were fuelled by the rising demand for African agricultural and mineral products which, consequently earned far better prices than before the war. In this context, there are many tales for an economic historian to tell—the rise of forced cotton cultivation in Mozambique helping to bring about a textile industry in Portugal, the tobacco boom in Southern Rhodesia, the dramatic spread of *robusta* coffee cultivation in Angola and the Ivory Coast, the rapid growth of tea production in highland Kenya, bauxite mining in French Guinea, iron ore mining in Liberia and then Mauritania, manganese mining deep in the interior of Gabon and, of course, the unprecedented mineral wealth produced on both sides of the British–Belgian frontier in the Copperbelt. Where regions had little to sell, more and more men were pulled out as labour migrants, and women as well as men came to try their luck in the rapidly growing cities.

If this was a period of very considerable strain, it was not really one of immiserization. Colonial revenues were placed to a greater extent into health and education systems, particularly in the more affluent colonies. Very significant proportions of the population became literate in the Gold Coast, southern Nigeria, highland Kenya, Northern Rhodesia, Senegal, Dahomey, and the Ivory Coast, for instance. And the demographic circumstances of Africa changed fairly dramatically. Decline in the population of many territories before the First World War had given way to moderate growth in the inter-War years. From the 1940s, a population explosion began to take place that would essentially last for half a century.

If the colonial powers had tried to attract settlers from the homeland to the colonies before the war, now they found that modest encouragement brought very rapid increases in the size of settler communities. This added to the brew of new social tensions as these settlers generally wanted land, infrastructure and assistance to create affluence and suitable social institutions in their new environment on an exclusionary basis. Their ambitions clashed head-on with the increasingly restive and ambitious African elite while playing on the fears of the masses. The British created new federations inspired by contemporary concepts of development—British East Africa, the Federation of Rhodesia and Nyasaland—that tried awkwardly to contain these forces, while settlers were at first very well represented in the representative institutions introduced by the French.

South Africa was also part of this ferment. The United Party government under General Smuts (1939–48) began to try to accommodate the rapidly growing African industrial workforce in terms of the beginnings of more progressive social legislation while holding the line of segregation against any real political change. Aside from the post-First World War years, it can be argued that most African resistance to the rising pressures of segregation had previously been rural, for instance in the case of the real presence of the Industrial and Commercial Union in the 1920s, but in this period, there is definitely a shift to the urban terrain—the creation of the African National Congress Youth League in Johannesburg, the much greater diffusion of the Communist Party and of attempts to organize black workers, the squatters' movement in what would become Soweto. The state became more and more committed to industrial policy, while the industrial economy became more varied and substantial, if still largely dependent on foreign technology, inputs, and investment.

In effect, Africa moved towards independence in this context. Expansion of the colonial economy and social services was quite dramatic, but did not lead to harmonious and slow political developments. There were several major armed struggles (Mau Mau in Kenya, Cameroun, Madagascar), but these were dealt with by the colonial authorities. Far more problematic were the challenges posed by demands that could not be met. Settlers could have been the engine to power deeper structural change, but their growing influence inflamed African opinion. Reform, not at first meant, quickly lead to independence, and put shrewd politicians in the drivers' seat who filled the new gap created for African leadership and skilfully used their leverage to demand more power. This greatly intensified the speed of political transformation.

It can also be argued that in the later 1950s, the development phase began to falter; outside South Africa, the prospects for full-fledged industrialization were still very limited. Prices for primary products began to be less interesting and the necessity of holding on to African colonies diminished. At first, after the war, Britain had used earnings from colonial raw materials to bolster the pound sterling, especially vis-à-vis the dollar. A decade later, however, British business clearly was starting to disengage from much of Africa (Fieldhouse 1994).

Of course, the colonial powers were involved in a game that also included players outside sub-Saharan Africa. British colonialism in Asia declined dramatically before the key decisions were made over Africa, while the French were very influenced by events in Indo-China, the Middle East, and North Africa. They were the most important actors on the colonial side; there was unwillingness to plan decolonization among the Portuguese and the Belgians, although the Belgians dramatically shifted their position at the end of the 1950s. Independence came to Africa in a context, for the most part, where the West wished to keep African resources from Communist control and where it was hoped that the new elites would follow through on colonial development plans and do the job that Europeans had failed to do (Cooper 1996). A high level of continuity in broad social and economic trends was anticipated and, to some extent, this is what did occur, at least in the first decade or so of national independence, which we can typically identify with the 1960s.

NEO-COLONIALISM: EXTENSION OF THE LONG CENTURY

If we stop at the point of African independence, that is to say around 1960-5, we are measuring a rather *short* century in fact. If we take the great West African savannah city of Kano, for instance, the period of colonial rule lasted less than sixty years, a period well covered within human memory for many elderly men and women. In Nairobi, independence followed a mere seventy years after the city's earliest foundations were laid on the expanding line of rail. Some parts of Africa—sections of the Somali desert, parts of the Sahara, the interior of northern Mozambique—were really only subdued by colonial forces after the end of the First World War and were subjected to colonial rule in any real sense for well under half a century. Claims for a long century make sense only if we consider that the post-colonial decades represent essentially continuation of the most important trends of the colonial period. This, of course, fits the view that neo-colonialism best characterizes this phase, that the broad patterns of class formation, state structure, of what is called development, changed largely from the point of view of the skin colour of those making the decisions, at least locally.

The pursuit of development in the colonial period was unquestioningly considered to be the prerogative of the colonial state. In some colonies, there were relatively well-developed merchants, with some potential to develop into capitalist accumulators, even industrialists, for instance in Nigeria. However, on the whole, it was only among the immigrant whites, or perhaps Asians, that local capitalists could be found. After independence, the state was expected to continue to play the main dynamic role, even in the conservative context of Kenya or the Ivory Coast, two model countries completely impervious to the lures of socialism. Development was pursued through the agency of parastatal companies generated by the state and dependent on generously laid on foreign aid. The Cold War made the aid game a race; deft African presidents could up the ante in aid by skilfully playing different countries and the two sides of the Iron Curtain against each other. Even were it possible for an autonomous capitalist class to form, there was much in the mind-set of the political leadership to prefer accumulation under the auspices and with the consent of the state through favoured contracts, the managing parastatals, and other such means.

With one or two exceptions (Botswana is the most remarkable), independent states became one-party structures, with power emanating from the top. This could create stability and a considerable willingness to expand expenditure on social services where the party had a strong record of anti-colonial organization or had historically confronted the interests of settlers. In other cases, undemocratic forms proved unstable, with military rule largely replacing the initially incumbent civilians (especially in West Africa). Allegiance often depended on common religious or ethnic or regional affiliation.

Often, the real politics bore little resemblance to the official ethos of progress and constitutional norms. Jean-François Bayart (1995) has referred here to the 'rhizome' state whose key operations take place beneath the ground on an effectively esoteric basis. Development efforts could be understood, to a large extent, in terms of furthering the interests of the state or some members of the elite (for instance, Ferguson [1994] using Lesotho as an example). And the new forms of locally vested power dazzled Africans: the impressive fictional work of Africa's first important novelists and playwrights (Achebe, Soyinka, Armah) was often dominated by the figure of the authoritarian president or general, his brutalities and delusions, while a society was being refashioned in his image.

In some cases, moreover, the immediate 'post-colonial' continuities crumbled rapidly. The Belgian state, for long utterly uninterested in decolonization, seems to have imagined that a very rapid independence process would guarantee that change would take place under watchful eyes in conservative hands. Instead, the Congo spun out of control in 1960, electing a first president unacceptable to the West in Patrice Lumumba. Lumumba was dethroned and murdered; major rebellions tried to avenge his death and establish a 'second independence'. Eventually, a kind of stability was restored under the control of Lumumba's erstwhile press officer, Joseph-Desiré Mobutu. Mobutu's grandiose and often ridiculous posturing was accompanied by a shrewd capacity to make himself useful to the West. Mobutu sustained power for decades on the strength of the Congo's minerals, but much of the colonial economy was in tatters and the colonial infrastructure irreparably destroyed. In the wake of disruption, hundreds of thousands of Congolese moved to the capital, renamed Kinshasa, where a limited colonial infrastructure now accommodated the population of a metropolis.

The nominally radicalizing president of Uganda, Apollo Milton Obote, was overthrown in 1971 by a military leader, Idi Amin Dada. Under Amin, responsible for thousands of murders, virtually all legal protection disappeared for those suspected of disloyalty by the state. Overnight, Amin expelled the Asian minority, previously dominant in the economy, dramatically reducing Ugandan capacity to trade and function effectively as an economy. With childish glee, Amin apparently defied Western opinion in crude humiliating forms of theatrical display in the years of power before his overthrow in 1979. Kampala, the Ugandan capital, by contrast to Kinshasa, regressed and grew very slowly compared to the projections made in Obote's time.

Lumumba's patron, Kwame Nkrumah, first president of the former Gold Coast, now Ghana, chose an ostensibly radical path. In the early

1960s, he began to look towards the Soviet Union and states such as Egypt, defying Western prerogatives as models, and tried to identify a socialist road to rapid industrialization and modernization. Tanzania under the presidency of Julius Nyerere, unifying the former Zanzibar and Tanganyika, promoted an egalitarian, peasant-based philosophy called *Ujamaa* and was very successful in attracting foreign aid from a variety of nations. Tanzania's Achilles heel lay in the very high level of aid dependence on which 'African socialism' rested.

One can best follow the progress of the radical model in the 1970s by looking further south to Mozambique. When Portuguese colonialism finally collapsed in the wake of the Portuguese dictatorship itself, it had already faced years of challenge in the form of armed struggle, to some extent articulated with parallel struggles throughout the southern African region. The former Portuguese colony of Mozambique, impoverished and suddenly bereft of its important settler element, was a major banner bearer of importance on the African left from 1975. Mozambique tried to incarnate an African version of the dream of creating a socialist path with the assistance of the Soviet Union and its allies through a great leap forwards dictated from the top.

This was even more starkly the case in Angola after 1975, where the state was able to tap into the resources of off-shore oil; in both cases, surrogate wars were created, feeding on the problems of the Soviet model, in order to cripple this possibility with Western and South African collusion. The radical path in Africa may seem superficial, compared to remarkable models such as Cuba or Viet Nam, but, given the absence of an indigenous capitalist class and the suspicion of the West, it did represent an effort to break with colonial models, dubbed neo-colonialism, and find some alternative road to empowerment in the modern world.

In Ethiopia, post-War modernization of the state and the economy had been relatively superficial. In the context of severe drought conditions causing major suffering, the empire was overthrown in 1975, bringing to power another ostensibly revolutionary government led by a soldier, Mengistu Haile-Mariam. Major land reforms did not provide the basis for a new system of production, and eventually, this regime too failed. The Horn has so far found only shaky beginnings to a new order. Ethiopia remains, under the surface, quite authoritarian, and it is unclear whether its ostensibly federal structure is sufficiently responsive to the ethnic question in what is an empire attempting to become a modern state without feudal remnants. Once Italian, Eritrea has successfully broken away from Ethiopia after a very long armed struggle. Ex-Italian Somalia is one of the classic models of 'state failure', with no coherent central government functioning other than a successful secession-created regime in the territory formerly occupied by the British and once joined to Somalia.

Yet, in retrospect, it is clear that this troubled period was more prosperous than it seemed to many at the time. Some of Africa's agricultural exports, notably coffee, continued to expand and thrive. Moreover, in many countries, mineral developments paid for unprecedented amounts of state expenditure. The most remarkable example, in Africa's most populous nation, was the discovery of oil in Nigeria, which began to be pumped three years before independence in 1960. In the 1970s, following a destructive civil war, Nigeria became a rich oil exporter with a temporary ability to finance its own development agenda.

The mineral boom was perhaps even more dramatic in some of the previously poorest African countries, such as Niger, a largely Saharan country now able to export uranium. Botswana, southern Africa's sedate democracy, was an arid and impoverished colony until, on the eve of independence, it began to export diamonds. If the post-colonial African one-party states proved essentially unsuccessful, it is important to realize that the nationalist impetus led to wide diffusion of education in many countries; that from virtually nowhere, a small industrial base began to emerge in the more significant countries; and that some capacity for real autonomy in the world began to emerge.

A Painful Rebirth Begins

In the course of the 1970s, it was however becoming clearer that the colonial inheritance in Africa was wearing thinner and thinner. Aid dependence was turning itself into indebtedness, and it was Africa's more soluble borrowers and apparently plausible developers, such as Kenya, the Ivory Coast, and Zambia, that now were falling down the hole. Once again, the tide was turning against Africa's primary products as technological changes updated the material basis for Western capitalism. Thus, copper, the mainstay of Zambia to an extreme extent, but of other African countries significantly, began to fall dramatically in value from 1974 onwards (for a perspective on this, see Ferguson 1999). Aid fatigue began to set in. The international balance of forces began to shift as the Cold War wore down in the 1980s, so that African countries lost a key bargaining chip in their dealings with the West. Moreover, faith in the possibility of a non-capitalist solution to Africa's development needs began to plummet together with the fortunes of the Soviet Union and its allies.

Western countries shifted rapidly after 1980 to try to force African countries to take up so-called structural adjustment policies if they wished to retain any lines of credit. The theory behind structural adjustment laid Africa's development woes on the state. The post-colonial state was seen as authoritarian, corrupt and wasteful, 'kleptocratic'. State-supported industrial development was based on protection and subsidies. Its role in the economy was now considered to be far too great; industries needed to be privatized or closed down if unprofitable. Farmers needed to be given prices for their produce without meddling from the state, social services needed to be cut down to affordable levels and, if otherwise unsupportable, sustained by private agencies, so-called non-governmental organizations, in this regard, successors to the Christian missionaries of the colonial era. Western support for African governments should depend on good governance, which meant at least the appearance of normal bourgeois freedoms and the alternation of political parties in power under the rule of law.

Undoubtedly, structural adjustment policies have forced something closer to Western norms on African political life. In a few countries, notably Ghana and Senegal, opposition parties actually have come to power constitutionally through the electoral process and military coups have become very much scarcer. However, it can also be argued that political parties are tolerated precisely because they rarely challenge the foundations of the new relationship with the West; they don't really offer an alternative to the dominant ideas.

At the same time, circumstances oblige the West to tolerate conditions that are far from the ideal in other cases. Favourite regimes for many Western countries were those in Uganda and, after the victory of a revolutionary army following the terrible massacres of 1994, in Rwanda. The government of Yoweri Museveni in Uganda, succeeding, as it did, the brutal dictatorship of Idi Amin and the even more brutal restored civilian government of Obote after 1981, brought back order and peace to southern Uganda and seemed to be a godsend to the governance preachers. Yet Museveni, while rebuilding the Ugandan economy, has not really allowed free elections based on party contestation to interrupt his administration. Both Museveni and his Rwandan counterpart, Paul Kagame, have meddled in the Congo in ways that certainly do not fit the prescriptions of Transparency International.

Nor has structural adjustment brought back rural prosperity; when the state can no longer effectively regulate or provide infrastructure, it often simply does not matter what 'farm gate' prices are; the African peasant cannot derive adequate income from what s/he produces or buy what s/he needs. If the parastatal model to industrialization from a low base was unsuccessful, de-industrialization is not necessarily a very successful alternative strategy; Africa cannot go forward if it is reduced to producing the same crops, for which an international advantage was shaped for it before independence, on a free market basis.

Having said this, it can also be noted that structural adjustment is a further step in loosening ties with the former colonial powers. What we might call the breakdown of neo-colonialism has provoked crises of extreme disorder in certain parts of Africa (the Democratic Republic of the Congo; Liberia/Sierra Leone/Guinea) as well as Somalia.

The real conditions under which structural adjustment is pursued do not genuinely lead to expansion of cash crop production in the old colonial way as some forms of accumulation typical of the colonial period have faded away. Instead, Africans are starting to pursue the quest for cash in novel and diverse ways. The past twenty years have seen a large-scale outpouring of Africans seeking fortunes outside the region, in Europe and America. Their departure can be mourned, but they may also bring skills and capital back to Africa that will eventually produce a more productive indigenous population. At the upper end, they include a far more varied and sophisticated skilled population than could be found in the past, but their talent now benefits Western countries as much as or more than Africa.

I have used the Muridiyya order as an example of African social structure adjusting to back up a classically colonial cash crop economy; in the heyday of the peanut crop, Senegalese farmers penetrated into less and less appropriate countryside to produce the country's main export as a mono-crop while Senegal became dependent on Asian rice imports. After 1980, the religious leadership refused to continue supporting this process. Instead, members of the order could be found all over the world, initially in West Africa and in Paris, now all over Europe, America and elsewhere, using more and more diffuse commercial activities to back their leaders. In Senegal, many of the Mourides have come to settle permanently in the holy city of Touba, abandoning village life for dependence on commerce and remittances (Guèye 2002). The Senegalese state, which once backed up some consumer industries strongly as a bulwark of state-led development, has now become dominated by free-market trading elements interested in cheap imports, not in import substitution industry (Boone 1992). One of Senegal's most distinguished living intellectuals said to me recently that for the first time in his life, he is hearing his contemporaries accept that capitalism in the globalized world is here to stay, and that they have an idea how to live with it and advance their own fortunes and that of their society within this framework, rather than searching for some major liberatory historical break. West African towns and cities are full of new houses built by the new migrants, whether in Ghana, Nigeria, or Francophone countries, and the situation is not dissimilar in the Horn. When will they start to invest effectively at home?

African agriculture in many areas yields declining crops for export to Europe, but is increasingly integrated into production for the local market. The Ivory Coast, for instance, with almost 40 per cent of its population urbanized, is largely dependent on foodstuffs grown internally to feed the capital Abidjan and other cities (Chaléard 1996). Local agriculture has been marketized in significant ways. In a sense, this is what those radicals who denounced dependence in the past had always called for.

The demographic context in Africa has also begun to change dramatically. Population increases, so steep in the generation after the Second World War, are beginning to level off substantially, especially outside West Africa. In part, this is due to a new unprecedented disastrous wave of AIDS but to give AIDS too much due is to mask the genuine tendency towards bearing fewer children. Moreover, African cities have stopped growing so dramatically. Much of the current growth seems, moreover, to be shifting towards towns and smaller cities, with less dominance by the state-centred capitals. Nonetheless, the present generation of youth may well live to see a continent where more than half the population lives in urban areas, a figure already attained in South Africa, and perhaps Zambia and Angola.

Despite alarmist literature that suggests that Africa is being written off the face of the modern world (to some extent, backed by frightening statistics of decline, typically taken in the 1980s), there are new forms of integration—globalization—noticeable. African land, given climate and soil conditions, is at times, of growing importance to world agrarian markets. African flowers, fruit, and vegetables are now flown in significant quantity to Europe. However, the conditions under which such products can be sold require corporate surveillance and intervention, if not ownership. Growers have a more direct relationship to control by large-scale capital, than was true in the colonial heyday of cash crop production. Many of the expanding producers are remnants of white settler populations. At the same time, in southern Africa, a so-called permanent 'food security crisis' is in play as subsistence supplies, now worth so little in cash terms, become less available.

Capitalist entrepreneurs of foreign origin are also prominent in the growth of tourism and of secondary industry, in locations where inexpensive industrial production exists. Mauritian investors, having transformed their sugar plantation island into a textile exporter, now set up factories in Madagascar for low-wage production; Lesotho attracts Taiwanese industrialists and locals of Asian origin in Kenya are also able to expand export markets. Africa is also and will remain a major source of oil, with massive wealth being accumulated in Angola, which may overtake Nigeria in this regard while new producers, such as Chad and Equatorial Guinea, come on-stream. Rentier states, for which offshore oil must be the ideal source of easy money, have a new lease of life.

A striking new feature of Africa at the end of the twentieth century was the emergence of post-apartheid South Africa. It can be argued that, just as with the 'neo-colonial' era elsewhere, apartheid was well able to nurture the development of South Africa as it had been structured in the 1950s and 1960s. Fuelled by the export of numerous non-precious metals especially, this was the heyday of import substitution industries employing large numbers of workers. Agriculture, forestry, and fishing took off with the help of state subsidies. Unemployment figures were relatively modest. In that phase, apartheid seemed pretty unbeatable.

But after about 1970, that South Africa ran out of steam. With economic growth stuttering, the failure to reconcile economic growth with real political devolution led to combustion—the emergence of a militant labour movement from 1973 and urban risings attracting the youth from 1976. Internal political movements, building up into the United Democratic Front formed in 1983, and notably, a powerful new trade union federation, were instrumental in preventing a long-term restoration of confidence and blocking the evolution of new forms of accumulation that excluded the black majority. South African capital, while not devastated by sanctions and the international movement to isolate the country, was anxious for a political solution that would allow it to escape the embrace of the Afrikaner nationalist state and re-integrate profitably with international partners.

In fact, the end of apartheid has been more striking for the growing movement of South African capital elsewhere than a major drive by outsiders to invest in South Africa. South African trading influences were never weak in Africa; conservative countries always traded with the South Africans, but after 1994, when the apartheid government ceded power to the ANC, elected into office, that influence expanded dramatically, coupled with investment and financial negotiation. The second South African president after Mandela, Thabo Mbeki envisions South Africa as an African state. The new South Africa is a combination of the post-apartheid vision, whereby an empowered black-dominated democracy emerges on the back of the revolutionary struggle together with essentially fairly conservative economic policies.

And South Africa tries to export its own balance of corporate partnership and black empowerment as policy more broadly. South Africa has become a notable investor, provider of infrastructure and crisis intermediary, complete with occupying soldiers, involved in a number of states in varied parts of the continent. And there has been, up to a point, a Pax Australafricana. Namibia, long administered by South Africa in defiance of the United Nations, became independent in 1990; South Africa voluntarily abandoned its control of the port of Walvis Bay and debt claims to its erstwhile colony. Peace broke out a decade ago in Mozambique with the armed opposition no longer able to access foreign aid. South Africa intervened clumsily, but successfully, to reverse a military coup in Lesotho. Finally, in 2002, Angola's generation-long and Cold War-spiked civil war came to end with the ignominious death of Jonas Savimbi.

A final point perhaps, if somewhat less tangible, is that Africans are becoming more and more able to access Western communications media, telephones, radios, and televisions. Through travel and through the media, cultural trends get diffused with amazing rapidity. Incorporation into a world of consumers, of people at least minimally 'wired', has extended very substantially. The terms under which Africans experience this world are often deeply unfair as well as chaotic and violent, but it is possible to posit the emergence of a new set of priorities and a new sense of belonging to larger world trends than before. The long century is over and a new one is beginning.

REFERENCES

Aluko, Olajide, (1974), 'Politics of Colonisation in British West Africa 1945–60', in J.F. Ade Ajayi and Michael Crowder (eds), *History of West Africa II*, Orient Longman, London.

Amin, Samir (ed.), (1984), *Modern Migrations in Western Africa*, Oxford University Press, London.

Ascherson, Neal, (1963), *The King Incorporated*, Allen & Unwin, London.

Bayart, Jean-François, (1995), *The State in Africa; The Politics of the Belly*, Orient Longman, London.

Boone, Catherine, (1992), *Merchant Capital and the Roots of State Power in Senegal, 1930–85*, Cambridge University Press, Cambridge.

Brown, Carolyn, (2003), *We Were All Slaves; African Miners, Culture and Resistance at the Enugu Government Colliery*, Heinemann, James Currey & David Philip, Portsmouth, NH, Oxford & Cape Town.

Chaléard, Jean-Louis, (1996), *Temps des villes, temps des vivres; l'essor du vivrier marchand en Côte d'Ivoire*, Karthala, Paris.

Cooper, Frederick, (1996), *Decolonization and African Society; The Labour*

Question in French and British Africa, Cambridge University Press, Cambridge.

Crush, Jonathan, Alan Jeeves, and David Yudelman, (1991), *South Africa's Labor Empire; A History of Black Migrancy to the Gold Mines*, Westview, Boulder.

Davis, Mike, (2000), *Late Victorian Holocausts; El Niño Famines and the Making of the Third World*, Verso, London.

Ferguson, James, (1994), *The Anti-Politics Machine; 'Development', Depoliticization and Bureaucratic Power in Lesotho*, University of Minnesota Press, Minneapolis.

—— (1999), *Expectations of Modernity; Myths and Meanings of Urban Life on the Zambian Copperbelt*, University of California Press, Berkeley.

Fieldhouse, David K., (1994), *Merchant Capital and Economic Decolonization: The United Africa Company 1929–89*, Clarendon Press, Oxford.

Freund, Bill, (1981), *Capital and Labour in the Nigerian Tin Mines*, Longman, London.

—— (1994), *The Making of Contemporary Africa: The Development of African Society since 1800*, Macmillan, London.

Guèye, Cheik, (2002), *La Capitale des Mourides*, Karthala, IRD & ENDA, Paris and Dakar.

Hochschild, Adam, (1998), *King Leopold's Ghost*, Houghton Mifflin, London.

Hopkins, Anthony G., (1973), *An Economic History of West Africa*, Orient Longman, London.

Low, D.A. and John Lonsdale, (1976), 'Towards the New Order 1945–63', in D.A. Low and Alison Smith (eds), *History of East Africa III*, Clarendon Press, Oxford.

Mamdani, Mahmood, (1996), *Citizen and Subject; Contemporary Africa and the Legacy of Late Colonialism*, Princeton University Press, Princeton.

Marseille, Jacques, (1984), *Empire colonial et capitalisme français; histoire d'un divorce*, Albin Michel, Paris.

Perrings, Charles, (1979), *Black Mineworkers in Central Africa*, Heinemann, London.

Phillips, Anne, (1989), *The Enigma of Colonialism; British Policy in West Africa*, James Currey, London.

White, Luise, (2000), *Speaking with Vampires; Rumor and History in Colonial Africa*, University of California Press, Berkeley.

Yudelman, David, (1983), *The Emergence of Modern South Africa; State, Capital and the Incorporation of Organized Labor on the South African Gold Fields, 1902–39*, Greenwood Press, Westport, CT.

5

Imperialism in Africa

Lance van Sittert

Critical scholarship on imperialism in Africa is of comparatively recent origin (Cain and Hopkins 1993; Robinson, Gallagher, and Denny 1961 for imperialism, Cooper 1994 and 2000; Miller 1999 for African historiography). For the first half of the twentieth century, during the era of grand colonialism, the European imperial powers were still great powers within the global system and dominated debates on their African empires, insisting on their white man's burden to 'civilize' the 'dark continent' and silencing or ignoring all dissenting opinions (Johnston 1898). Only with the decline of Europe after 1945 and the disintegration of their empires into new nation-states did an alternative critical discourse on imperialism find voice and flourish, although a virulent strain of colonial apologia survived and enjoys something of a renaissance in the present (Gann and Duignan 1969–75; Bruckner 1986; Ferguson 2003). The chief articulators of popular anti-imperialism were initially indigenous nationalists who designated imperialism as the enemy and diagnosed its chief sin as racism, promising that by wresting political control over the colonies from these evil foreign hands, the subjects-cum-citizens of new nation-states could divert the cornucopia of modernity back to source (Anderson 1991; Chatterjee 1986; Davidson 1992).

Cold War clientelism and deepening debt, however, soon gave the lie to first-wave African nationalism's boast to have defeated imperialism and delivered 'independence' and spurred a search for explanations of what was now increasingly seen as 'neo-colonialism'. This was sought in the 1970s in so-called dependency or underdevelopment theory borrowed from Latin America, which suggested that Africa's historical insertion into the global economic system under the aegis of informal and formal imperialism as a raw material supplier was incapable of amelioration by flag independence or import substitution industrialization, but required the radical act of disengagement and pursuit of economic cooperations with like-minded states, a salvation increasingly believed to lie down a socialist road (Amin 1972; Rodney 1972). Second-wave African nationalism's attempts to pursue such a path from the mid-1970s was brutally aborted by military and foreign aid offensives linked to the resurgence of the Cold War in the 1980s and an all-pervasive 'Afro-pessimism' marked this decade's scholarship across the political spectrum (Rimmer 1991; Anyang' Nyong'o 1992; Leys 1994; Crowder 1987). Foreign powers or imperialism, it was widely agreed, remained the key determinant of Africa's destiny.

The end of the Cold War and discovery of 'civil society' in the 1990s encouraged a further re-evaluation of imperialism, which rejected the old orthodoxies of a single (European) road to development and Africa's developmental pathology, to insist instead on an African road pioneered by indigenous agency. Central to this re-reading of imperialism was a thoroughgoing critique of the implicit normative perspective and concomitant assumptions of the post-independence academic scholarship generated in the old imperial heartlands around the north Atlantic rim. In this view, imperial hegemony over Africa was more apparent than real, involving the Africanization of European models, not vice versa. A shift in focus from 'high' to 'low' politics was required to reveal the African road to modernity, which, whatever its pathologies, was unquestionably an indigenous product, albeit one regularly and repeatedly hybridized with European imports (Bayart 1983; Chabal 1996; Chabal and Daloz 1999; Bayart 2000; Mbembe 2001).

In taking imperialism as its focus, this chapter thus rehearses a very old theme in the comparatively new critical scholarship of Africa, and seeks to steer a course between two extremes of seeing foreign influence as either determinant or irrelevant, the former denying all indigenous agency and the latter any foreign culpability. To do so, it takes, as its lodestar, the no longer fashionable idea of Marx that 'Men [sic] make their own history, but not of their own free will; not under circumstances they themselves have chosen, but under the given and inherited circumstances with which they are directly confronted' (Fernbach 1974: 146). In short, imperialism in Africa's long twentieth century was the product of a dialectic between foreign and indigenous agency, rendering neither the past nor the future in any sense pre-determined.

'PACIFICATION', C. 1884–1914

Imperialism's long twentieth century in Africa is conventionally deemed to have begun with the 1884–5 conference in Berlin between all those European nation-states with imperial interests or ambitions in the west of the continent, which established the ground rules for occupation in order to preclude conflicts in Africa triggering wars in Europe. Henceforth, for a claim to African empire to be recognized required both notification of a 'sphere of influence' and demonstration of 'effective occupation' (Phimister 1995).

Berlin regulated and accelerated, but did not initiate a process of European conquest of African protectorates already gathering momentum since at least the final quarter of the nineteenth century. The impetus to formal empire would appear to have originated in the rise of competitor nation-states and industrial economies to Britain's around the north Atlantic rim in the latter half of the nineteenth century, aggravated by a protracted trade depression in the global economy. Britain's hitherto informal African empire, based on its unrivalled supremacy in manufacturing production and maritime power, thus gave way to a host of more or less formal empires which were avowedly protectionist, reserving colonial raw materials and markets exclusively to national production in Europe (Andrew and Kanya-Forstner 1971; Hopkins 1973' Clarence-Smith 1979; Cain and Hopkins 1993).

The establishment of formal European empires, the so-called scramble for Africa, lasted down to the First World War and involved innumerable pacifications of recalcitrant subjects unwilling to recognize the new suzerainty created by Berlin in small wars fought throughout the continent. Despite the ubiquitous use of scorched earth and the maxim gun, indigenous alliances were as important as military conquest in creating Europe's African empires, and the majority of soldiers who beat the bounds of the new European satrapies were African. Indeed, formal imperialism might more usefully be thought of as a graft on to pre-colonial African social formations, either incorporating their ruling elites if willing, or replacing them with others who were, than their wholesale substitution with European models (Ajayi 1968, 1969; Crowder and Ikime 1970; Afigbo 1972; Peel 1983; Mamdani 1996). Nor was this an innovation of the scramble, but rather the continuation of a process that dated back to the very beginning of European commerce with Africa. Conquest merely formalized and elaborated it under the rubric of indirect rule (Lugard 1922). Europe's African empire was thus shaped by Africans as well as Europeans and hence reflected both the relative power and weakness of the latter.

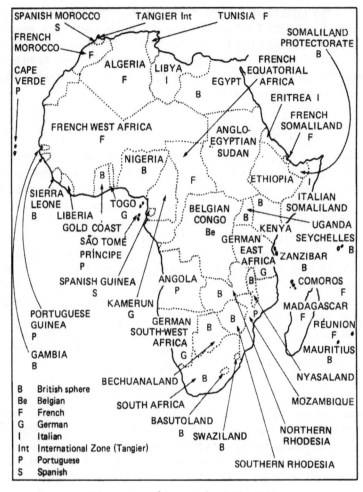

Map 5.1   African Colonies in 1914

Source: Freund 1998: 120.

Efforts to avert war among Europe's industrializing nation-states finally failed, and the 1914–18 conflagration both spilled over into their African empires and re-coloured the map, as defeated Germany's colonies were divided up between victorious Britain and France. All the European nation-states recruited soldiers for the war in their African empires from among both settlers and indigenes. In addition, south-central Africa was a major theatre of the war itself, as armies of South African settlers and native levies loyal to Britain conquered the German colonies of South-West and East Africa. The lost African empire and fantasies of its recovery and expansion animated the fascist movements in inter-War Germany and Italy and lead directly to the latter's invasion of Abyssinia in 1936 to avenge the famous defeat at Adowa forty years earlier and further Mussolini's reincarnation of the Roman Empire.

GRAND COLONIALISM, C. 1918-39

The degree of integration of the African colonies into wider imperial systems—centred on the national industrial economies of Europe—varied, depending on the relative strength of the colonizing power and the resource endowments of the individual colony. Thus, prior to the First World War, both the Portuguese state and Belgium king, without the means to develop their new African fiefdoms, sublet vast tracts of central Africa to private concession companies. The latter sought to maximize the returns on their rentals by asset-stripping the captive populations and resources in their domains before expiry of their tenure. Labour and production were thus forcibly reoriented into export commodities, and the infamous 'Red Rubber' scandal that terminated Leopold's private rule in the Congo Free State more closely approximated the norm, than the aberration it was purported to be by the Congo Reform Movement (Harms 1975; Vail and White 1980; Clarence-Smith 1985).

Unlike in the temperate zones of the American and Australasian colonies, European settlement in Africa floundered, except in the Mediterranean climates at the northern and southern extremes of the continent, and where altitude muted tropical climate on the South African Highveld, Zimbabwe Plateau, and Kenyan Highlands. Even there, settlers failed to attain demographic majority and proved expensive, inefficient, and unmanageable surrogates. They demanded infrastructure, subsidies and colour bars that inflated their costs to the colonial administrations and antagonized indigenous populations forced to pay for their privilege. Indeed, their remorseless demand for African land, labour, and subjugation ultimately impoverished and destabilized the imperial marches, which they settled by smothering indigenous production and alienating African allies (Sorrenson 1968; Palmer 1978; Berman and Lonsdale 1992-4).

Mineral deposits were eagerly prospected as a potential lure to foreign capital and revenue cows for colonial administration. The vast south-central African mineral complex, lying roughly along the Witwatersrand–Copper Belt–Katanga axis and brought into production over the half century after Berlin, exerted a massive centripetal pull on capital, labour, and commodities throughout the continent south of the Congo River, as did its smaller West African cousin in that region. The lion's share of the profits from mining production were confiscated by foreign shareholders, but the trickledown of expenditure, wages and revenue catalysed growth in commercial agriculture, urbanization, transport, and energy infrastructure as well as public administration in Africa (Van Onselen 1976; Perrings 1979; Freund 1981; Higginson 1989).

Throughout much of West Africa, however, formal empire depended not on the innovations of concession companies, settlers, or mineral extraction, but the old stalwart of African cash crop production that sustained the 'legitimate commerce' of British free trade imperialism during the first two-thirds of the nineteenth century. What formal conquest did was to skew the terms of trade in favour of European merchants by freeing them from the extractions of indigenous rulers and middlemen, giving them direct access to primary producers and modernizing internal transport systems (Berry 1975; Manning 1998).

Regardless of typologies of difference based on the nature of economic activity or administrative style, there were certain features common to Europe's African empires during the inter-War period. The first was the establishment of a cash-based economy through the direct (forced labour and cultivation) and indirect (taxation) coercion of African subjects as well as its powerful solvent effect on the kinship base of pre-colonial social formations and, in particular, the authority of older men (Freund 1994). Second was the ubiquitous insistence on Africans' essential ethnicity and the use of tribal categories in all aspects of their administration and, hence, the inability to recognize newly emerging 'detribalized' groups such as workers and educated professionals (Vail 1989; Waller and Spear 1993). Third was the ultimately contradictory nature of the colonial project, curtailing the market to shore up the eroding base of the traditional native authorities necessary for administration. Finally then, there is the highly uneven nature of grand colonialism and the hybrid nature of its final product, producing scattered islands of capitalism in vast seas of subsistence peasant production (Warren 1980; Cooper 1999).

END OF EMPIRE, C. 1939–60

The Second World War profoundly disrupted Europe's African empires, already badly shaken by the Great Depression, forcing the reinvention of the colonial project and, when this failed, its gradual abandonment in favour of a return to more informal means of suasion.

The demands of the northern hemisphere war economies for labour and raw materials fundamentally reorganized people and production in the African empires, irreparably rupturing the tribal categories and tributary networks of inter-War indirect rule by creating new detribalized urban populations and entrepreneurial classes. The emergency also compelled the expansion of administrative superintendence over colonial economies, further eroding the position of native authorities. Similarly, in the settler colonies, the war lent new importance to settler production and role in administration, fuelling demands for greater political autonomy. These wartime realignments of people, production, and political power constituted an internal crisis for European colonialism, exacerbated by the economic crisis occasioned by the end of the War. The European colonial powers' ability to address this crisis was severely constrained by their own economic devastation and loss of great power status as a result of the conflict (Killingray and Rathbone 1986).

Britain and France emerged from the War impoverished and heavily indebted to the US. America also acquired a substantial economic interest in Africa during the War and, as the pre-eminent capitalist economy on the planet, no longer saw the need to tolerate its exclusion from the continent through the protectionism of imperial preference. This economic interest was glossed as historic anti-colonialism, with the US styling itself as the first self-liberating colony, but acquired a new ideological urgency with the commencement of the Cold War. America worried that Europe's African empires, by showing an unacceptable face of capitalism, were recruiting grounds for communism, fears enhanced by the Soviet Union's search for influence through support for anti-colonial nationalisms in the South. The steadily multiplying new forums of international opinion spawned by the UN were also utilized by both superpowers and the new Asian nation states to maintain the anti-colonial pressure on Europe's African empires. This constituted the external crisis of European colonialism after 1945 (Louis 1977; Pearce 1982).

The response of the European colonial powers to the post-War crisis in their African empires was determined by their own economic weakness. African labour and raw materials were crucial to their own national reconstruction and servicing the American debt, and hence, withdrawal was impossible. Rather, colonialism was reinvented as development to blunt the teeth of its African enemies and placate its international critics, while allowing the continued utilization of African resources for European recovery. To this end, metropolitan revenue was redirected to Africa, for the first time, to finance limited social welfare spending as well as ambitious infrastructure and agricultural expansion plans, all superintended by the enlarged wartime administrations, now redirected to the task of post-War development. The aim was to buy off key elements of the urban underclass with collective bargaining schools, houses, and clinics, while allowing the countryside to be re-engineered into a patchwork quilt of cash crop zones tightly configured around expanding rail and road networks radiating out from the deep water ports. With the towns quiescent and the countryside developing, Europe's newly 'responsible colonialism' would extend the life of its African empires indefinitely (Havinden and Meredith 1993; Cooper 1997a).

The optimism of Europe's second coming to Africa after 1945 was largely based on its importation of new scientific approaches to both labour and production devised in Europe, but now deemed universally applicable. Administrators, armed with industrial psychology, for the first time recognized African workers organized in trade unions from among the detribalized masses thronging the cities and sought to coopt them through social welfare spending. Similarly, agricultural science was deployed by colonial administrations in the countryside to save the soil and redeem production from the purportedly dead hands of the African which peasantry, was forcibly resettled, re-educated or rejected in favour of mechanized state farming. The second colonial occupation suffered predictable shipwreck on its own racist hubris. Industrial relations and social welfare provisions encouraged rather than contained urban demands, while temperate northern hemisphere agricultural science and technology failed spectacularly in the tropical environments of the African empires, sowing dragon's teeth of discontent among the peasantries forcibly subjugated to their authoritarian dictates (Cooper 1997b; Van Beusekom and Hodgson 2000).

By the mid-1950s, it was becoming increasingly clear that the reinvention of colonialism had failed to either contain the political challenge of anti-colonialism from within and without, or significantly revolutionize the economies of Europe's African *satrapies*. If anything, 'development' appeared to have exacerbated difficulties on both fronts; seeding the countryside with anti-colonialism and squandering scarce resources on flagship white elephants. The first wave of decolonization in the decade to the mid-1960s was a direct response to this failure, and led to the negotiated transfer of both formal political control and responsibility for development of Britain and France's non-settler colonies to African nationalist movements (Flint 1983; Cooper 1996).

The home-grown variants of nationalism, which flourished in post-War colonial Africa, were fashioned by the first generation of native intelligentsia raised under imperial tutelage, which came of age during the

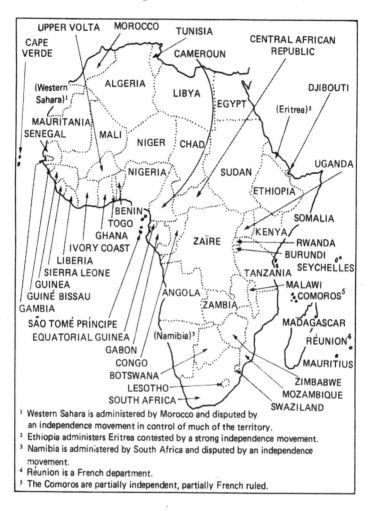

Map 5.2 Independent Africa

Source: Freund 1998: 206.

War and used European models, gleaned from their mission educations and personal pilgrimages to the imperial metropolis to re-imagine the colonies as nation-states. They seized the moment, provided by anti-colonialism abroad and massive wartime urbanization and post-War development at home, to fashion an insurgent anti-colonial populist politics in the cities, which sought the transfer of political control to indigenous hands (Berman 1991, 1998; Allman 1993; Rathbone 1999).

Although decked out in a bewildering array of pre-colonial trappings, intended to proclaim their indigeneity and novelty of purpose, the process of decolonization, now glossed as independence, in effect saw the continuation and acceleration of colonial development as national development, guided by the same assumptions, aims and, in many instances, experts (Cooper 1996; Tignor 1998).

ILLUSIONS OF INDEPENDENCE, C. 1965–80

Development, of whatever ideological stripe, offered African nationalism a unifying ideology in place of anti-colonialism, and apparent state-led shortcut to modernity. As an isolated urban minority at the head of a broad cross-class alliance beset on all sides by alternative imagined communities of class, ethnicity, and religion, the African educated elite embraced the cult of the state—promoted with equal enthusiasm by modernization theorists and scientific socialists—as the means to simultaneously realize both their ideological and accumulation ambitions. They thus took over the administrative mechanisms and blueprints of colonial development and pursued them with a paternalistic hubris similar to their European predecessors, but a far greater zeal, fired by the purported popular legitimacy conferred by election victories and their subsequent claim to embody the will of 'the people'. The post-War Long Boom in the global economy (c. 1947–72), during which the demand and price for African raw materials followed a broadly upward trend, and generous development funding from east and west for pliant Cold War clients, further encouraged nationalist hallucinations of import substitution industrial revolutions built on the backs of export cash-cropping or mining (Lewis 1955, Beckman 1976; Killick 1978; Bates 1981; Iliffe 1983; Sender and Smith 1986; Ferguson 1990).

The indigenous nationalisms of the settler colonies traversed a different route to independence via armed insurrections against the revanchist intentions of resident European minorities to maintain their privilege at African expense. Only in south-central Africa were settlers able to prevail—those in Kenya and Algeria being forced to accommodate themselves to indigenous majority rule by the early 1960s. In South Africa and its Namibian colony, Afrikaner nationalism gained ascendancy on the back of a plan to defeat black nationalism by shattering it into a myriad ethnic fragments. Settlers in Rhodesia and the Portuguese colonies of Angola and Mozambique also moved to suppress nationalism among the African populations in their territories through the concomitant promotion of ethnicity and use of military force. In all these colonies-cum-settler nation- states African nationalist movements moved over into armed resistance against settler minorities in the early 1960s. Whereas the latter styled themselves outposts of Western civilization and received American protection as proxy guardians of mineral resources and transport routes deemed strategic to the Cold War, African nationalist movements on the subcontinent sought allies in the east for their guerrilla wars against the white south. The fruits of the Long Boom in south-central Africa were thus denied African nationalism and confiscated instead by the settler minority, which in South Africa and Rhodesia attained a standard of living rivalling that of the north Atlantic rim by the 1970s (Bowman 1973; Loney 1975; Posel 1991).

The development paths of both the surviving settler states and first-wave nationalist movements to the north were finally undone by the global crisis occasioned by oil price hikes engineered by the Oil and Petroleum Exporting Countries (OPEC) from the mid-1970s. Oil price inflation triggered an international recession and the end of the post-War Long Boom simultaneously bringing the curtain down on independent Africa's one-crop and mineral economies' independence honeymoon. The demand and price for African raw materials slumped in inverse relation to the continent's oil bill, and state-led development disappeared into the widening maw between export earnings and import costs. The global recession also prompted a sea change in economic orthodoxy, away from the cult of the state to a new market fundamentalism as well as resumption of the Cold War. Under these radically altered circumstances, the first wave of nationalisms and white enclaves faltered and fell to new variants of one-party, personal, or military authoritarianism, which largely dispensed with internal mandates in favour of superpower clientelism (Arrighi 2002; Fieldhouse 1986; Johnson 1977; Price 1991; Luckham 1994).

As the always febrile trappings of independence and democracy of the first wave disintegrated, to reveal a comprador class at the helm of a clint state, a second wave of African decolonizations in the mid-1970s seemed to offer an alternative socialist road to development modelled on the East, rather than the West. The implosion of Portugal's African empire and Smith's settler state in Rhodesia after protracted guerrilla wars brought to power nationalist movements radicalized by their immersion in the peasantry. Though their ideological pedigree was doctrinaire scientific socialism, rather than the bastardized African variants cobbled together by the more imaginative of the first-wave nationalists, their socialist agenda was ultimately the same—state-led industrialization on the back of the peasantry to build an indigenous capitalist class, albeit one that addressed each other as 'comrades', rather than 'brothers'. The second-wave's denouement was far swifter and more brutal than that of the first, a product both of its own hubris and sustained external attack by client states of the West under the rubric of the reinvigorated Cold War (Clarence-Smith 1980; Astrow 1983; Saul 1985; Stoneman and Cliffe 1989; Hodges 2001).

Thus, apartheid South Africa, with American support, invaded Angola in 1976 in support of anti-MPLA elements of the nationalist movement, fought Frelimo in Mozambique via the MNR, originally organized by the Rhodesian intelligence service in the dying days of the Smith regime, supported dissidents hostile to ZANU in south-west Zimbabwe in the early 1980s, and everywhere attacked SADCC states hosting ANC operatives. The American-sanctioned 'destabilization' of southern Africa literally destroyed or forced the hasty abandonment of a socialist development path and, once again, underscored Africa's continued vulnerability to external diktat despite its supposed independence. In the harsh new world of the last quarter of the twentieth century, military attack was only one type of neo-colonialism, which took on the even more all-pervasive and intrusive form of structural adjustment in the 1980s as the African debt crisis deepened (Hanlon 1986; Vines 1991).

BACK TO THE FUTURE, C. 1980–2000

Contemporary analyses of the crisis in African development were shaped by the new free market orthodoxy, that gained ascendancy in the wake of the ending of the Long Boom, and the prescribed remedy, enforced through the new financial leverage enjoyed by international financial institutions, governments, and banks owing to Africa's ballooning debt. The former insisted that independent Africa's one-crop and mineral economies had failed, not because they were inherently unviable except in the unique moment of the Long Boom, but due to mismanagement. Flirtation with the economic heresies of socialism, according to this diagnosis, compounded the pervasive veneration of the state as prime economic orchestrator and actor. Burgeoning state intervention in the economy smothered market forces and efficiency, a situation further aggravated by the corruption born of diminished political accountability. The solution, as divined by the IMF, was to shrink the state and thereby liberate the invisible hand of the market to magically restart the stalled engine of development through the alchemy of the price mechanism (Freund 1994; Arrighi 2002).

The vulnerability of African nation-states to the new free market fundamentalism of the north Atlantic rim was determined by their growing debt burdens. The initial shortfalls in the trade balance of payments during the 1970s were made good by borrowing on the assumption that the conditions of the Long Boom were the norm, rather than an aberration, and would imminently return. This view was shared by private banks in the North eager to off-load massive deposits of OPEC petrodollars and thus overlook the usual requirements of due diligence in financing African debts. The belated realization that Africa's economic problems were permanent, led to a drying up of easy private credit and an increasing dependence on the IMF which, acquired huge leverage over national economies and became the continent's international credit guarantor as more and more African countries exceeded their borrowing rights and became subject to conditionality. The IMF's primary objective in Africa was to enforce debt service, and its efforts to restart African development—styled 'structural adjustment'—have always been directed primarily towards this goal (Lawrence 1986; Ravenhill 1986; Ravenhill and Callaghy 1993; Bienefeld 2000).

In practice, structural adjustment required African nation-states to exploit their supposed comparative advantage within the global system as raw material producers. The humiliating revival of the colonial export economies was compounded by the concomitant decimation of fledgling industries through the removal of protection and urban support bases by privatization, rationalization, removals of subsidies and price controls as well as reductions in social welfare spending. The IMF, through the mechanism of structural adjustment, literally turned the clock back— economically and socially—to the colonial era, in the interests of Africa's creditors, but, it should also be added, with the complicity of its nationalist rulers. The latter, despite occasional populist flourishes, proved remarkably willing to impose austerity measures on their populations, in return for continued foreign financing, and adept at ring-fencing their own and their clients' interests against its ravages. They could also always rely on generous military aid from one or the other patron in the Cold War to ensure the bitter medicine did not politically destabilize their fiefdoms. It was no coincidence that the darling of the IMF and alleged proof of structural adjustment's success in the 1980s was the Ghana presided over by Rawlings' junta (Gibon, Bangura, and Ofstad 1992; Van der Walle 2001; Herbst 1993; Gyimah-Boadi 1993; Arrighi 2002).

The relative stability engineered by IMF structural adjustment and Cold War *realpolitik* proved transient, and with the end of the Cold War, Africa became increasingly marginal to the geopolitical calculations of the only surviving superpower, and many of the client states sustained by the conflict disintegrated along their ancient internal fault-lines of alternative imagined communities, with rump states cohering around resource enclaves, if at all (Abdullah 1997, Adam 1992, Richards 1998, Ellis 1999, Ferme 2001, Mkandawire 2002). Post-Cold War instabilities were amplified by the imposition of the new political conditionality of democracy, alongside the old economic panacea of the market, in the belief that both these fruits of capitalism's purported victory in the Cold War were now the inalienable right of all humankind. Donor democracy in Africa served the dual function of explaining the failure of 1980s' economic conditionality (the delinquency of the unaccountable African state) and reinforcing the international financial institutions' traditional anti-statism by redirecting finance away from the state to so-called civil society. The third-wave decolonizations of Namibia (1990) and South Africa (1994) are the preferred African poster children for export democracy, but their dark doppelgangers in the abortive Angolan peace process (1992–8) and Rwandan genocide (1994) are equally exemplary instances of the externally imposed civil society fad of the final decade of the twentieth century (Allen 1992, Johnson and Schlemmer 1996, Marais 1998, Hodges 2001, Mamdani 2001).

THE MORE THINGS CHANGE, THE MORE
THEY STAY THE SAME

Nearly one hundred and twenty years on from the conference in Berlin, on the threshold of another imagined new era—the twenty-first century—as the nationalists of the third wave once again tout an imminent African renaissance and United States of Africa, this time confected from a neoliberal recipe, a certain pattern of process is discernable. Its frame was set by the high colonial period during the first half of the twentieth century, which more or less forcefully annexed the resources and populations of the African empires as captive raw material suppliers and markets for European industrial economies. The classic one-crop or mineral open economy has proved a remarkably difficult mould to break, and remains the enduring orientation of African national economies down to the present. The second half of the twentieth century witnessed three successive waves of indigenous nationalisms attempt to slip these historical bonds nonetheless.

The first wave of the Long Boom pursued state-led import substitution industrialization on a modernization theory or African socialist blueprint, financed with subventions from the export sector and ex-colonial-cum-Cold War patrons. This effort, soon in trouble, was finally ended by global recession in the mid-1970s, which destroyed both the demand for African raw materials and the cult of the state. The second wave arose simultaneously with the demise of the first, propelled by the efforts of nationalist movements in southern Africa to break the chains of dependency with the hammer of scientific socialism. This wave, even more so than the first, was directly attacked, for its ideological heresy in the context of a resurgence of free market fundamentalism around the North Atlantic rim and resumption of the Cold War, and destroyed within a decade. Suitably chastened, the final post-Cold War wave has sought the holy grail of development through democracy and neo-liberal orthodoxy.

Each of these efforts has been made at immense cost, and the third wave currently seeks to rise from amidst the wreckage of its predecessors strewn all around it. The early achievement by the first wave of social welfare gains and fledgling industrial bases (coming off very low colonial baselines) were systematically disintegrated by the subsequent debt crisis and triage imposed by the IMF. The similar gains made by the second wave via an alternative route were even more meagre, and were swiftly and thoroughly annihilated by the sustained military assault of America and its southern African surrogates and their proxies. Ironically, although the pious orthodoxy of the neo-liberal third wave makes it virtually immune to external attack, its singular failure to deliver comparable popular gains to the first two, leaves it more exposed to internal challenges than its predecessors, and more encumbered by democracy and anti-statism in trying to manage them.

REFERENCES

Abdullah, Ibrahim, (1997), 'The Bush Path to Destruction: The Origins and Character of the Revolutionary United Front (RUF/SL)', *Africa Development*, 22, 45–76.

Adam, Hussein, (1992), 'Somalia, Militarism, Warlordism or Democracy?' *Review of African Political Economy*, 54, 11–26.

Afigbo, A.E., (1972), *The Warrant Chiefs*, Longman, London.

Ajayi, J.F.A., (1968), 'The Continuity of African Institutions Under Colonialism', in T.O. Ranger (ed.), *Emerging Themes in African History*, East African Literature Bureau, Nairobi, 189–200.

—— (1969), 'Colonialism: An Episode in African History', in L.H. Gann and Peter Duignan (eds), *Colonialism in Africa*, Volume 1, Cambridge University Press, Cambridge, 497–509.

Allen, Chris, (1992), 'Restructuring and the Authoritarian State: 'Democratic Renewal' in Benin', *Review of African Political Economy*, 54, 43–58.

Allman, J.M., (1993), *The Quills of the Porcupine: Asante Nationalism in an Emergent Ghana*, University of Wisconsin Press, Madison.

Amin, Samir, (1972), 'Underdevelopment and Dependence in Black Africa:

Origins and Contemporary Forms', *Journal of Modern African* Studies, 10, 503-24.

Anderson, Benedict, (1991), *Imagined Communities: Reflections on the Origin and Spread of Nationalism*, second Edition, Verso, London.

Andrew, C.M. and A.S. Kanya-Forstner, (1971), 'The French Colonial Party: Its Composition, Aims and Influence', *Historical Journal*, 15, 99-128.

Anyang' Nyong'o, Peter, (1992), *30 Years of Independence in Africa: The Lost Decades?* Academic Science Publishers, Nairobi.

Arrighi, Giovanni, (2002), 'The African Crisis: World Systemic and Regional Aspects', *New Left Review*, 15, 5-36.

Astrow, Andre, (1983), *Zimbabwe: A Revolution that Lost its Way*, Zed Press, London.

Bates, R.H., (1981), *Markets and States in Tropical Africa: The Political Basis of Agricultural Policies*, University of California Press, Berkeley.

Bayart, J.F., (1983), *The State in Africa: The Politics of the Belly*, Longman, London.

—— (2000), 'Africa in the World: A History of Extraversion', *African Affairs*, 99, 217-67.

Beckman, Bjorn, (1976), *Organising the Farmers: Cocoa, Politics and National Development in Ghana*, Scandinavian Institute of African Studies, Uppsala.

Berman, Bruce, (1991), 'Nationalism, Ethnicity and Modernity: The Paradox of Mau Mau', *Canadian Journal of African Studies*, 25, 181-206.

—— (1998), 'Ethnicity, Patriotism and the African State: The Politics of Uncivil Nationalism', *African Affairs*, 97, 305-41.

Berman, Bruce and John Lonsdale, (1992-4), *Unhappy Valley: Conflict in Kenya and Africa*, 2 volumes, James Currey, London.

Berry, Sara, (1975), *Custom, Cocoa and Socioeconomic Change*, Clarendon Press, Oxford.

Bienefeld, Manfred, (2000), 'Structural Adjustment: Debt Collection Device or Development Policy?' *Review*, 23, 533-82.

Bowman, L.W., (1973), *Politics in Rhodesia*, Harvard University Press, Cambridge, MA.

Bruckner, Paul, (1986), *Tears of the White Man: Compassion as Contempt*, Free Press, New York.

Cain, P.J. and A.G. Hopkins, (1993), *British Imperialism: Innovation and Expansion, 1688-1914*, Longman, London.

Chabal, Patrick, (1996), 'The Africa Crisis: Context and Interpretation', in R.P. Werbner and Terence Ranger (eds), *Postcolonial Identities in Africa*, Zed Books, London, 29-54.

Chabal, Patrick and J.P. Daloz, (1999), *Africa Works: Disorder as Political Instrument*, James Currey, London.

Chatterjee, Partha, (1986), *Nationalist Thought and the Colonial World: A Derivative Discourse*, Zed Press, London.

Clarence-Smith, Gervase, (1979), 'The Myth of Uneconomic Imperialism: The Portuguese in Angola, 1836–1926', *Journal of Southern African Studies*, 5, 165–80.

—— (1980), 'Class Structure and Class Struggle in Angola in the 1970s', *Journal of Southern African Studies*, 7, 109–26.

—— (1985), *The Third Portuguese Empire*, Manchester University Press, Manchester.

Cooper, Frederick, (1994), 'Conflict and Connection: Rethinking Colonial African History', *American Historical Review*, 99, 1516–45.

—— (1996), *Decolonization and African Society: The Labour Question in French and British Africa*, Cambridge University Press, Cambridge.

—— (1997a), 'Modernising Bureaucrats, Backward Africans and the Development Concept', in Frederick Cooper and Randall Packard (eds), *International Development and the Social Sciences: Essays on the History and Politics of Knowledge*, University of California Press, Berkeley, 64–92.

—— (1997b), 'The Dialectics of Decolonization: Nationalism and Labour Movements in Post-War French Africa', in Frederick Cooper and A.L. Stoler (eds), *Tensions of Empire*, University of California Press, Berkeley, 406–35.

—— (1999), 'Africa in a Capitalist World', in Darlene Clark Hine and Jacqueline McLeod (eds), *Comparative History of Black People in Diaspora*, Indiana University Press, Bloomington, 391–418.

—— (2000), 'Africa's Pasts and Africa's Historians', *Canadian Journal of African Studies*, 34, 298–336.

Crowder, Michael, (1987), 'Whose Dream was it Anyway? Twenty-five Years of African Independence', *African Affairs*, 86, 7–24.

Crowder, Michael and Obaro Ikime (eds), (1970), *West African Chiefs: Their Changing Status under Colonial Rule and Independence*, Africana Publishing Company, New York.

Davidson, Basil, (1992), *The Black Man's Burden: Africa and the Curse of the Nation State*, James Currey, London.

Ellis, Stephen, (1999), *The Mask of Anarchy: The Destruction of Liberia and the Religious Dimension of an African Civil War*, New York University Press, New York.

Ferguson, James, (1990), *The Anti-Politics Machine: Development, Depoliticization and Political Power in Lesotho*, Cambridge University Press, Cambridge.

Ferguson, Niall, (2003), *Empire: The Rise and Demise of the British World Order and the Lessons for Global Power*, Basic Books, New York.

Ferme, M.C., (2001), *The Underneath of Things: Violence, History and the Everyday in Sierra Leone*, University of California Press, Berkeley.

Fernbach, David (ed.), (1974), *Karl Marx Political Writings Volume II: Surveys from Exile*, Vintage Books, New York.

Fieldhouse, D.K., (1986), *Black Africa: Economic Decolonization and Arrested Development*, Allen and Unwin, London.

Flint, J.E., (1983), 'Planned decolonization and its Failure in British Africa', *African Affairs*, 82, 389–412.

Freund, Bill, (1981), *Capital and Labour in the Nigerian Tin Mines*, Longman, London.

—— (1994), *The Making of Contemporary Africa: The Development of African Society since 1800*, London, Macmillan

Gann, L.H. and Peter Duignan (eds), (1969–75), *Colonialism in Africa, 1870–1960*, 5 volumes, Cambridge University Press, Cambridge.

Gibon, Peter, Yusuf Bangura, and Arve Ofstad, (1992), *Authoritarianism, Adjustment and Democracy: The Politics of Economic Liberalization in Africa*, Scandinavian Institute of African Studies, Uppsala.

Gyimah-Boadi, Emmanuel (ed.), (1993), *Ghana Under PNDC Rule*, CODESRIA, Dakar.

Hanlon, Joseph, (1986), *Beggar Your Neighbours: Apartheid Power in Southern Africa*, James Currey, London.

Harms, Robert, (1975), 'The End of Red Rubber: A Reassessment', *Journal of African History*, 16, 73–88.

Havinden, Michael and David Meredith, (1993), *Colonialism and Development: Britain and Its Tropical Colonies, 1850–1960*, Routledge, London.

Herbst, Jeff, (1993), *The Politics of Reform in Ghana, 1982–91*, University of California Press, Berkeley.

Higginson, John, (1989), *A Working Class in the Making: Belgian Colonial Labour Policy, Private Enterprise and the African Mineworker*, University of Wisconsin Press, Madison.

Hodges, Tony, (2001), *Angola from Afro-Stalinism to Petro-Diamond Capitalism*, James Currey, Oxford.

Hopkins, A.G., (1973), *An Economic History of West Africa*, Longman, London.

Iliffe, John, (1983), *The Emergence of African Capitalism*, Macmillan, London.

Johnson, R.W., (1977), *How Long Will South Africa Survive?* Macmillan, London.

Johnson, R.W. and Laurie Schlemmer, (1996), *Launching Democracy in South Africa: The First Open Election, April 1994*, Yale University Press, New Haven.

Johnston, H.H., (1889), *A History of the Colonization of Africa by Alien Races*, Cambridge University Press, Cambridge.

Killick, Tony, (1978), *Development Economics in Action: A Study of Economic Policies in Ghana*, St Martin's Press, New York.

Killingray, David, and Richard Rathbone (eds), (1986), *Africa and The Second World War*, St Martins Press, New York.

Lawrence, Patrick (ed.)., (1986), *World Recession and the Food Crisis in Africa*, James Currey, London.

Lewis, W.A., (1955), 'The Economic Development of Africa', in C.W. Stillman (ed.), *Africa in the Modern World*, University of Chicago Press, Chicago, 97–112.

Leys, Colin, (1994), 'Confronting the African Tragedy', *New Left Review* 204, 33–47.

Loney, Martin, (1975), *Rhodesia: White Racism and Imperial Response*, Penguin, Harmondsworth.

Louis, W.R., (1977), *Imperialism at Bay: The United States and the Decolonization of the British Empire*, Clarendon Press, Oxford.

Luckham, Robin, (1994), 'The Military, Militarization and Democratization in Africa: A Survey of Literature and Issues', *African Studies Review*, 37, 13–75.

Lugard, Lord, (1922), *The Dual Mandate in British Tropical Africa*, Frank Cass, London.

Mkandawire, Thandika, (2002), 'The Terrible Toll of Post-colonial "Rebel Movements" in Africa: Towards an Explanation of the Violence against the Peasantry', *Journal of Modern African Studies*, 40, 181–215.

Mamdani, Mahmood, (1996), *Citizen and Subject: Contemporary Africa and the Legacy of Late Colonialism*, Princeton University Press, Princeton.

—— (2001), *When Victims Become Killers: Colonialism, Nativism and the Genocide in Rwanda*, Princeton University Press, Princeton.

Manning, Patrick, (1998), *Francophone Sub-Saharan Africa 1880–1995*, second edition, Cambridge University Press, Cambridge.

Marais, Hein, (1998), *South Africa: Limits to Change: The Political Economy of Transition*, Zed Books, London.

Mbembe, Achille, (2001), *On the Postcolony*, University of California Press, Berkeley.

Miller, J.C., (1999), 'Presidential Address: History and Africa/Africa and History', *American Historical Review*, 104, 1–32.

Palmer, Robin, (1978), *Land and Racial Domination in Rhodesia*, Heinemann, London.

Pearce, R.D., (1982), *The Turning Point in Africa: British Colonial Policy, 1938–1948*, Frank Cass, London.

Peel, D.D.Y., (1983), *Ijeshas and Nigerians, c. 1890s–1970s*, Cambridge University Press, Cambridge.

Perrings, Charles, (1979), *Black Mineworkers in Central Africa*, Heinemann, London.

Phimister, Ian, (1995), 'Africa Partitioned', *Review*, 18, 355–81.

Posel, Deborah, (1991), *The Making of Apartheid 1948–61: Conflict and Compromise*, Clarendon Press, Oxford.

Price, R.M., (1991), *The Apartheid State in Crisis: Political Transformation in South Africa, 1975–1990*, Oxford University Press, Oxford.

Rathbone, Richard, (1999), *Nkrumah and the Chiefs: The Politics of Chieftaincy in Ghana, 1951–1960*, Ohio University Press, Athens.

Ravenhill, John (ed.), (1986), *Africa in Economic Crisis*, Macmillan, London.

Ravenhill, John, and Thomas Callaghy (eds), (1993), *Hemmed In: Responses to Africa's Economic Decline*, Columbia University Press, New York.

Richards, Paul, (1998), *Fighting for the Rain Forest: War, Youth and Resources in Sierra Leone*, James Currey, London.

Rimmer, Douglas (ed.), (1991), *Africa Thirty Years On*, James Currey, London.

Robinson, Ronald, John Gallagher and Alice Denny, (1961), *Africa and the Victorians*, St Martin's Press, New York.

Rodney, Walter, (1972), *How Europe Underdeveloped Africa*, Bogle-L'Ouverture, London.

Saul, John (ed.), (1985), *A Difficult Road: The Transition to Socialism in Mozambique*, Monthly Review Press, New York.

Sender, John and Sheila Smith, (1986), *The Development of Capitalism in Africa*, Methuen, London.

Sorrenson, M.P.K., (1968), *Origins of White Settlement in Kenya*, Oxford University Press, Oxford.

Stoneman, Colin and Lionel Cliffe, (1989), *Zimbabwe: Politics, Economics and Society*, Frances Pinter, London.

Tignor, Robert, (1998), *Capitalism and Nationalism at the End of Empire: State and Business in Decolonising Egypt, Nigeria and Kenya, 1945–1963*, Princeton University Press, Princeton.

Vail, Leroy (ed.), (1989), *The Creation of Tribalism in Southern Africa*, James Currey, London.

Vail, Leroy and Landeg White, (1980), *Capitalism and Colonialism in Mozambique*, Heinemann, London.

Van Beusekom, Monika and Dorothy Hogdson (eds), (2000), 'Lessons Learned: Development Experiences in the Late Colonial Period', *Journal of African History*, 41, 29–130.

Van de Walle, Nicolas, (2001), *African Economies and the Politics of Permanent Crisis, 1979–1999*, Cambridge University Press, Cambridge.

Van Onselen, Charles, (1976), *Chibaro: African Mine Labour in Southern Rhodesia*, Pluto Press, London.

Vines, Alex, (1991), *RENAMO: Terrorism in Mozambique*, James Currey, London.

Waller, Richard and Tom Spear, (1993), *Becoming Masai*, James Currey, London.

Warren, Bill, (1980), *Imperialism: Pioneer of Capitalism*, Verso, London.

6

The Middle East in the Long Twentieth Century

Faruk Tabak

The long twentieth century has witnessed the passing, sequentially, of dynastic and colonial empires. Among the dynastic empires that faced dismemberment after the Great War was the Ottoman Empire, and its passing gave birth to a score of newly-founded states in the Middle East, most of which were hastily placed under the aegis of the so-called great powers. The resultant fracturing of networks that criss-crossed and integrated different quarters of the empire and the forging of new networks within the parcelized, colonial world of the inter-War era served to rebuild the economic infrastructure of the region on different foundations than before. The dissolution of colonial empires in the aftermath of the Second World War, in turn, vested the erstwhile colonial and mandate states with independence, with slight adjustments to the territorial partitioning inherited from the preceding period. Though the previously demarcated borders remained largely in place, this did not mean that, *grosso modo*, the political map of the Middle East did not undergo profound modification after the Great War.

Economically, the region's performance during this politically tumultuous period has been all but impressive. For one, its share of world capital and merchandise flows currently stands at a level lower than that at the turn of the twentieth century. So does its relative wealth, when measured as a proportion of that commanded in the world economy's core zone. The 'regions of recent European settlement', Latin America, and East Asia have all experienced bouts of upward mobility at different times during the course of the century, even though these phases of mobility were eventually cut short and at times brusquely. The Middle East, by contrast, has been exempt from this. A corollary to this exemption has been the persistence in the widening income gap between the region and the world economy's core zone. Widening income disparity has remained stubbornly unchanged during the course of the long twentieth century despite the breadth of the political metamorphosis that has remapped the region. The striking discordance between the magnitude of political change in the region and the worsening of its relative economic standing vis-à-vis the North is the subject matter of this chapter.

As the Great Depression of the nineteenth century set in from 1873 and a new round of imperial rivalry commenced—much to the chagrin of London whose unrivalled global supremacy during the mid-Victorian period thus came under growing challenge—the sweep and nature of Pax Britannica underwent veritable change. The onset of imperial rivalry, or 'great power bickering', as Polanyi termed it, codified in 1878 with the Berlin Treaty, unleashed a massive wave of colonization, especially in Africa. Indeed, what stood at the heart of the escalating imperial rivalry was the partitioning of Qing China and Asia, more so than of the Ottoman and Russian Empires. At the end of the twentieth century, developments remarkably similar to those that unfolded at its beginning have placed East Asia, once again, at the centre of hegemonic rivalry. China's growing integration into the world economy, facilitated immensely by the phenomenal developmental success of the Four Tigers since the 1970s, has further tightened the region's hold on world economic flows. Yet, at the beginning of the century, the Ottoman Empire, however distant from the principal arena of rivalry, was not exempt from the changing global political configurations that followed the signing of the Berlin Treaty. The Sublime Porte and, later, the young Turkish Republic reaped benefits from the political opportunities occasioned by Berlin's growing challenge to London. Similarly, the weakening of American rule has engendered a world very different from that at its height, and the resurgent rivalry has failed to create, at least thus far, such a space of opportunity for the Middle East. Put differently, the erosion of Pax Americana could not possibly have brought about a political climate more different from that ushered in by the waning of Pax Britannica at the end of the nineteenth century.

At the dusk of British rule, Berlin's bid for power bolstered a lasting alliance between Kaiser Wilhelm II and Sultan Abdülhamid and, later, the Young Turks, owing largely to the landlocked nature of the German realm—hence the hegemonic rival's much-touted need for *lebensraum*, breathing room. Endearing the alliance to the Sultan and undergirding the German strategy in the region was the preservation of the territorial integrity of the empire with the express purpose of utilizing it as a point of entry into the Indian Ocean and, by extension, Asia. Since the rapprochement took place at a time when Britain and France were both inclined to force the passing of the sick man of Europe, Germany's easterly march, its *Drang nach Osten*, provided political breathing room, not only for the Kaiser, but also for the Sultan (Keyder 1987: 55–9). In the closing decades of the twentieth century, the return of rivalry, looming yet again in the East, has had its repercussions on the states in the region. Among others, the influx of capital flows into China, and the Pacific rim generally, and the region's appearance as an increasingly vital hub of world manufacturing is taking its toll on the rest of the periphery, including the Middle East, albeit not as brutally as in Latin America. But more crucially, the mobility of capital, resumed since the mid-1960s, and the globe-spanning inter-enterprise system put in place by American hegemony have combined to undermine the territorial basis of rivalry (Arrighi 1994) that had previously provided the Sublime Porte with room to manoeuvre. Therefore, from a political point of view, the region's role today is much more diminished than it had been a century ago.

From an economic point of view too, the empire was favourably positioned at the beginning of the century to benefit from the existing rivalry as it was able to extract financial and commercial concessions from the great powers. Presently, no such fortuitous conjuncture exists. The Sublime Porte, despite signs of periodic malaise exhibited by the Ottoman economy, gained access to funds that would otherwise have been denied it. In other words, the political leverage, however limited, which flowed from the stratagem of playing one power against the other, also yielded economic returns, however paltry. Neither the empire in its dying days nor the independent successor states that came into being with its disintegration fared any worse than colonial states that were steeped in and shaped according to the demands of the world system and the rule of the market. In fact, the newly established and nominally independent states in the Middle East, though still fettered by the commercial restrictions inherited from their imperial predecessor (for example, 1929 in the case of Turkey and 1930 in the case of Egypt), fared marginally better than most other states in the periphery. Certainly, the breakdown of the world economy from the late 1920s provided a brief reprieve to most peripheral states whose economic performance in the 1930s and 1940s proved to be slightly better than the expansionary period from 1896 to the 1920s. In the case of the Middle East, the region's comparatively better performance was not simply confined, as in other parts of the periphery, to the period following the Great Crash of 1929 (Bairoch 1977), but to the period that stretched from 1896 to 1945. Not surprisingly, the colonial and mandate states in the region, from Lebanon to Algeria, increasingly subject to the imperatives of imperial blocs after the breakdown of the world market, experienced more taxing times than the nominally sovereign states which had the luxury to profit from the autarchy that followed the breakdown.

The relatively slow pace of growth in income disparity between the core and Middle Eastern economies during the fall of British rule can thus be viewed as a by-product, in part, of imperial rivalry, which exempted the region from the exigencies of the marketplace. At the onset of the weakening of American rule, the situation appears, on surface, to be completely different. The region's share of world capital and merchandise flows has shrunk further, and now stands at a level lower than that at the turn of the twentieth century. Not heavily reliant on private capital flows like Latin America or South Africa, or lacking proximity to Pax Nipponica's vital sphere of operation like East Asia, the Middle East finds itself marginalized and exempt, by default, from the demands of the world economy in a manner reminiscent of the closing decades of the empire. Yet, the presence of oil-wealth in the region, even though most of it is geographically concentrated on its margins and stored outside it, has functioned so far in a manner similar to the way inflows of funds accompanying imperial rivalry did earlier.

As opportunities presented by rivalry at the dawn of the nineteenth century fashioned their own mechanisms of compliance, best exemplified by the exactions of the Public Debt Administration that served as a proxy of the rule of the market, so now do the intricate webs of dependence created by oil-wealth. Undoubtedly, the inflow of petro-dollars has provided the region with a precious *lebenstraum*. Notwithstanding this reprieve, however, the region's exemption from the punishing discipline of capital markets has been but complete. The influx of oil-wealth into the region has, instead, demanded and extracted a series of economic rearrangements from the states in the region. All the same, despite the resumption of widening world income disparities between the core and the periphery in the last two decades or so, the region's share of world's wealth has shrunk relatively less than its counterparts. In other words, the region's success, if it can be called that, has been to fare less poorly than most other peripheral regions. So world-economically, the decades following the heyday of Pax Britannica and Pax Americana have created conditions that could be considered more analogous than not.

That the Middle East has not fared as poorly as some other quarters of the periphery should not, however, obscure the fact that it has lost, during the course of the long twentieth century, significant ground vis-à-vis the core in terms of its share of global wealth, despite the respite bestowed on it by hegemonic rivalry and oil-wealth. Aggregate figures for the two most populous countries of the region, Egypt and Turkey, illustrate that their GNP per capita as a proportion of the GNP per capita of the world economy's core zone declined from 14.9 per cent in 1938 to 5.6 in 1988 (Arrighi 1991: 49). In fact, the historical pedigree of this contraction can easily be traced back further than the inter-War period: in the case of Egypt, for instance, its per capita income which stood at 17 per cent of that in the US in 1903–13, had fallen to 4.7 per cent by 1984 (Hansen 1991: 47, Sutcliffe 2002: 113). The brief hiatus in this persistent deterioration coincided, not unexpectedly, with the heyday of American hegemony. Yet, as will be discussed at length below, the dynamics behind the hiatus were more conjunctural than structural. This is why the trend has resumed without delay upon the conclusion of the expansionary period of 'the thirty glorious years,' from 1945 to 1975. That, by and by, the region's economic standing, vis-à-vis the core has diminished may seem to be at odds with the tempo and nature of political change, that not only created a score of independent states in the wake of the decolonization process of the post-1945 period, but also witnessed a shift in hegemonic command.

Ironically, the persistence of economic trends for most of the twentieth century, in spite of the shift in hegemonic lead, flows from the fact that Pax Britannica's success in carving out new states was brought to full fruition by Pax Americana's success in deepening the process of 'stateness'. The consolidation of bureaucratic structures during the period of modernization in the 1950s and 1960s and the 'statizing' nature of import-substitution policies that remained in place until the late 1970s deepened the order put in place by British rule. After all, Pax Americana 'furthered the reach, framework, and penetration of the world system' that was brought to 'global dominion' by Pax Britannica (Hopkins 1990: 409–11). And the reconstruction of the global economic space rendered these new polities increasingly dependent on mobile capital, allowing the resumption of trends of the inter-War era. Despite the collapse of one world order and the ascent of another, the continuity in global political trends buttressed world economic trends, including the growing disparity in incomes. In fine, the political upheavals and large-scale economic transformations that stemmed from the rise of American hegemony have deepened the sway of ceaseless economic devolution in the periphery that has characterized the long twentieth century.

In both cases, the income gap between the world economy's core and peripheral zones widened much faster during periods of hegemonic decline and imperial rivalry than periods of hegemonic maturity. The downfall of Pax Britannica and Pax Americana, which generated the so-called 'two waves of globalization', found their immediate manifestation in the accelerating pace of contraction in the region's relative wealth. And in these periods of imperial rivalry, the Middle East's economic trajectory was determined, first, by the rise not only of mono-crop economies specializing in tropical crops, but also of cereal-growing temperate settlements, and later, by the ascent of the Pacific rim. Of course, the consolidation of American hegemony had its ramifications on the political reconfiguration of the region, but from an economic point of view, the transformations it has wrought have been negligible. Indeed, gains that accrued during hegemonic moments, at the height of British rule in 1850–73, and of American rule in 1945–73, have quickly been reversed, and the growth in income disparity promptly resumed.

In this chapter, then, it is the persistence of this trend—the widening of the income gap between the Middle East and the world economy's core zone during the twentieth century—that will be at the centre of investigation. Three processes, it will be argued, enhanced this trend, and each process will be examined in a separate section. The section, 'From Lebensraum to Petro-dollars', will take stock of the transformations experienced by the region during periods of imperial rivalry and compare these changes with those that accompanied periods of hegemonic maturity. The brevity and momentary nature of the changes inaugurated in the region by the two periods of hegemony will be contrasted with the deep and slow-moving nature of changes associated with periods of rivalry. That the gains associated with the period of hegemony were promptly wiped out will explain in part the resumption of the world systemic trends that were in place at the beginning of the twentieth century. The section, 'From Formal to Informal Empire', will scrutinize the nature of the transition from the British to the American order, two orders that came to envelop the twentieth century: it will maintain that a transition from formal to informal empire tends not only to reproduce, but to deepen trends already at work. It will subsequently depict the nature of the developmental path the region followed at the height of American hegemony, and will argue that the region's import-substitution industrialization replicated trends dominant in the periphery, but in essence, its dynamic was fundamentally different than that of its successful counterparts elsewhere. The gains registered during this exceptional period of growth reflected less the region's successful adherence to the American world order, and more the reverberations of the 'golden age' of the twentieth century. Finally, the last section 'From Plantations to Sweatshops', will then address some structural reasons—among them, the character of the rural sector—as to why the region's economic performance was destined to be less satisfactory than expected. If the absence of large-scale commercial agriculture was a deterrent to the region's successful incorporation at the beginning of the century, at its end, it is the absence, *ceteris paribus*, of a sizeable rural sector which could partake in subsidizing the industrial sector that serves as an impediment to the region's ability to fully participate in the intensifying competition, and not the incapacity of the states to keep up with the tempo of global change, as most studies of the region would argue.

FROM LEBENSRAUM TO PETRO-DOLLARS

Hegemony, by definition, is a short-lived and ephemeral moment. And it is during these moments that the reconstruction of the world system's economic and political space, subject to fracture during wars of imperial rivalry, takes place. The 'hegemonic moment', therefore, invariably brings about a period of generalized prosperity. This worldwide prosperity, too, is, by extension, short-lived and ephemeral. For the world economy's agglomerative power, that routinely flows from its construction de novo— eventually starts to dissipate past the hegemonic moment. The systemic order, built under the watchful eyes of the hegemon, gets swiftly revamped by the mobility that capital regains upon the restoration of the unity of the world economy. Periods of hegemony then, due to their brevity, provide us with poor indicators of long-term economic performance, since capital, deprived of its habitual room for manoeuvre, perforce finds itself reliant on the hegemon's ability to restore its mobility by establishing the unity of the world market. Periods of rivalry, by contrast, register better long-term trends not simply because they span a longer time period, but more crucially, they unfold under the shadow and aegis of capital, reincarnated by the reconstruction of the unity of the world market.

Historically, then, that the generalized prosperity of the world economy at the height of Pax Britannica and Pax Americana, in the mid-nineteenth and mid-twentieth centuries, respectively, was not endowed with longevity is not surprising. Certainly, it was at the peak of British hegemony, and during the reconstruction of the Continent, that the world economy's peripheral regions, from British India to the newly-decolonized Spanish America, partook, as producers of raw materials and agricultural goods, in the mid-Victorian expansion. Their share of world economic flows increased considerably, and significant rates of growth were registered, among other things, on an income per capita basis. By the century's end, however, the peripheral zone's share in world trade had fallen from its heights in the late 1840s, from 23 to 18 per cent; so had its GNP per capita (Hanson 1980: 20 Zimmerman 1962). To be sure, growth resumed following the end of the Great Depression in 1896, but thenceforth, it was the temperate settlements which assumed an increasingly pivotal role in global economic flows, as attested to by the debate about the divergence, from the opening decades of the twentieth century, in the fortunes of the temperate settlements and the tropical world, to the injury of the latter (Lewis 1978).

Similarly, it was in the heyday of Pax Americana, during the reconstruction of war-torn Europe and Japan, that a large part of the peripheral world not only gained its independence from colonial overrule, but also partook in the spectacular expansion of the thirty glorious years. In the minds of many, in fact, there was no doubt that the 1970s was most deserving of the sobriquet 'the development decade'. The momentary rise of the so-called newly industrializing countries, in this view, was no less than the economic counterpart of the political emancipation wave of the 1950s and 1960s. Income per capita in the periphery increased at an annual rate of 3 per cent between 1950 and 1973, differences in performance notwithstanding. Growth increased from 2 per cent in the 1950s to 3.4 per cent in the 1960s (Wee 1978: 58). By the century's end, the gains registered in the periphery before the late 1970s have, once again, mostly disappeared (Arrighi and Drangel 1986: 37–40). In 1990, the share of Africa, Asia, and Latin America in world trade was substantially lower than it had been before 1945, owing to a major decline in the relative importance of tropical raw materials in world trade compounded by deterioration in the terms of trade of the Third World exports from the 1970s. Latin America's share of world exports fell from 12.4 per cent in 1950 to 3.9 per cent in 1990; that of Africa from 5.2 to 1.9 per cent, as Asia's share increased from 13.1 to 14.0 per cent (Leys 1996: 22–3; Bagchi 2000: 286). And this time, East Asia is performing a function similar to that of the temperate settlements a century ago. The Pacific rim has in effect assumed a pivotal role in global economic flows, at the expense of the rest of the peripheral world.

Hence, the advent of imperial rivalry in the 1870s, and later in the 1970s, reversed the trends witnessed by the periphery during the hegemonic moments of 1850–73 and 1945–68/73. To wit, during the waning of British hegemony, the incomes of the world economy's peripheral regions, when measured as a percentage of that of the core zone, all dwindled, with one noticeable exception. Between the commencement of the Great Depression of the nineteenth century and the Great War, Africa's GNP per capita, as a proportion of that of the core, fell from 0.2 to 0.15; that of Asia, from 0.26 to 0.17. The exception was Latin America, whose share rose from 0.34 to 0.36, thanks largely to the meteoric rise of Argentina, a member of the temperate settlements. Even the global upswing that spanned from the 1890s to the 1920s failed to arrest the almost inexorable drop in incomes of the peripheral world. This relative descent in incomes in the periphery lasted well into the 1940s, again with the exception of Latin America, where the shift from export of tropical crops to import-substitution industrialization had already started in the 1930s. Between 1913 and 1950, colonial mining and plantation economies either stagnated or shrank: GNP per capita in Asia, the centrestage of plantation economies, dropped, again as a proportion of that in the core zone, from 0.17 to 0.12, and Africa's GNP remained unchanged at 0.15, whereas that in Latin America rose from 0.36 to 0.44 (Maddison 1995; Amsden 2001: 9).

At the end of the twentieth century, a similar scenario was unfolding. The onset of the waning of America's might was having its debilitating impact on most quarters of the periphery. Africa's per capita income, as a proportion of incomes commanded in the core zone, went on to decline from 0.11 in 1973 to a mere 0.07 in 1995; and that of Latin America from 0.35 to 0.28. Yet again, there was one exception. Not surprisingly, the exception this time was and remains East Asia, whose spectacular performance has lifted Asia's per capita income from 0.14 to 0.18 of that of the core (Amsden 2001: 9). Overall, then, periods of rivalry have proven to be times when the world economy's income distribution gets attuned to the demands of capital, and the traces of economic recovery ushered in by the hegemonic moment becomes at once a relic of the past.

Like most quarters of the peripheral world, the Ottoman Empire, too, partook in the phenomenal expansion of the world economy during the mid-Victorian period, as did the Middle East a century later, in the prosperity of the thirty glorious years. In the 1850s and 1860s, and especially during the American Civil War, cotton and grain from the Ottoman dominions found their way into the world markets in ever-growing quantities. A century later, in the 1960s and 1970s, most states in the Middle East, echoing worldwide trends, adhered to the widely popular import-substitution industrialization strategy, increased the share of manufacturing as a percentage of GDP, and registered gains on an income per capita basis (Issawi 1982: 109). In both instances though, periods of impressive growth were cut short by the economic downturns that ensued. By the turn of the twentieth century, the Ottoman Empire's share in world trade, despite the advent of railroads and a proliferation in the number of concessionary companies, had failed to surpass 2 to 3 per cent of the total (Rostow 1978: 70). At the close of the twentieth century, the picture was not all that different: the region's GNP, as a proportion of the core zone, had shrunk from 11.1 per cent in 1980 to 7.1 per cent in 1988 (Arrighi 2002: 15) at a time when revenues from oil had not even sunk to their lowest levels. Equally significant, the region's share in world capital flows—that have grown during the last quarter century from US$ 3 billion to US$ 200 to US$ 250 billion—has been almost negligible. Throughout the 1990s, the sums injected into the region have not exceeded a mere 1 per cent of total capital flows—as well as of the region's total GNP (Owen and Pamuk 1999: 233; McMichael 2000: 216).

That the gains registered at the zenith of hegemonic rule were rapidly wiped away during the last quarters of the nineteenth and twentieth centuries stemmed from similar reasons. The expansionary thrust of the late nineteenth century opened up the temperate settlements to cultivation and made possible their full integration, as agricultural producers, into global networks of production and trade as it expanded the number of suppliers of tropical and other plantation crops. By the 1930s, the regions of recent settlement had all moved up higher on the ladder of global wealth. Conversely, the Empire's role as a major agrarian producer was undermined by the phenomenal rise of temperate settlements as the granaries of the world economy, despite all the measures introduced to facilitate the flow of Ottoman agricultural goods into world markets. The economic landscape shaped during the mid-Victorian expansion therefore suffered the erosive effects of the re-division of labour on a global scale. The globe-spanning nature of Pax Britannica, especially after the 1880s, increased the number of sites of production in the periphery, which itself was expanding in tandem with the growth in the sway of colonial empires, and lowered returns on economic activities in which these regions were specialized.

The Ottoman Empire's lacklustre performance from the 1870s to the 1930s did not derive from its inability to compete with producers in Asia or Latin America specialized in tropical crops, though plans to introduce some tropical crops into the Mediterranean and establish therein large agricultural holdings were never scarce; they were, as will be discussed below, seriously entertained time and again. It was the ascent of temperate settlements in a relatively short span of time that radically altered the economic climate of the world economy and the Ottoman Empire's integration into it. Ottoman wheat exports consequently fell from 7 per cent of the total in 1878–82 to less than 1 per cent in 1911–13. The turnaround came 'after 1890 when North American wheat entered world markets and world wheat prices began to fall' (Hansen 1991: 303–4). With the increase in the number of cotton producers worldwide, the share of raw cotton in Egypt's exports declined from 90 per cent in 1910–14 to 70 per cent in the 1930s as the volume of the country's trade declined from an index of 150 in 1913, with the base year 1938 as 100, to 61 in 1933 (Issawi 1982: 26–7, 31).

In a strikingly similar scenario, the expansionary thrust of the late twentieth century, too, came to be associated almost exclusively with the emergence and rise of the countries around the Pacific rim, whose economic might has been amplified beyond measure by the incorporation of China. Whereas in the 1970s, the gains that accrued from industrialization were distributed among a relatively wide variety of locales (inter alia, South Africa, Brazil, and Mexico), a quarter century later, East Asia became the *locus classicus* of the world's manufacturing activities—as Brazil and South Africa were undergoing economic and social tumult as a result of this relocation. In brief, the upward mobility which the age of Pax Americana had started to deliver is cut short again, only to expose the frail basis of the prosperity the post-1945 period heralded in the peripheral and semi-peripheral regions of the world economy. Not as industrialized nor as reliant on capital flows as either Brazil or South Africa, the region finds itself in a situation where the threat of punishment by world capital markets lacks force. So far, there has been no rush by the states in the region to dismantle their existing social infrastructure, however mediocre, in the hopes of attracting capital: this has allowed them to largely escape the kind of economic upheaval faced by most states in the periphery (Walton and Seddon 1994). Accordingly, the region's relative impoverishment has been less steep than that of its counterparts. Whereas Latin America's GNP per capita as a proportion of world GNP per capita declined by 17 per cent between 1975 and 1999 and that of sub-Saharan Africa by 50 per cent, the contraction in the Middle East and North Africa was only by 3 per cent (Arrighi 2002: 15).

If, on the surface, the start and the close of the twentieth century produced similar scenarios in most parts of the peripheral zone, this should not obscure the significant differences between the two periods as well. In fact, the repercussions of the onset of the waning of Pax Britannica from the 1870s and of Pax Americana from the 1970s could not have been more diametrically opposed than in the Middle East. Today, the relocation of the workshops of the world and the growing re-centring of the world economy in the Pacific rim and its environs render the benefits which world markets are expected to cargo in to the states and peoples of the region a rather distant and suspect prospect, a situation partially remedied by the proximity of oil-wealth. But given the mercurial character of oil markets, the resources at the region's disposal may not prove to be as long lasting as that provided by hegemonic rivalry previously.

In the last quarter of the nineteenth century, growing imperial rivalry over the Ottoman Empire gave the Sublime Porte precious breathing room in its dealings with the great powers in matters of debt and bankruptcy. Owing largely to Germany's *Drang nach Osten*, inflow of capital in the form of public debt continued unabated despite the Empire's alleged economic ill-health. By 1914, Germany's share in the Empire's public debt and private investment had outstripped that of Britain: London held 14 per cent of the Empire's public debt, and 13 per cent of private investments, whereas Germany's share reached 20 per cent in the former category, and 30 in the latter. The picture could not have been any different from that in 1881. Then, London's share in the Empire's public debt consisted of 30 per cent of the total, as opposed to the insignificant sums extended by Berlin. Its share of direct investments in 1895 was 24 per cent of the total, while the German share stood at 19 per cent (Issawi 1982: 64–71). Surely, the rivalry at the end of the nineteenth century allowed the Porte to momentarily escape the 'market discipline' the great powers would have liked to impose on it.

In the last quarter of the twentieth century, as a new round of imperial rivalry gradually set in, the Pacific-bound movement of US and Europe-based transnational corporations, this time centred on China, once again, provided the states in the Middle East with similar room to manoeuvre, but this time by exempting them from the competitive pressures of the world economy. Ironically, if the *lebensraum* the German challenge allowed the Empire to breathe easier than its colonial counterparts elsewhere, today the returns to the policy of not precipitously dismantling the economic and political structures of the import-substitution era have not been insubstantial: the breathing room furnished by the proximity of oil-wealth has allowed the region to fare comparatively better, however dismally, than those who have done otherwise. This freedom of action is partly owed to the petro-dollars circulating in the region. Between 1973 and 1989, the Gulf states provided US$ 140 billion to the countries in the Middle East: the figure includes workers' remittances and US$ 50 billion of official assistance (Henry and Springborg 2001: 39, 46). Not heavily reliant on world capital markets, the region's indebtedness remains, with the exception of Turkey, lower than either Latin America or South Asia. Between 1988 and 1998, debt service ratios to GDP and to exports of goods and services have increased in the region from 13 to 15, whereas the rise in Latin America was from 25 to 37, and in South Asia, from 19 to 25 (Henry and Springborg 2001: 53).

That these developments have unfolded during a period when oil prices were stumbling and migration to the oil-rich districts of the region was severely curtailed, is not without significance. After all, the region has not been as dependent on private capital inflows as, say, Latin America; and it has not consequently suffered from the retrenchment in the 1980s of the world economy's capital flows. By the same token, the reversal of this trend in the 1990s has failed to give its economy a boost. Nor has the Middle East, unlike Africa, been completely bypassed by capital owing to the dissemination of oil wealth in the region. The fall in oil prices since the 1980s has dramatically reduced the volume of capital entering the region since total revenues accruing to the states diminished from US$ 250 billion in 1981 to US$ 110 billion in 1998 (Henry and Springborg 2001: 39, 46). But even this dramatic fall has hitherto failed to undo the economic networks that came to interlink the region during the oil boom (Chaudhury 1997).

It needs to be emphasized that the rewards of this exclusion were not evenly distributed in the region. At the turn of the twentieth century, the end of the Great Depression did not boost the fortunes of the Empire. Surely, there was a recovery during the Edwardian *belle époque*, but the economic constitution of the Empire remained unaffected by the resumption of growth. Even though economic growth in the region remained delphic in the inter-War period, there were telling differences in the performance of the states of the post-Ottoman era. In the mandate and colonial economies, per capita production and income declined until the 1950s, as attested to by the cases of Syria and Lebanon. In Egypt, on the other hand, GNP per capita increased by 1 per cent in 1913–28, and by 1.5 per cent in 1929–39, or increased by 2.6 per cent during 1923–46 (Hansen 1991: 46; Owen and Pamuk 1999: 34, 244; Issawi 1982: 25, 107–8). Broadly, non-colonial states that enjoyed autarky in the interwar period performed better than colonial states which behaved according to the dictates of the market.

Currently, those states which have acquiesced to the dictates of the market, Turkey and Egypt foremost, have shown poorer performance than states in the region that have eschewed them. Not paradoxically, this contrarian stance has slowed down the pace of de-industrialization in the region. Whereas manufacturing as a percentage of the region's GDP relative to the world average remained unchanged between 1990 and 1999 at 69, it fell steeply in Latin America from 112 to 101, and in sub-Saharan Africa from 87 to 75 (Arrighi 2002: 19). In fact, despite the steady pace of contraction of its relative wealth, the region has managed, in the period from 1960 to 1999, to fare better than its counterparts in the South in that income per capita in the region has declined relatively less steeply than in either Latin America or Africa. The decline in the number of people living on less than US$ 1 per day demonstrates that the region fared slightly better, in relative terms, at a time when the number is inexorably increasing in some other parts of South. The proportion of population living below US$ 2 per day, on the other hand, has increased from 25 to over 30 per cent of the population, mostly due to increases in Egypt, Turkey, Morocco, and Yemen—not surprisingly, in places where neo-liberal reforms have been the order of the day.

The rule of the market, as represented by the colonial stranglehold and later by adherence to the recipe of liberalization, did not serve the states in the region well. Those states that remained outside the hold of lending agencies performed better. Both periods of rivalry therefore served to exempt the region from the immediate vagaries of the marketplace to a considerable extent. Owing to the great power bickering of the nineteenth century and the oil-wealth of the twentieth, the Ottoman Empire and the contemporary states in the Middle East found themselves not as hard pressed, as their counterparts elsewhere, by the demands of the market. The presence in the Ottoman Empire of German capital from the 1880s, and in the Middle East of oil-wealth from the 1980s, has kept the region within the reach of, but not under the direct suzerainty of world economic forces.

Nonetheless, despite the respite, the region's income as a proportion of that of the core zone continued to fall, albeit at a slower rate than in other parts of the periphery. The resumption of persistent economic devolution in spite of the region's impunity from unfettered market rule, attests to the presence of deeply rooted processes at work that taxed the region all the same. There were two basic reasons as to why ceaseless economic devolution became the order of the day. The first reason pertains to long-term change and involves the extension and deepening of the world system via the spread of stateness. And the second pertains to short-term change, and entails the region's nominal, rather than effective incorporation into the economic order crafted by US hegemony. The following section will correspondingly dwell on these dual reasons and track their impacts on the trajectory of the region.

FROM FORMAL TO INFORMAL EMPIRE

The political panorama in the Middle East changed hue with the passing of colonial empires. The gravitas London and Paris had in the region in the first half of the century may not have receded instantaneously with the withdrawal of colonial empires from it. Nevertheless, the most ostensible and telling demonstration of the former colonial rulers' exclusion from the new balance of power was the failure of the triple aggression against Egypt in 1956, fundamentally because it was not endorsed by the new hegemon, the US. Two years later, in 1958, the solution to the crisis in Lebanon did not involve the intermediation of the former imperial powers, but rather, the deployment of American military might. Throughout the Middle East, new alliances, from the Baghdad Pact to SEATO, were struck under the leadership of Washington. In a decade or so after its independence, the region, that had long remained within the gravitational field of London and Paris, found itself under the long shadow of Washington.

To be sure, the region could not escape the geopolitical strains created by the world system's duopolistic power structure, and became an arena of contestation during the Cold War. Granted, the bipolar divide began to lose some of its demarcative function after 1973 with the launching of *infitah* in Egypt. Yet, in political and economic terms, most states in the region, as peripheral states elsewhere, whether of the Soviet or the American bloc, followed similar paths in the Cold War era. In terms of the actual political structures, most states in the region were 'either one-party states or military dictatorships' most of the time. In terms of actual economic structures, the role private local enterprise and foreign capital performed in the region, as elsewhere, has varied to a certain extent, but more often than not, state enterprises have occupied the pride of place. Also, the region's states, whatever their political proclivities, obtained aid in the form of direct grants and loans. What is more pertinent from our vantage point is that they all adhered to the idea and implemented strategies of national development (Wallerstein 1992: 112–14).

Initially, the achievement of independence from colonial rule, if and when coupled with the strategy of national development, was expected to grant deliverance from the global division of labour fashioned under British rule. Putting aside momentarily whether or not this economic strategy would automatically have undone the division of labour that neatly divided the world into producers of manufactured goods on the one side and of agricultural goods and raw materials on the other, it needs to be underscored that the twin processes of industrialization and urbanization inscribed in it, triggered massive social change. And both processes gained noticeable pace at the zenith of American hegemony. Given the scope and sway of the social and political transformations undergone by the third world in the post-1945 period, the transition from British to American rule occurred incommensurably swiftly, if not smoothly. In the Middle East as well, the transition from the centrality of London (and Paris) to that of Washington occurred as speedily as elsewhere in the Third World.

The speed of the transition from formal to informal empire resulted from the fact that the institutional infrastructure laid by Britain and her rivals, in extending the reach and extent of 'stateness' to distant parts of the globe via colonization, was later skilfully utilized by Pax Americana. The transformations associated with American rule, grand though they may have been, merely deepened and legitimated the command of states, owing in large part to the consolidation of bureaucratic structures under indigenous rule and the 'statizing' nature of import-substitution policies. Although the economic consequences of the transition to a new hegemonic rule were momentous, the period of transition that generated them, as emphasized above, was incommensurably short in span. Briefly exploring the nature of this transition is of germane import in stressing the persistence of the trend of widening income disparity—between the core zone and the Middle East in particular and the South in general—during the long twentieth century. So what follows next is a brief discussion on the nature of the process that abetted Washington to supplant London, and the impact this had on the ongoing redistribution of world wealth.

From the un-embarrassment of riches underlying the Edwardian belle époque to the embarrassment of the wartime Lend-Lease Act, London, as the heart of the world economy, found its much-coveted position taken over by New York rather precipitously. Her steady and relative loss of power, that ultimately culminated in the eventual dethronement of the City from the apex of the world system, commenced roughly with the start of the Great Depression in 1873 and ended with the completion of the War in 1945, in approximately three-quarters of a century, to be precise. Following up on the throes of the massive colonization wave, which picked up pace in the 1880s and abetted the consolidation of the interstate system worldwide, the new American imperial order found a political environment supportive of its coming of age, as attested to by the lasting popularity of the Wilsonian doctrine even in most distant quarters of the globe. The young Turkish Republic, for example, wanted to solidify its independence from continental rivals by declaring its willingness to be placed under American mandate, but to no avail. Since the emergent order tended to undermine the hold the colonial empires of the previous era established over the peripheral regions of the world system, the post-1945 period proved to be fertile ground for the implantation of American command.

Historically speaking, the swiftness of the transition was not unique. Amsterdam's ascent to the pinnacle of the world system was equally brisk. It, too, took place against a backdrop of an immense colonial enterprise, then undertaken by the Portuguese and Spanish empires from the latter half of the fifteenth century. She overtook Antwerp with impressive speed and agility, from the 1550s to 1625, in three-quarters of a century. The shift in the centre of gravity of the world economy was so sudden that it was almost as if the 'Spanish' Antwerp, a Portuguese and German creation, had 'changed into Amsterdam'. Her climb to eminence, too, had repercussions reminiscent of the decolonization wave of the latter half of the twentieth century: as a result of Amsterdam's rise, 'Portugal lost her empire in the Far East and very nearly lost Brazil as well' (Braudel 1984: 34, 187). World historically, the modernity and weightlessness—at times ascribed to the American (and Dutch) empire(s) and denied to the British (and Iberian) empire(s)—were owed in no small part to the systemic compliance successfully compelled by the former colonial empires in the regions newly incorporated into the world system (Arrighi 1994).

It was this systemic expansion that set the stage and allowed for the relatively precipitate transition from the colonial order of Pax Britannica to the imperial order of Pax Americana, the defining transformation of the long twentieth century. The primary process that lent support to the strengthening of states worldwide was, of course, colonization. For it recast existing polities in the mirror of modern states, and framed transborder operations as imperial operations. The transfer of political power to local elites in the wake of de-colonization struggles thereby entailed a change in cast, but not necessarily in the direction of the process itself. If anything, the transfer of power lent credibility to the newly established states that its colonial precedent badly lacked. Witness the land redistribution policies in the Middle East in the 1950s and 1960s that were devised to eradicate the legacy of colonialism and institute new relations of rule. In effect, the growth of local bureaucracies and the fulcral position the newly sovereign states occupied in the creation of a national economy all advanced the deepening of stateness: it multiplied state-mediated transactions, to be precise. Doubtless, the state-to-state character of most aid programmes during the Cold War was also instrumental in enhancing the nascent bureaucratic apparatus.

More crucial to the process of deepening stateness was the role assigned to statal agencies in overseeing and underwriting the import-substitution strategy. By the 1950s, the secular trends of the world economy in place since the Great Crash, namely, the declining share of agriculture in world trade (from 46 per cent in 1950 to 13 per cent in 1988), the secular decline in the terms of trade for raw materials, minerals, and agricultural goods (30, 14, and 27 per cent lower in 1990 than 1960) acted in tandem to create an environment receptive to widespread adherence to industrialization programmes. The relatively low raw material content (per unit of output) of the major industries of the period (as opposed to those of the preceding period—that is, textiles, clothing, food processing), when accompanied by the predominance of import substitution industrialization in many locales of the world economy, tended to disfavour the growth of world trade. But this did not signal that the world markets played a subordinate role to statal command: transfer of technology and expertise, producers' goods, primary, and intermediary goods, and at times, direct investment went on to interlink, in an ethereal fashion, the deceptively segmented world market. The ensuing chronic balance of payments problem and the unavailability of foreign exchange to carry on the importation of capital and intermediate goods plagued the region at the height of its industrialization push (Keyder 1985; Richards and Waterbury 1996).

Stated differently, the strategy of import substitution, designed in part to undermine the basis of the Victorian division of labour, as is to be expected, eased the transition to US rule. The resumption of transnational expansion of US corporate capital after the War was contingent upon the reconstruction of the war-devastated core zones where the hegemon's capital resources were tied and the sustenance of the economic momentum gathered in the non-core zones during the inter-War period, especially in the Americas—the Western hemisphere, that is, the primary field of operation of US corporate capital until the late 1950s. In 1950, Canada had 30 per cent of US direct investments, but the pride of place was held by Latin America, which accounted for 39 per cent (Whichard 1981: 43), where industrial production which had doubled from 1937 to 1950, rose by a further 70 per cent between 1950 and 1959. Outside the core zone, the only peripheral region that came to be included within the compass of US-based transnational corporations was thus Latin America. In other parts of the periphery, where industrialization also became the order of the day, mobilization of local resources proved to be the only viable formula to finance the undertaking. Revenues accruing from the wave of nationalization that followed the withdrawal of colonial powers, of the Canal and concessionary companies in Egypt, transfer of resources from agriculture to the industrial sector, as in Turkey, and inheritance of rights over large tracts of *dominium eminens* in most parts of the region, ensured the continued growth of manufacturing, and to good effect. The annual rate of growth in Middle East manufacturing was 13.5 per cent in 1950–9 and 10.6 in 1960–73 (Issawi 1982: 162–3).

That core capital was tied up in select theatres of the world economy until the 1960s further fuelled seemingly autarchic industrialization policies in the periphery. And the presence of a worldwide movement towards industrialization, coupled with urbanization, helped give the strategy a semblance of pervasiveness and ubiquity. This semblance of universality notwithstanding, the presence of corporate capital in Latin America placed the continent on a path different than the rest of the peripheral world, where corporate capital was conspicuously absent, with the exception, later, of the Four Dragons. In fact, the absence of core capital in the periphery in the 1950s and 1960s, that stemmed from the need to re-establish the unity of the world market by rebuilding Europe and Japan, induced the hegemon to prescribe *étatist* regimentation in the Middle East, as it did in Syria in 1954 and in Turkey in 1958 via the World Bank, on the diagnosis that only the government had the resources to address problems arising from sustaining the momentum of industrialization.

The *locus operandi* of core capital, confined largely to the core zone and the western hemisphere, was neatly mirrored in the structure of merchandise trade, especially in manufactured goods. Ceaseless was the rise during the long twentieth century in the volume of intra-core trade in manufactured goods. The trade expansion in this category, that accounted for 50 per cent of total trade expansion in 1913, reached 60 per cent in 1929, and 70 per cent in the 1950s, a far higher proportion than had ever before been achieved (Maizels 1963: 84). Capital and merchandise flows therefore short-circuited in a narrow and confined arena of the world economy. During the reconstruction of world markets on the basis of mobility of capital rather than goods, and the take-off of industrialization in the periphery, the ratio of exports to GDP in the core, even in the 1960s, at the zenith of the US imperial order, was at an all time low (Lipietz 1987).

Indeed, the share of the US in world trade was higher in the inter-War period, approximately 15 per cent, falling to 11 per cent during the 1960s. So did the share of export of manufactures. In the meanwhile, the policies of import substitution in non-core regions of the world economy corroborated the predominance of intra-core trade: despite a rise in the share of manufactures from 19 per cent of world trade in 1960 to 42 per cent in 1974, the share of non-core regions in world trade fell from 21.3 per cent in 1960 to 17.7 per cent in 1970. Of the total exports of these areas, the share of primary products (excluding oil), in turn, fell from 80 per cent in 1960 to 54 per cent in 1974. Resultant trade deficits were covered in part by aid and development assistance extended by rival powers, and by remittances sent by migrants overseas and invisible exports (Keyder 1985).

The highly protected domestic markets of the era helped transnational companies to benefit from the protective barriers in sites where they had located their subsidiary plants. In addition to the procurement and processing of natural resources, the exploitation of potential markets, heavily fractured and highly protected before and during the War, paved the way

to the reorganization of production (and services) across national boundaries—a reorganization corroborated later by attention to differentiation
of labour costs. With the resumption of the mobility of capital in the late
1960s, there was a change in the destination of FDIs. In Asia, the share
devoted to the Philippines and India declined to the benefit of Singapore,
Hong Kong, Malaysia and Taiwan. Likewise in the Middle East, until the
mid-1950s, over three-quarters of investments were made in places other
than Iran; by 1972, this share was only 15 per cent. In harmony with the
direction and volume of capital flows, the manufacturing activities from
the 1970s came to be highly concentrated in the Pacific rim, within the
magnetic field of Pax Nipponica and Pax Americana (Cummings 1987). In
the combined exports of the non-core zone, the share of the Four Dragons
rose from 9.1 per cent in 1963 to 22.0 per cent in 1973, and 32.2 per cent in
1980, at the expense of other regions: this was particularly pronounced in
south Asia (whose share plummeted from 10.7 per cent in 1963 to 5.6 per
cent in 1980), and North Africa and Middle East, where the drop was from
4.5 to 2.4 per cent (Balassa 1987).

So even though the import-substitution strategies of the era found echo
in all quarters of the periphery, including the Middle East, there was a
structural difference between the experiences of the countries of Latin
America and the Pacific rim on the one hand and the rest on the other.
Surely, Turkey and Egypt, in particular, followed strategies similar to
those in Latin America, since the relative autonomy they attained after
independence in the inter-War period permitted both to initiate the
strategy earlier than other states in the region. On the face of the momentum gained by industrialization in the 1950s and 1960s, the similarities in
the paths followed by the states in the Middle East and Latin America
seemed negligible. In retrospect, the retrenchment of American capital in
the western hemisphere during the collapse of the world market and the
restoration of core economies in the 1940s and 1950s forced US-based
transnational corporations to weave dependencies within the hemisphere
through their affiliates and subsidiaries. As suggested by theories of
'dependent development', it was the interplay of forces between local
capital, the state and foreign capital that determined the mode and dynamics of industrialization.

In the Middle East, the sources that served to finance the undertaking
were much more varied, yet none of these sources commanded longevity.
Remittances sent back home by workers abroad, earnings from invisible
exports, transfers of oil money, and employment of agricultural surpluses
in fostering industrialization were all subject to serious disruptions, and
dependent on conjuncture. For instance, with the end of the Cold War,

development assistance made available to states in the region declined precipitously, the region's share fell from 30 per cent of the total in 1977 to 17 per cent in 1990 and 9 per cent in 1997, 'reflecting the region's diminished importance in the world' (Henry and Springborg 2001: 31-2). In contradistinction to Latin America and the Pacific rim, where the transnational expansion of core capital was operative and created a dynamic which was *sui generis* to these regions, in the Middle East, the downturn in the world economy and the end of the Cold War induced a crisis. The inundation of world financial markets with petro-dollars in the 1970s veiled the full extent of the weaknesses inherent in the region's economic structure. But the retrenchment of capital resources at the core in the 1980s exposed it fully.

The insularity of industrialization in the Middle East in the 1980s was in stark contrast with that in Latin America and East Asia in the context of the inter-enterprise system. In the absence of transnational capital, the region's inter-industry trade index is substantially lower than in Asia and Latin America: the weighted average for the region (excepting Turkey) is 0.081 and for Turkey, 0.284. In the cases of Mercosur and APEC, the index stands at 0.519 and 0.903 respectively (Henry and Springborg 2001: 42-3). In Latin America, this interdependence allowed the momentum to last into the 1990s, despite a drastic reduction in the volume of private capital inflows. Nonetheless, once capital regained its global sweep, Latin America, too, became a less valued field of operation than before (Mahon 1996). Of late, the region has been losing ground, undoing the Brazilian 'miracle'. With the end of the hegemonic maturity that lasted from 1945 to the 1970s, during which the economic and political health of most peripheral states was restored and capital's mobility hampered, the divergence in income disparity between the core and the peripheral zones recommenced or accelerated with capital's newly found mobility.

In brief, if the centering of world economic flows in the temperate zone at the turn of the twentieth century and in the Pacific rim at its end have placed the region in a disadvantageous position, so did the concentration of American capital in the core and the western hemisphere in mid-century. There was a momentary rise in the fortunes of the regions of recent settlement during the first quarter of the twentieth century, and in the fortunes of Latin America from the 1930s to the 1970s. The fall of the British Empire brought a reversal of fortunes in the temperate settlements, leaving its members to lose most of the gains they accrued during the inter-War period, and capital's 'liberation' to gain worldwide mobility from the 1970s brought a similar reversal in the fortunes of Latin America. The Middle East experienced fast economic growth from the 1950s to the

1980s, and industrialized like most other regions of the periphery. Yet, at a structural level, there were differences between its mode of industrialization and those of the regions that registered success. And this difference stemmed from the fact that the Middle East never became an integral component of the space of capital flows fashioned by American rule. So even when the difference between it and the core zones in terms of income was momentarily arrested or decelerated in the 1940s and 1950s, it was more due to the overall growth of the world economy than the region's successful insertion into it.

Overall then, the territorialization of political rule during the long twentieth century did not yield economic returns as anticipated in the period of decolonization, but instead deepened the income gap between the core and the periphery, the Middle East included. In this outcome, the region's nominal incorporation into Pax Americana was equally responsible. During the long twentieth century, from the 1870s to the present, the region has continued, with the exception of the 1970s, to lose ground vis-à-vis the core. So far, we have laid emphasis on world-systemic aspects of the Middle East's trajectory more so than regional aspects, which follow next.

FROM PLANTATIONS TO SWEATSHOPS

The dynamic underlying the periodic bouts of upward (and downward) mobility that dotted the long twentieth century, as inventoried in the preceding section, was world systemic in nature. This, of course, does not imply that regional aspects of the process were negligible, but that instances of mobility were tied, in varying degrees, to the rise (and at times decline) of the three hegemonic powers, the UK, the US, and Japan. Despite the centrality of world-systemic trends in laying out the principal coordinates of economic mobility, the main emphasis most analyses place in their evaluations of the economic performance of the Middle East qua economic region remains principally on the political pedigree and make-up of the states that inhabit it, and more importantly, their failure to keep up with the tempo of global change. Since politics is deemed to be the driving force of the region's social dynamic, construction of a rigorous political taxonomy is expected to provide a meaningful point of entry, if not an impeccable guide, to the origins of the differing economic trajectories that blanket it today (cf. Henry and Springborg 2001; Owen 1992). Laying emphasis primarily on state structures stems from the diagnosis that the region's states have served as veritable obstacles to change, remaining either unresponsive to or defensive in the face of the major transformations currently revamping the world economy. When set against the expectations of the withering away of strong states, the deeply rooted character of political command in the region strikes an anomalous note. This not only sets the region apart from its counterparts in the South, but also accounts for its relatively poor economic performance. For it is taken for granted that political streamlining would inevitably bolster economic growth and insure economic mobility. Yet, in light of the pivotal part played by world-systemic trends in generating mobility, the issue should be broached from a wider angle.

Historically speaking, what has left indelible marks on the region's economic constitution were periods of rivalry and hegemonic decline, more so than periods of hegemony which, in essence, bypassed first the Ottoman Empire, and later the Middle East (Wallerstein 1985). The ends of British and American rule created analogous scenarios in that they spared the region from the vicissitudes of the market. This was most evident in the sparseness in the region of plantation-like units of production at the turn of the twentieth century and of inter-enterprise/corporate networks interlinking economic activities within the global space of flows. In other words, in terms of the region's economic infrastructure, the transformations that Pax Americana has been undergoing since the 1970s resemble in form, if not in essence, those Pax Britannica witnessed from the 1870s.

By the last quarter of the nineteenth century, the suppression of slave trade in the Atlantic, largely complete in the 1860s, had already furthered the dissemination and proliferation of the plantation complex throughout the length and breadth of the Indian Ocean, from the Mascarene Islands to Assam and Malaysia. No longer based on slave labour par excellence, the plantation complex thrived in this new clime owing to the abundance of coolie labour. Correspondingly, production of tropical goods expanded spectacularly over the course of the next half-century, from Brazil to Ceylon, cutting down their prices more than those of manufactured goods until prices collapsed catastrophically in the late 1920s (Topik and Wells 1998). As a result, the stellar performers of the mid-nineteenth century, producers of sugar, coffee, and indigo, were easily displaced by competitors from the Pacific Ocean and South America.

At the century's end, industrial production in the periphery—that had been mostly confined to a few locales on both sides of the Atlantic (like Brazil, Argentina, and South Africa) until the 1970s—is, in a similar manner, spreading east, into the environs of the Pacific rim. To a considerable extent, the easterly relocation of manufacturing operations is following the tracks of the spread of the plantation complex. Today's counterparts of the plantations are, of course, the factories and sweatshops that have come to dot many peripheral region. And expectedly, the abundance of cheap labour still plays a cardinal role in the transfer and outsourcing by transnational corporations of their manufacturing operations overseas.

That the spatial fix of both waves of relocation of economic activities was to be found in Asia is not the only feature of the process that unites the high ages of Pax Britannica and Pax Americana. So do the outcomes generated by the momentum of the very same process. At the turn of the twentieth century, the effective extension in sites of production of tropical goods from the Atlantic to the Indian Ocean, when coupled with the ability of putting indentured labour to work, placed downward pressure on the prices of these goods, setting in train continual deterioration in terms of trade of the exports of the peripheral world. Today, a similar crowding in manufacturing in the world economy's peripheral regions, that has been in the making since the 1930s owing to the dispersal of import-substitution industrialization, is bringing about an outcome reminiscent of the fate of prices of tropical goods in the first quarter of the century. The impressive spread of industrialization outside the core zone has rendered the activity itself less remunerative today than at the turn of the century, when suppliers were still limited in number (Arrighi and Drangel 1986).

With the downward pressure on prices in both instances, due to the territorial expansion of the world system after the 1870s and 1970s and the resultant proliferation in production sites, regions that hosted these peripheral economic activities saw their fortunes shrink. The impressive gains of the first few decades, when the relocation of these activities was initially taking place, were eventually wiped out: witness the star performers of the late nineteenth and early twentieth centuries whose fortunes, even before the Great Crash, were abruptly reversed, and failed to recover well into the 1950s. In the latter half of the heyday of tropical trade, from the 1870s to the 1930s, personal incomes in Latin America, Asia, and Africa, when measured as a proportion of the incomes commanded in the core zones of the world economy, went on to shrink or stagnate at best, until the collapse of the world market (Latham 1981). The situation somewhat changed in the dramatic environment of the 1930s. A similar scenario of divergence between the fortunes of the core and peripheral zones has again been at play since the late 1970s. As depicted in the first section of this chapter, incomes commanded in the periphery as a proportion of those in the core have again been shrinking, resuming the persistent and deepening income equality between the core and the periphery (Korzeniewicz and Moran 1997).

At the height of Pax Britannica, the rural producers in the Ottoman dominions were not alienated from their landholdings and, hence, could not be turned into either coerced labour, as in the case of plantation economies, or commercialized, market-dependent farmers, as in the regions of recent settlement (cf. Friedmann 1978), definitely worked against it, although admittedly, this was not the only factor that determined the region's developmental trajectory. But the overwhelming number of the smallholding peasantry that survived, even when the ownership of land was concentrated in a few hands, mostly outside of Anatolia, after the passing of the 1858 Land Code, oftentimes turned into shareholders rather than farm hands. If the region's inability to create supplies of surplus labour worked against it in its attempts to be an integral part of the Victorian division of labour, today it is the very success of the processes unleashed by Pax Americana that taxes its economic performance. The share of the rural population has fallen from 80 to 90 per cent of the total population in 1913 to below 50 per cent in most parts of the region today; in Turkey, for instance, the percentage is fast approaching one-third of the total population, an average closer to that in Latin America.

The survival of the small peasantry was intimately linked to the ability of the Ottoman imperial bureaucracy to collect, without intermediation, part of the agricultural surplus in the form of tithe. At the height of British hegemony, the centrality of this bureaucracy was reinforced by the passing, in 1858, of the Land Code. Despite the burgeoning of centripetal forces in the form of provincial notables, the overwhelming dominance of the small-holding peasantry remained intact, and the enterprising and commercially-minded landed elites had to bring under tillage previously uncultivated land, rather than dislodge petty producers from their holdings (Keyder 1987). And even when title deeds were obtained by powerful local interests—instead of their rightful owners, the direct producers—the existing organization of production remained unaffected (Gerber 1987). Simply put, what changed was the destination of rent paid by the peasant, from the central seat of power to new landholders, and not the agrarian structures themselves, nor the manner in which the surplus was extracted from direct producers.

The Empire was thus manned by small rural producers, unlike the plantation economies that needed importation of labour on a large scale. Against the background of the high land–labour ratio that silhouetted the Empire's landscape, it proved difficult to subjugate rural labour to the exigencies of capital. Even after the migratory movements and influx of populations following the Crimean War and successive wars in the Balkans, the land–labour ratio remained high. In other words, the Empire never played host to unlimited supplies of labour à la Lewis. In fact, there were labour shortages in Egypt at the height of the cotton boom, and even though, at times, the idea of importing labour into Anatolia or Iraq was seriously entertained, it failed to materialize. The difficulties the imperial powers encountered in the implantation of new structures of agrarian production were compounded by the fact that there was not much 'foreign' ownership of land.

The attempts by British officials to establish large-scale agricultural units failed, with the exception of Egypt. The relatively populous quarters of the empire were placed under close scrutiny by these powers as potential sites for large-scale commercial agriculture. The success obtained in Egypt and Algeria could not have been replicated elsewhere, but similar projects were entertained for certain parts of Anatolia as well. It was not only in the field of cereal husbandry that the great powers could not refashion the region in the form of large estates. Tropical goods encountered a different fate. The Mediterranean was, after all, not ecologically rich and diverse enough to allow for the full acclimatization of tropical crops. Geographically speaking, it was the Mediterranean shore of the Empire that was heavily canvassed and at times contested. The French government intended to introduce tropical crops into the littoral regions of the Empire, and turn the region into a large-scale supplier of sugarcane, coffee, tea, silk, and other items, but without success. Only the introduction of cotton and tobacco proved somehow durable. Ironically, the experiment eventually had to yield to the forces of nature reigning in the Mediterranean, and grains and wine continued to prevail at the expense of tropical crops (Issawi 1982: 35).

In brief, in the Ottoman dominions, unlike most quarters of the periphery at the turn of the twentieth century, large commercial estates were scarce, with the notable exception of Egypt. The prevalence of smallholding peasantry implied two developments which ran counter to the trends unleashed by the decline in British power. First, in the absence of specialization inherent in plantation economies, the Empire's exports remained highly variegated: wheat, tobacco, barley, raisins, figs, raw silk, raw wool, and opium. These eight crops comprised 51 per cent of the Ottoman exports in 1878–80, and 44 per cent in 1913. When cereal exports decreased sharply because of the inundation of world markets with wheat originating in the temperate settlements, tobacco rose to first place, and cotton was promoted to a higher rank at an impressive pace. The crop-mix remained more varied in the inter-War period as well (Issawi 1982: 31–2). But the share of any commodity in the total value of Ottoman exports rarely exceeded 12 per cent. Second, the lebensraum described in the first section of the chapter permitted the Empire to finance its exports more easily than its colonial counterparts in the periphery (Frank 1976). This helped the petty-holders to escape the clutches of world-market specialization instituted elsewhere, limiting the volume of exports. In most of the final fifty years of the Empire's existence, its imports exceeded its exports, allowing the survival of this agrarian structure.

The absence of institutionalized coercion mechanisms, such as those that distinguished plantation or colonial economies, was a formidable obstacle in the region's attractiveness for the commercially minded. Yet, even when that happened, albeit incompletely in the eyes of some, as in plantation-like 'izbas in Egypt (Richards 1979), the vicissitudes of the cotton trade, like any other, failed to insure long-term and sustained development. On the contrary, the declining share of cotton exports in British trade brought along stagnation. In fact, except for a short period in the opening decade of the twentieth century, the share of cotton in Egyptian exports declined steadily. At its height in 1910–13, Egypt's total trade may well have constituted as much as 50 per cent of its GDP, a figure just larger than that of Britain (Owen and Pamuk 2000: 5). The inter-War experiences of the other colonial or mandate states in the region, such as Syria, Transjordan, and Iraq, were similar in that as dependencies of larger colonial entities, control over flows of goods remained in the hands of imperial authorities, and they did not have the luxury Turkey had in terms of turning inwards on the face of shrinking, and then collapsing, markets. Overall, colonial Egypt, with its world famous long-staple cotton, performed more poorly than did the young Turkish Republic.

The establishment of colonial rule and the integration of rural notables into the colonial apparatus sanctioned the formation of large estates. Yet, not only were these estates rarely constituted as instances of gutsherrschaftlicht, but more significantly, the timing of their consolidation could not have come at a worse time in the face of falling demand for and prices of agricultural goods from the 1920s, culminating in the subsequent collapse of the world market. With the notable exception of Turkey, their vulnerability to fluctuations in world markets was at its height. So the tenuous hold of rural notables over large stretches of land failed to turn into the solid hold of grundherrschaftlicht. If landlord and merchant interests reigned, and the close association between colonial and notable rule left its stamp on the political life of the colonial (and mandate) states during the Thirty Years' War from 1914 to 1944, the early days of the independent states generated a momentum different from that of Turkey. A series of land reforms reversed the trends of the inter-War period. In this, they were helped by the needs of the industrialization strategy: it provided the urban–industrial sector with steady supplies of raw materials to be transformed into manufactured goods and the labouring classes with food inputs. In Egypt, the decline in cotton exports allowed an early start to industrialization. In Turkey, the absence of a landholding class allowed the bureaucrats to steer the economy according to their wishes.

Under Pax Americana, the popularity of import-substitution industrialization with the urban–industrial sector at its hearth contributed to the hollowing out of the countryside due to the impressive pace of industrialization and the relatively higher incomes it offered to migrant labour. The food aid programmes of the post-War period also contributed to this fate by facilitating to the evacuation or emptying of rural areas (McMichael 2000). As a result, the share of rural labour in the reserve army of labour has fallen precipitously.

In the Middle East, too, with the decades, not only has the region become more urbanized and come to house cities such as Cairo and Istanbul, and numerous others, but also its countryside has gone through a three-pronged process whereby its landscape has changed beyond recognition. First, the urban–industrial emphasis of the import-substitution era, by subjugating agrarian prices to the needs of the industrialization drive and thereby keeping them below world prices, turned agriculture into a less lucrative economic activity than before, contributing to the massive outflow of labour that fed urbanization. Today, agriculture's contribution to Turkey's or Egypt's GNP hardly exceeds 10 per cent. Second, when the outflow of rural labour found its way into the hard-currency zones— Europe in the case of Turkey in the 1960s and 1970s, and the oil-rich emirates in the case of Egypt, Syria, and Jordan in the 1980s—the inflow of remittances exempted their rural sectors from market pressures, or, in their absence, forced them to undertake activities that served rich markets, which meant devoting more land to horticulture, among others, than to cereal culture. And third, the stipulations regarding agriculture in the IMF stand-by or austerity programmes, the reduction of subsidies in particular, further exposed agricultural production to the vagaries of the world market. The region's shrinking rural populations and agricultural share of GNP, seen as signs of development just a few decades ago, are now starting to take their toll.

These three developments have placed agriculture in an increasingly vulnerable situation. In the absence of a vibrant agricultural sector that feeds into a wide range of networks dovetailing into the urban–industrial complex, subsidizing a competitive industrial sector through it becomes a virtual impossibility. In the process, the region, which was a net exporter of cereals until the 1940s, has of late turned into a large importer. In 1978, imports of cereals amounted to nearly 23 million tonnes, costing over US$ 4.2 billion. Turkey was the only significant exporter. More generally, the Middle East now has by far the highest per capita food imports among developing nations (Richards and Waterbury 1996).

The agricultural hinterland serving the regions hosting the robust industrial growth of the last two decades—the Four Dragons and South China—contains three-quarters or more of the region's total population. Arguably, urban islands set in a vast sea of agrarian populations, providers of benefits not shouldered by companies and sources of cheap labour that is not 'unbound', have facilitated the process immensely. This *differentia specifica* cannot, by itself, account for the miraculous rise of East Asia, as it cannot account for the present state of the Middle East. But certainly, the possibilities the region has on offer in terms of outsourcing and subcontracting, two strategies preferred by corporate capital in extending its compass to the periphery (Tabak 1996), are compounded by the modal distribution of its populations. This mode of accumulation has transferred costs of reproduction from the firms onto the shoulders of the workers themselves, and has made Asian labour more attractive to firms' outsourcing strategies. In the Middle East, the mediocre growth prospects offered by urbanization, the inability of the rural population to 'switch back', either to subsistence-like activities or to commercial agriculture, the declining pace of informalization, and the reduced ability of agricultural pursuits to provide for large numbers of people, all contribute to the weakening of the rural sector and its ability to underwrite urban growth. Hence, if at the end of the nineteenth century, the availability and accessibility of plantation labour was an asset that attracted capital flows and direct political control in the form of colonialism, at the end of the twentieth century, it is the availability of rural networks of subsidy to buttress the industrial sector that facilitates the remuneration of capital. This, the Middle East lacks, as the Ottoman Empire lacked the former.

At the turn of the century, a similar story is unfolding. The path Turkey travelled in the inter-War period, when compared with that of Egypt, an economy with a colonial past and intimately integrated into the world economy, fared worse than quasi-autarchic Turkey in the long run. During the fall of British rule then, Egypt's 'development without growth' stood in contrast to Turkey's fast recovery after 1923 (Hansen 1991: Chapter 3). Since the 1970s, the two states that have strived to keep up with global trends and followed the precepts of opening up—Egypt from 1973 and Turkey from 1981—unsuccessful though these attempts may have been or seen to be, have not particularly benefited from it. From 1970 to 1988, the per capita income in the region as a percentage of the core zone fell from 8.1 to 7.1; in the case of Egypt and Turkey aggregate, the drop was from 7.7 to 5.6 (Arrighi 1991: 49). And as mentioned earlier, the proportion of the population living below US$ 2 per day in the region rose, predominantly due to increases in Egypt, Turkey, and Morocco. Put differently, the colonized regions of the empire (namely, Egypt and Algeria), reshaped economically and politically under the watchful eyes of colonial powers, went through a period of tremendous change. Once the world these regions were forced to inhabit crumbled, with the passing of the hegemon (and colonial empires), the success of the former era could not be sustained. At present, a similar parting of ways can again be seen within the region. Today, the fortunes of Turkey, an early convert to the programme of liberalization, and Egypt, the first to initiate opening-up, do not tower over the region as success stories: income inequality in both places have widened considerably, and both are heavily indebted. Once again, those who have played the game by the rules set by the hegemon have failed to fare better than those who have not.

This is at variance with the widely held view that the states in the Middle East have not been adequately proactive in meeting challenges posed by the changes in the global economic landscape since the 1980s, as have some of their counterparts been in the South (Henry and Springborg 2001: 132). In line with the orthodox recipes offered for success by the World Bank, the concentration and consolidation of state power from the 1960s, which were seen as welcome developments against the backdrop of political volatility that marked the region in the first decades of its decolonization process, are now seen as a formidable obstacle to change. Yet, regional aspects of the Middle East's economic trajectory, important though they may be, were dwarfed by world–systemic aspects of long-term processes that undergirded bouts of mobility. As argued above, if the centrality of the temperate settlements from the 1870s and of the Pacific rim from the 1970s redefined the region's relative position in the new global division of labour, it was the centrality of the Western hemisphere in the mid-century that performed the same function. And these bouts of mobility were more closely associated with the hegemonic cycles of the world system than regional dynamics per se. The breathing room the region was given during periods of rivalry may have altered the pace of economic devolution, but not its direction. The Middle East is not the only region in the South to experience a widening income gap with the core. In recent decades, a deepening income inequality between the core and peripheral zones has been the norm, not the exception. Whether the lifting of incomes in East Asia (and its hinterland), the singular exception to this trend thus far, will be able to place the North–South relations on a new footing, still remains to be seen.

REFERENCES

Amsden, Alice, (2001), *The Rise of the Rest: Challenges to the West from Late-industrializing Economies*, Oxford University Press, New York.

Arrighi, Giovanni, (1991), 'World Income Inequalities and the Future of Socialism', *New Left Review*, 189, 39–65.

——, (1994), *The Long Twentieth Century: Money, Power and the Origins of Our Times*, Verso, New York.

——, (2002), 'The African Crisis', *New Left Review*, 15, 5–36.

Arrighi, Giovanni and Jessica Drangel, (1986), 'The Stratification of the World Economy: An Exploration of the Semiperipheral Zone', *Review: A Journal of the Fernand Braudel Center*, 10(1), 9–74.

Bagchi, Amiya Kumar, (2001), 'Fluctuations and Turbulence of the World Economy', *Review: A Journal of the Fernand Braudel Center*, 24(2), 253–99.

Bairoch, Paul, (1977), *The Economic Development of the Third World Since 1900*, University of California Press, Berkeley.

Balassa, Bela, (1987), 'The Importance of Trade for Developing Countries', *Banca Nazionale del lavaro*, December.

Braudel, Fernand, (1984), *Civilization and Capitalism, 15th–18th Century, Vol. 3: The Perspective of the World*, Harper and Row, New York.

Chaudhury, Kiren, (1997), *The Price of Wealth: Economies and Institutions in the Middle East*, Cornell University Press, Ithaca.

Cummings, Bruce, (1987), 'The Origins and Development of Northeast Asian Political Economy: Industrial Sectors, Product Cycles, and Political Consequences', in Frederic C. Deyo (ed.), *The Political Economy of New Asian Industrialism*, Cornell University Press, Ithaca, NY, 44–83.

Frank, Andre Gunder, (1976), 'Multilateral Trade Imbalances and Uneven Economic Development', *Journal of European Economic History*, 5, 407–38.

Friedmann, Harriet, (1978), 'World Market, State, and Family Farm: Social Basis of Household Production in the Era of Wage Labour', *Comparative Studies in Society and History*, 20(4), 545–86.

Gerber, Haim, (1987), *The Social Origins of the Modern Middle East*, Lynne Rienner, Boulder.

Haber, Stephen, (1997), 'Economic Growth and Latin American Historiography', in Stephen Haber (ed.), *How Latin America Fell Behind*, Stanford University Press, Stanford, 1–33.

Hansen, Bent, (1991), *The Political Economy of Poverty, Equity, and Growth: Egypt and Turkey*, Oxford University Press, New York.

Hanson II, J.R., (1980), *Trade in Transition: Exports from the Third World, 1840–1900*, Academic Press, New York.

Henry, Clement M. and Robert Springborg, (2001), *Globalization and the Politics of Development in the Middle East*, Cambridge University Press, New York.

Hopkins, Terence K., (1990), 'Note on the Concept of Hegemony', *Review: A Journal of the Fernand Braudel Center*, 13(3), 409–11.

Issawi, Charles, (1982), *An Economic History of the Middle East and North Africa*, Columbia University Press, New York.

Keyder, Caglar, (1985), 'The American Recovery of Southern Europe: Aid and Hegemony', in Giovanni Arrighi (ed.), *Semiperipheral Development*, Sage Publications, Beverly Hills.

—— (1987), *State and Class in Turkey: A Study in Capitalist Development*, Verso, London.

Korzeniewicz, Roberto P. and Timothy Moran, (1997), 'World Economic Trends in the Distribution of Income, 1965–1992', *American Journal of Sociology*, 4, 1000–39.

Latham, A.J.H., (1981), *The Depression and the Developing World, 1914–1939*, Rowman and Littlefield, New Jersey.

Lewis, W.A., (1978), *Growth and Fluctuations, 1870–1913*, Allen & Unwin, London.

Leys, Colin, (1996), *The Rise and Fall of Development Theory*, Indiana University Press, Bloomington.

Lipietz, Alain, (1987), *Mirages and Miracles*, Verso, New York.

Maddison, Angus, (1995), *Monitoring the World Economy, 1820–1922*, Development Centre of the Organisation for Economic Co-operation and Development, Paris.

Maizels, Alfred, (1963), *Industrial Growth and World Trade*, Cambridge University Press, Cambridge.

Mahon, Jr. James E., (1996), *Mobile Capital and Latin American Development*, Pennsylvania State University Press, Pennsylvania.

McMichael, Philip, (2000), *Development and Social Change: A Global Perspective*, second edition, Pine Forge Press, Thousand Oaks, CA.

Owen, Roger, (1981), *The Middle East in the World Economy, 1800–1914*, Methuen, New York.

—— (1992), *State, Power and Politics in the Making of the Modern Middle East*, Routledge, London.

Owen, Roger and Sevket Pamuk, (1998), *A History of Middle East Economies in the Twentieth Century*, Harvard University Press, Cambridge, MA.

Pamuk, Sevket, (1988), 'The Ottoman Empire in a Comparative Perspective', *Review: A Journal of the Fernand Braudel Center*, 11(2), 127–49.

Richards, Alan, (1979), 'The Political Economy of Gutswirtschaft: A Comparative Analysis of East Elbian Germany, Egypt, and Chile', *Comparative Studies in Society and History*, 21(4), 483–518.

Richards, Alan, and John Waterbury, (1996), *A Political Economy of the Middle East*, second edition, Westview Press, Boulder.

Rostow, W.W., (1978), *The World Economy, History & Prospect*, University of Texas Press, Austin.

Sutcliffe, Bob, (2002), *100 Ways of Seeing an Unequal World*, Zed Books, London.

Tabak, Faruk, (1996), 'The World Labour Force', in Terence K. Hopkins and Immanuel Wallerstein (coordinators), *The Age of Transition. The Trajectory of the World System 1945–2025*, Zed Books, London, 87–116.

Topik, Steven C. and Allen Wells, (1998), 'Latin America's Response to International Markets During the Export Boom', in Steven C. Topik and Allen Wells (eds), *The Second Conquest of Latin America*, University of Texas Press, Austin.

Wallerstein, Immanuel, (1985), 'The Relevance of the Concept of Semiperiphery to Southern Europe', in Giovanni Arrighi (ed.), *Semiperipheral dDvelopment*, Sage Publications, Beverly Hills, 31–39.

—— (1992), 'The Concept of National Development, 1917–1989: Elegy and Requiem', in I. Wallerstein, *After Liberalism*, (1995), The New Press, New York, 108–122.

Walton, John and David Seddon, (1994), *Free Markets and Food Riots: The Politics of Global Adjustment*, Blackwell Publishers, Boston.

Waterbury, John, (1993), *Exposed to Innumerable Delusions: Public Enterprise and State Power in Egypt, India, Mexico, and Turkey*, Cambridge University Press, New York.

Wee, Herman van der, (1986), *Prosperity and Upheaval: The World Economy, 1945–1980*, University of California Press, Berkeley.

Whichard, Obie G., (1981), 'Trends in U.S. Direct Investment Position Abroad, 1950–79', Survey of Current Business, Vol. XIV, No. 1, 15–38.

Zimmerman, L. F., (1962), 'The Distribution of World Income, 1860–1960', in Egbert DeVries (ed.), *Essays on Unbalanced Growth*, Mouton, The Hague, 39–54.

7

Southeast Asia

Imperial Possession and Dispossession in the Long Twentieth Century

Maria Serena I. Diokno

A broad and inherently diverse region, Southeast Asia in the twentieth century has been a zone of contrasts: of Burma at one end as a doubly colonized state (it was not until 1923 that a Burmese passed the Indian Civil Service examinations, held not in Burma, but in London and India), and of Thailand at the other end, which was never directly colonized; of the Philippines, often described as more 'Latin' than 'Asian' unlike her Southeast Asian neighbours, or Viet Nam, 'sinicized' long before other parts of China had become part of that huge country; of the vast expanse of federated Indonesia, compared to the island states of Singapore and Brunei, and so on. Contrasts like these tend to make generalizations about Southeast Asia difficult and are best understood when examined in light of the sources of regional diversity.

The first contrast, for example, speaks of varied political experiences under colonial rule. The terminology here is interesting, for similar terms have been used to denote different modes of colonial control on one hand, such as 'direct' and 'indirect' rule, and types of colonialism on the other, such as 'direct' (formal) and 'indirect' (informal) colonialism. For example, in British Malaya, 'indirect' rule in Kedah, Kelantan, Terengganu, and Johore allowed the indigenous power structure to remain intact (at least in form) and protected Malay religion and custom, but required indigenous rulers to heed the instructions of British Advisers in all other areas of community life. However, other parts—such as Perak, Pahang, Selangor, and Negri Sembilan—were directly governed by the British Resident-General. To a certain extent, indirect and direct rule was also applied by the Dutch in Indonesia, with the regencies in Java and Madura headed by Dutch-appointed Regents, while in the so-called native states in the outer islands, indigenous rulers were recognized.

Viewed another way, however, these forms of European rule were simply expressions of colonial power calibrated to suit different local conditions. Whether under direct or indirect rule, there is no question that Malaya was a British colony and Indonesia a Dutch colony, as was Burma under the British, Viet Nam under the French, and the Philippines under the US. In contrast to these examples of direct colonialism, Thailand was never a colony, that is to say, at no time was the monarchy supplanted by foreign rule, not even indirectly as in British Malaya. But the Thai monarchy was subjected to intense colonial pressure from the French and British as these powers expanded on both sides of the kingdom. From 1855, when the kingdom was opened to British trade, to 1909, when the monarchy ceded its southern periphery to Britain, Thailand entered into about a dozen treaties with various European nations, hoping to ward off potential encroachments closer to the centre. Such external pressure has been described as indirect or informal colonialism in contrast to outright colonies elsewhere in the region.

The second contrast refers to cultural distinctions in the region as reflected in such labels as 'Latin' or 'sinicized' Southeast Asia. In fact, these labels are products of specific (and different) historical experiences. Having been colonized by Spain for more than three centuries, for instance, predominantly Catholic Philippines has stood out in stark contrast to Buddhist Southeast Asia on the mainland and Muslim island neighbours. Hence the perception of some that the former Hispanic colony is more 'Latin' and less 'Asian' than the rest. Similarly, the label, 'sinicized' Viet Nam, results from China's overlordship of Viet Nam centuries past. Long after the experiences that gave rise to them have passed, the labels remain as interpretive descriptions open to challenge and debate.

The contrasts seem endless. In terms of sheer physical size, Indonesia towers over the island states of Singapore and Brunei. In truth, these contrasts are not merely spatial; they are political as well. The contemporary boundaries of Southeast Asian states were delineated by rival empire-building by the West and the attainment of independence by Southeast Asian peoples. Starting from the old colonial centre of Batavia, the Dutch spread out to the rest of the islands of Indonesia. The terms, Lower and

Upper Burma, denoted more than geographical areas; they also signified the direction of British territorial conquest, from the Irrawaddy Delta region as the core, and then extending upward to the Shan, Kachin, and Chin states. On the other hand, Singapore was originally conceived as part of the larger state of Malaysia, but unresolved differences on the eve of independence resulted in the formation of not one but two independent nations.

There is nonetheless a spectral sense to the region that gives it a unifying character: in a comparative way, as Benedict Anderson (1998) points out with respect to Thailand, Indonesia and the Philippines, the sense of incompleteness as evidenced by unfinished and ongoing projects of nation- and community-building; and in terms of seeming repetitions of patterns or movements, at times suggesting a seamless continuity from the colonial past to the purportedly independent present. The history of imperialism in Southeast Asia is in this sense, then, a narrative in progress, with certain events in the present bearing the unmistakable mark of past empires, and other events finding solidarity elsewhere in the region. Three examples are discussed in this chapter: the path to modernity as progress, best exemplified by the sponsorship of education by Western rulers in the region; the struggle for modernity as freedom, this time on the part of indigenous elites and peoples; and the transformation of local economies and their integration into world trade networks as an important element of empire-building. In each country in the Southeast Asian region these developments took place at different points in time. For this reason the long twentieth century is a useful time frame; its encompassing length allows comparisons to be made across colonial borders.

MODERNITY AS A DOUBLE-EDGED WEAPON

The disparity between humanitarian rhetoric and coercive assimilation was an enduring theme of the imperial project. Previous centuries had seen how conquest began with the very act of renaming the colonies through the imperial trope: Netherlands East Indies, British India, French Indochina, the Philippines (named after Spanish King Felipe II). Dispossessed of their names and stamped with the identities of their colonizers, empires were launched; in the words of Paul Carter, 'the imperial project of permanent possession through dispossession' [1] (Carter 1995: 377) had begun. By the 1900s, the philosophy of conquest and foreign rule was well established as

---

[1] Paul Carter used this phrase with reference to the naming of Hartog Island in Australia, 'Cape Inscription' in 1801.

the rhetoric of humanity. In Burma, British colonial officials insisted that theirs was 'the task of education and government ... not as a tyrant but as a trustee for civilization in order to ... build up those conditions of liberty and opportunity for the individual in which the people can learn to govern themselves' (Cady 1958: 198–9) while in the Philippines, American colonizers peddled the idea of 'benevolent assimilation', asserting that American sovereignty and the rights and freedoms of Filipinos were not incompatible. Like their British counterparts, American rulers argued that their purpose was 'to guarantee them [Filipinos] a rightful freedom; to protect them in their just privileges and immunities; to accustom them to free self-government in an ever-increasing measure; and to encourage them in those democratic aspirations, sentiments, and ideals which are the promise and potency of a fruitful national development.' (Schurman 1900: 4). Never mind that these colonies were seized by means of war, Burma in a three-part series in the nineteenth century, and the Philippines through the inaugural war of the twentieth century. The tragedy of the present is that the concept of liberative assimilation lives on, this time applied by means of precise, technologically-advanced weapons of war.

The philosophy of humanitarian conquest was at once creative and destructive. For the good of the colonized peoples, a social, political and cultural order had to be invented either to mirror the image of the superior colonizer or at least bring the natives up several notches though never quite at par with Western rulers and residents in the colony. 'Little brown Americans', the phrase American officials used to describe Filipinos, is perhaps an extreme case. But to create an image in the imperial likeness or raise local levels to colonially accepted standards, the indigenous had to be broken down bit by bit (or so empires thought), renamed and reinvented by means of language and education, and given an incremental taste of power while safeguarding Western strongholds.

The durability of imperialism in post-War (independent) Southeast Asia and the legacy of the symbiotic collaboration between the elites of the colonial and colonized societies explain, in large part, the longish, perhaps unduly extended, character of the century past. On one hand, education and the offer of self-administration were attractive incentives to local elites. Urged by imperial governments to forego independence momentarily, indigenous rulers were invited to take part in the Western-sponsored march to progress. From the Shan princes to the Malay sultans, education served as the path to modernity. Sandwiched between competing colonial powers, the kingdom of Siam, too, responded avidly to the attraction of Western modernization. Decentralized rule, efficient administration and the welfare of the colonized were hailed as the 'keynotes of the new era' of colonialism, (Furnivall 1967: 230) best exemplified by the Dutch ethical policy in Indonesia toward the end of the nineteenth century.

The promise of advancement in the civil service and acquisition of the tools of self-rule were crucial to the agenda of modernity. From traditional symbols of power, local authorities were transformed into bureaucratic elites, albeit as lower-level functionaries with limited responsibility for the political administration of the colony. Away from their rural origins and increasingly oriented toward the West, these modern educated elites performed the additional task of mediating between the peasants and their European rulers. As Emerson put it in his treatise on imperial rule in Malaysia, 'For the bulk even of the most enlightened and sympathetic colonial civil servants the fact is ever present that they are rulers of a dependency: their role is to govern while that of the people is to obey. This conception does not in the least exclude sincere efforts to improve the conditions of the natives and to lead them into a happier and more secure existence, but it does exclude the acceptance of the natives as equal collaborators in this work.' (Emerson 1979: 484–5).

On the other hand, the tools of modernity were double-edged. Having exposed educated Southeast Asian elites to Western notions of liberty, how could imperial rulers deny them the benefits enjoyed by Western peoples at home? In an article written in 1913, 'If I were Temporarily to be a Dutchman', Suwardi Surjaningrat wrote: 'In my opinion, there is something out of place—something indecent—if we (I still being a Dutch-man in my imagination) ask the natives to join the festivities which celebrate our independence. First, we will hurt their sensitive feelings because we are here celebrating our own independence in their native country which we colonize.... Does it not occur to us that these poor slaves are also longing for such a moment as this, when they like us will be able to celebrate their independence? ... If I were a Dutchman, I would not organize an independence celebration in a country where the independence of the people has been stolen' (Anderson 1983: 107–8).

The contradiction between colonial pronouncements of public good and the loss of freedom resulting from conquest understandably became the subject of nationalist movements in the region. Andres Bonifacio, leader of the first war of liberation in the region, summed up Spanish colonial rule in the Philippines as follows: 'More than three hundred years have elapsed since then, and for that length of time we have been bounti-fully supplying the needs of Legaspi's countrymen, we have been feeding them lavishly, even if we had to suffer deprivation and extreme hunger; we have spent our wealth, blood, and life itself in their defence; we even went so far as to fight our own countrymen who refused to submit to them; and likewise, we combated the Chinese and the Dutch who attempted to wrest the Philippines from them.'

'Now, for all this, what is the tangible concession that has been bestowed upon our country in exchange for what we have done? What do we see in the way of keeping faith with their promise that was the cause of our sacrifices? None but treachery is the reward for our munificence, and instead of keeping their promise that we would be led to the path of knowledge, they have blinded us and contaminated us with their meanness of character and forcibly destroyed the sanctity of our country's customs. We have been nurtured in a false belief and the honour of our people has been dragged into the mire of evil. And if we dare beg for a little love, they retaliate by banishing us and tearing us away from our beloved children, wives, and aged parents. Every sigh that escapes our breast is branded as a grave sin and is immediately punished with brute ferocity' (Bonifacio 2002: 96).

RELIGION, LANGUAGE, AND FREEDOM

Articulations of nationalist awakening expectedly varied throughout the region. In some parts, such as Burma, Indonesia, and Malaysia, religion played a significant role in the development of nationalist thought, religion being a source of distinction between the colonized and their colonizers. The pagoda controversy in Burma in 1917 sparked the coalition of Buddhist groups in the colony, giving the Young Men's Buddhist Association (formed in 1906) strong political colour hitherto unseen. One of the earliest leaders to demand home rule was U Ottama, a *pongyi* (Buddhist monk) who had spent some time in India as a member of the Indian National Congress. Meanwhile, at the village level, local nationalist associations (*wunthanu athins*) had sprouted in most districts of Burma by 1924, boycotting Chettyar moneylenders and British taxes and, in some areas, setting up shadow governments (Moscotti 1974: 21–34). In Malaysia and Indonesia, religion, too, became a vehicle for claiming self-identity. One strand of Islam was modernizing, as exemplified by the Malay periodical, *Al-Imam* (1906–8), which argued that Islam was not antipathetic to Western knowledge and that religion had to be stripped of superstition and outmoded rituals. Known as the *Kaum Muda* or Young Faction, these reformists stood in direct contrast to the more traditional Old Faction *Kaum Tua*, the religious elite insistent upon the established social order. A politicized *Kaum Muda* later found expression in anti-colonial, pan-Malayan and pan-Islamic nationalism (Roff 1967: 56–90).

In quite a different way, religion also became an arena of early opposition in heavily Catholic Philippines. Critical of abuses by Spanish friars, Filipino reformers writing in Spain and the colony denounced the 'monastic supremacy' of the religious orders in the Philippines. In his exposition of the political and economic power of the Spanish friars, Marcelo del Pilar complained that the religious orders did 'nothing but ... provoke the Filipinos to repent of their loyalty to Spain and proclaim to the world the tyranny and inefficiency of the Spanish government' (del Pilar 1974: 191–2). Conscious of European notions of liberty and equality, these highly educated (*ilustrado*) Spanish-speaking reformers demanded that the Philippines be granted the rights and privileges enjoyed by the provinces of Spain. Assimilation into Spain was the means rather than the end to the enjoyment of such entitlements as representation in the *Cortés* (Parliament) and freedom of speech and assembly. Fundamental to the reform of the colony was education—not narrow religious indoctrination by the friars, but education in agriculture, science, and other areas that would prepare the country for modern life. As Graciano Lopez-Jaena put it, 'After five years at the university, a lad goes out speaking enough Latin to confound his fellow townsmen, and knowing correctly what is substance and accident, first matter and substantial form, but hardly has he notions of geography, mathematics, physics, chemistry, etc., unless he has studied those subjects by himself and privately'. Lopez-Jaena added, 'if all these subjects are conspicuous by their absence, on the other hand, never absent are the rosary, *trisagion*, the thousand and one novenas of the saints, the Virgin and the martyrs with which the tender minds of the children are nourished spiritually and viciously' (1974: 119).

Language was another aspect of the development of nationalist consciousness. Like their French counterparts in Viet Nam, Spanish colonialists did not want Filipinos to learn Spanish in school so as to prevent the influx of advanced ideas from Europe. But unlike the French, who opted to promote *quoc ngu* (Vietnamese romanized script) as the language of Vietnamese civil servants, Spain did not support the official use of Tagalog either, or any other Philippine language for that matter. When the Americans took over from Spain, they made it their mission to teach English (and obliterate Tagalog) so that, as explained by the superintendent of public instruction in 1903, the Filipino would be liberated 'from that degraded dependence upon the man of influence of his own race which made possible ... insurrection' (Stanley 1974: 85). In contrast, in Viet Nam the French-sanctioned use of *quoc ngu* enabled the language to develop into an instrument of Vietnamese nationhood. So potent had *quoc ngu* become in the 1930s that any suggestion that the language was second class (a 'patois' according to some) provoked strong criticism from Vietnamese journalists and intellectuals (Marr 1981: 136–7).

The growth of the Malay language and its application in the service of nationalism were also unwittingly triggered by the British colonial reform of Malay education in 1917. The Winstedt Report called for a strong Malay school system in the villages that would equip the rural population with vocational and agricultural skills. The best rural graduates were then sent to the Sultan Idris Training College (founded 1922) where they were taught to become teachers. The task of the College graduates was to return to the village schools and, using Malay as the medium of instruction, teach Malay literature, history, indigenous crafts and manual skills. In this manner the grounds for the development of Malay consciousness were laid down. The Malay press, meanwhile, took shape in the form of religious reform journals such as *Al-Imam*, secular daily newspapers such as *Utusan Melayu*, and periodicals like the *Majalah Guru* that catered to educated Malays (Roff 1967: 126–77).

With political liberty as the reverberating focus of nationalist movements throughout the region, freedom acquired new meanings in local articulations. Against pressure from European powers, the Chakkri kings, Rama IV to Rama VI (1851–1925), used the written Thai language to assert their authority and accommodate new usages demanded by a modern bureaucracy in dealing with external aggressors. The traditional meaning of *tai* since the twelfth century—non-slave subjects of the king—posed a contrast to slavery, long a part of Thai social structure. In 1890, as part of the reforms undertaken by King Chulalongkorn, his brother Prince Damrong put forth the argument that slavery was the anti-thesis of Thainess. About two decades later, an interesting juxtaposition emerged between the current Thai word for freedom, *seriphap*, which stresses one's control over oneself, and *itsaraphap*, the traditional word for the power of one over another. To resolve the conflict between these two concepts, Rama VI (1910–25) defined Thai nationalism as the unity of 'nation, religion, and king'. With Buddhism as the moral guide, the Thai monarchy served as the foundation of stability as well as defender of the faith (Aphornsuvan 1998: 161–86). In 1939 Major General Luang Phibunsongkhram changed the name of the country from Siam to Thailand, and the word *thai* acquired dual meaning: ethnicity, or the Thai people who comprised the nation, and freedom or independence from external control. The identity project apparently remains unfinished; in the 1960s and as recent as the mid-1990s, calls have publicly been aired by some members of Thai society for a return to the name 'Siam'.

The Javanese, on the other hand, distinguish between sovereign freedom, which they consider outer or ordinary freedom (*kemerdekaan lahir*), and an inner kind of freedom (*kemerdekaan batin*) enjoyed by one 'who has liberated himself from every worldly temptation'. A god-given right, the latter was therefore universal; it was also necessary to 'overcome whatever is not pure' (Reid 1998: 153). Interestingly, the recognition of inner freedom as an essential component of liberty is also found in the thinking of the *Katipunan* (Highest and Most Respectable Society of the Sons of the People), which launched the Philippine revolution against Spain in 1896. In the 'Teachings of the Katipunan' Emilio Jacinto wrote, 'If he who guides moves toward evil, they who are guided likewise move toward evil' (Rule X); and 'He who is noble prefers honour to personal gain; he who is mean prefers personal profit to honor' (Rule V).[2]

OF FREEDOM AND REBELS

The dichotomy between internal and external sovereignty, however, posed a danger to the cause of liberation from colonial rule. Two examples from the Philippine struggle are instructive. The first is that of the *Katipunan*, which viewed freedom as three inter related objectives: the political goal of independence from Spain, the moral objective of 'internal transformation' of the people, and the civic goal of mutual defence of the oppressed. Against the conventional or pragmatic approach of setting these goals apart in neat compartments so that each could be achieved separately and in phases, the *Katipunan* leaders fused the external (independence from Spain) and the internal (transformation of society); one was not to be postponed or sacrificed in favour of the other. As military battles against Spain loomed high on the revolutionary agenda, the founding philosophy of the movement gradually lost steam, replaced by more pragmatic considerations of military strategy and political command of the revolution. The split in the *Katipunan* resulted in the fall and eventual execution of its founder, Andres Bonifacio. In part, the division within the movement can be explained by differing perspectives of freedom: one, focused on the 'external transformation' of society and the necessity of military strategy and skill in order to defeat the colonial enemy; and the other, melding external (sovereign) freedom with the liberation of the self (*loob*) from untoward, selfish habits and attitudes. As Ileto explains, the former tended to view the latter as evidence of a 'folk' and, by implication, an inferior mind (Ileto 1979: 135–9).

---

[2] Translated and cited in T.A. Agoncillo, (1956, reprinted 2002), *The Revolt of the Masses*, University of the Philippines Press, Quezon City.

The treatment of these goals as separate, rather than as an integrated whole, made it convenient to postpone independence while social transformation and development took place. This was the line taken by the Federal Party, which was formed by disgruntled members of the Filipino elite who had joined the revolution and then (unhappily) faced the prospect of war against the US. Trinidad Pardo de Tavera, a leading Federalista, explained: 'Political independence does not make a people safe from slavery: the law can not protect the individual of inferior capacity from the native or foreign individual of superior capacity.... It is only a social transformation that can shield us from this danger' (Stanley 1974: 71). Hence, independence could wait until the people were good and ready.

Similarly, early in his career as editor of the newspaper, *La Cloche Fêlée* (The Cracked Bell), Nguyen An Ninh, who later figured prominently in the Vietnamese nationalist movement, argued that Viet Nam was plagued equally by social and political problems that independence alone would not solve. The people needed a rejuvenation of spirit built on solid Vietnamese culture and intellect (Duiker 1976: 140). However, barely two years later (in 1925), and quite unlike Pardo de Tavera, Nguyen An Ninh realized that, to succeed, social transformation and cultural revitalization needed a free, not hostile, environment: 'When a race is trapped to the point of having a choice only of death or of slavery,' he warned, 'to face death is the more courageous.... If the masses brave death rather than accept injustice, and if the colonialists do not want to renounce their policies of oppression and unscrupulous exploitation, it is the duty of the most courageous and devoted Annamites to dream of methods of struggle which correspond to present needs, and to organize a resistance which can combat oppression' (Duiker 1976: 142).

On the other side of the struggle, imperial officials applied labels to Southeast Asian rebels and revolutionaries aimed at a single message, that lawlessness and criminality were the stuff of which revolutions were made. Filipino rebels, for example, were called *tulisanes* or *ladrones* (bandits) by Spanish administrators, and later, brigands by the Americans; Vietnamese rebels were labelled pirates by the French. (During the emergency period in the late 1940s and 1950s, Malayan Communist Party guerrillas were officially labelled terrorists.) In 1900, US Commissioner William Taft justified the treatment of Filipino revolutionaries who refused to submit to American forces as outlaws—'either hang or transport them as they are captured'—because 'resistance to American authority is nothing but a conspiracy of murder and assassination' (Stanley 1974: 65). In the final drive to acquire full control of Viet Nam in the late nineteenth century, Colonel Lyautey declared, 'One must be completely convinced: this is piracy and not an insurrection', to which the guerrilla leader De Tham replied in 1892: 'We are not pirates, but rebels who defend their country against the invader; we respect the dead and do not mutilate the wounded' (Lamb 1972: 253).

GLOBAL TRADE AND LOCAL ECONOMIES

The political assimilation of Southeast Asian peoples was accompanied by the integration of their local economies into the world trade. Southeast Asia's experience in maritime trade was, of course, not new. Long before colonial rule, the region was an arena of shifting networks of trade and cultures criss-crossing the seas. This experience in maritime trade, along with the presence of influential immigrant populations, mainly Chinese and Indian, has given Southeast Asian economic history its most enduring features. One view, that of Ian Brown, is that under imperial rule, the Southeast Asian peasant essentially held on to established agricultural practices,

not embarking on a new form of economic activity, making a decisive break with the past, but simply doing on a much larger scale what he, or she, had always done. In the early modern period, individuals and communities had commonly practiced a marked degree of occupational and crop specialization, produced surpluses, and exchanged and sold in both local and distant markets. In the modern period, they merely seized the opportunity to serve larger markets on a larger scale, to exploit more thoroughly the advantages of specialization (Brown 1997: 278).

On the other hand, specialization had its drawbacks. In the case of Siam, for example, specialization in rice as a response to strong external demand after the mid-nineteenth century resulted in the decline of the homemade textile industry (also because foreign imports were cheaper) and the production of household consumption goods such as sugar. Chatthip and Suthy conclude that part of the increase in rice exports was made at the expense of other locally made products (Nartsupha and Prasartset 1981: 5). A familiar story occurred on Panay island, where the once thriving textile industry of Iloilo suffered with specialization in sugar production in the nearby island of Negros. Alfred McCoy describes the effect of the shift from textile production to sugar exports: 'The capital, commercial skills, and labour dislocated by the precipitous decline of the weaving industry were quickly absorbed into Negros' expanding sugar economy.... As the city's entrepreneurs moved across the Guimaras Strait to take up sugar lands, the urban districts of Jaro and Molo lost their dynamism and became quiet suburbs of the foreign entrepôt that began to grow at the mouth of the Iloilo River. Jaro's population plummeted from 30,200 in 1856 to only 11,200 some 30 years later.' (McCoy 1982: 307).

Moreover, to 'seize' the opportunity connotes a sense of power on the part of the peasantry, power that existed within limits and came to life in various (no doubt, creative) ways, but within the framework of colonial economies and under the political authority of imperial states. If the economic history of the region tends to highlight the role of Western firms and play down that of the Southeast Asian cultivators, it is largely because the former is well documented, while evidence on the latter, particularly statistical data, is incomplete, sketchy, uneven, and, at times, not reliable.

Nevertheless, there is no question that Western firms played a significant role in Southeast Asian economies. Whether in the extraction and processing of agricultural crops or mineral products, or their purchase and sale for export, these companies' major interests were the vast natural resources of the region: rice, sugar, coffee, abaca, teak and other timbers, oil, tin, rubber and so on. To carry out their operations and maximize profits, some engaged in far-reaching banking operations extending from the major colonial centres to rice fields and upland teak areas. Most firms began modestly as individual proprietorships or partnerships, sometimes among friends and kin. Examples are, the largest rice firm in colonial Burma, Steel Bros. and Co., founded by William Strang Steel, and the teak firm Foucar Bros, which started with Ferdinand Foucar (Braund 1975: 17–18). In the Philippines, those responsible for putting up Russell and Sturgis, the most important firm in the nineteenth century, were related by blood or marriage: Thomas Handasyd Perkins, Thomas T. Forbes, George Robert Russell and Henry P. Sturgis (Legarda Jr 1999: 256). The friendship between Thomas Scott, a partner in Guthrie and Co., Singapore and T. H. Hill of the Malay Peninsula Coffee Co. led to the formation of the Kamunting (Perak) Rubber and Tin Co., Ltd.; similarly, the establishment of the Highlands and Lowlands Para Rubber Co. (London) was traced to the personal connection between W. W. Bailey, a planter in Selangor, and J. M. Allinson, manager of Barlow and Co., Singapore (Drabble 1973: 79–81).

In addition, Western companies were directly linked to the major financial and shipping centres in Europe and the US. British firms in Manila, for example, had head offices in Liverpool, Glasgow, or London, with senior officers often moving there after serving in the Philippines. Registered as joint stock companies in Europe or India, the large European rice and timber milling firms in Burma had financial arrangements with the Imperial Bank of India, then the government's banker, and with exchange banks in Rangoon that financed the sea-borne trade, such as the Chartered Bank of India, Australia, and China, the Hong Kong and Shanghai Banking Corp., and Lloyds Bank. In Malaya, rubber firms such as Guthrie and Co. and Edward Boustead and Co. were called 'agency houses' because of their association with firms in London (Drabble 1973: 78–9). The connection with London, the world's financial centre at the time, gave European firms a huge advantage. The introduction of bills of exchange by British firms in the Philippines, for instance, was made possible by the London connection (Legarda Jr 1999: 256–60).

By making advances to cultivators before harvest time, Western firms were able to control the supply and, not infrequently, the prices of export crops. As merchant bankers, Anglo-American firms in the Philippines accepted deposits of religious orders and private individuals, thereby financed trading operations, and advanced loans to sugar, coffee, and abaca growers based on the estimated value of the crop and buying it in advance. Agricultural advances were done through various intermediaries, among them Spanish *mestizos* and Chinese, extending from the principal financiers to the Filipino cultivator (Legarda Jr 1999: 277–82).

Similarly, the rice brokerage system in Burma was financed by advances from large, mostly British, millers, though not from private deposits but from credit supplied by banks in Rangoon and the port towns. Through layers of brokers, starting with the firm's head broker, advances were passed on all the way down to 'jungle brokers' in rice fields. Unpaid advances eventually ended up as loans (*sabape*) that covered successive harvests.[3] Large Western firms in Rangoon also made advances to small Burmese rice millers through future delivery contracts. To succeed, the forward prices of milled rice in the early part of the season had to be considerably higher than those for ready produce, and small millers had to comply with contract dates and deliveries of agreed sales (Solomon 1931: 81). The importance of these advances was in fact used to counter charges of foreign exploitation of peasants. For example, an article in an official weekly argued: 'None dispute the richness of Burma soil, but what would the cultivators have done without Indian coolie labour and advances of money obtained from paddy brokers, which they had in turn received from foreign rice firms?'.[4]

UNION OF INTERESTS

Western firms in Southeast Asia also branched out into other valuable, though at times unrelated, business interests. By means of the managing

---

[3] *Report on the Marketing of Rice in India and Burma*, 1941, Manager of Publications, Delhi, 283.

[4] 'Foreign Exploitation Bogey', *Rangoon Gazette Weekly Budget*, 18 May 1931: ii.

agent system, the agent partly financed, promoted, and completely managed other industrial interests, even if he was not a substantial shareholder. Also, varied agricultural production cycles allowed several processing operations to take place at different times of the year. Thus, some rice mills in Burma doubled as saw or oil-pressing mills although the biggest rice mills (in terms of capacity) were devoted completely to rice. Indeed, although the firms usually described themselves as commission merchants in the export and import trade, many of them had broader reaching interests. A considerable number (especially among the important firms) served as shipping and insurance agents and owned various subsidiary enterprises, including property. Ker & Co. in Manila, for example, was the agent of the British & Foreign Marine Insurance Co., Union Marine Insurance Co. and Sun Fire Office; and Smith, Bell & Co., of the Commercial Union Assurance Co., and Imperial Fire Assurance Co. In addition to being the agent of the Colonial Maritime and Fire Insurance Co. of Batavia, Russell & Sturgis owned a cold storage plant and a coffee plantation and was the local representative of Baring's Bank (Legarda Jr 1999: 275–6).

Elsewhere similar practices took place. Apart from rice and teak, Steel Bros. reminded their forest staff that ' "Steels" are interested in everything in the Province [of Burma] and that we do business in many other lines than forestry'.[5] These interests included concessions for all minerals except oil, shareholdings in the Indo-Burma Petroleum Co., the Pyinma Development Co. (a mining firm), and the Burma Cement Co., and ownership of cotton and oil mills, a ginning factory and baling press, a tin-making plant, soap and candle-making factories, rubber estates, a flour mill and a lac factory. In addition, Steels were agents of shipping lines such as the Bibby Line, Henderson Line, India-Natal Line, and Indo-China Steam Navigation Co., and insurance firms like Lloyds and eighteen other life, fire and marine insurance companies. To supplement their trading operations, Steels also dealt in cotton, vegetable oils, and other produce.

Furthermore, in most Southeast Asian colonies, Western firms belonged to influential business associations that protected their trade and mercantile interests. Those in Burma, for instance, belonged to the (European) Burma Chamber of Commerce, which had representation in the Burma Legislative Council, Port Trust Board, Municipal Council, and various government sub-committees on rice, timber, imports, and shipping. So successful was the Chamber in its lobbying efforts that it was able

---

[5] Steel Bros. and Co., Ltd., (1932), 'Steel's Products', in *Forest Department Standing Orders*, 1 July 1932: 103.

to block the Burma Alienation Land Bill of 1908. 'The [European] Group, though small', noted Sir Arthur Bruce, commercial adviser to the colonial government, 'was compact and, on occasion, in the struggle for power between the Burmese political parties, might find itself holding the balance of power.'[6]

In Malaya, the colonial government provided the legal and institutional environment for private enterprise. For example, the General Land Code (1879) authorized the government to grant leases 'on exceptionally favourable terms' to persons or firms that 'introduce improved systems of working mines by the agency of European machinery under skilled European superintendence' (Wong 1965: 54). The Mining Code (1895) treated mining land as a commodity that could be freely purchased and used as collateral for loans although not for speculation, and gave miners security of tenure from the state and from rival claimants (Wong 1965: 55). The net effect of these measures was to rob Malay chiefs of their traditional power over the mines and to dislodge Chinese miners who had monopolized the industry for much of the nineteenth century.

But in the Philippines, the situation was different. Described in the late nineteenth century as an 'Anglo-Chinese colony with the Spanish flag', (Wickberg 1965: 72) a Spanish supporter lamented: 'Sad thing that Spanish country. If one looks at the currency, Mexico appears; if one looks at its predominant population who intermingles with the indigenous masses, China appears; if one looks at its more valuable commerce, England, Germany and North America appear' (Quioquiap 1894: 177). As Benito Legarda (1999: 256) rightly observes, economic activity (non-Spanish Western) and political control (Spanish) did not rest in the same hands.

Neither was the colonial government interested in creating the conditions in which private industry could thrive. Hence, Anglo-American companies in the Philippines were unlike other firms in Southeast Asia that enjoyed political influence by means of representation in high-level government bodies, or benefited from colonial laws and regulations receptive to private enterprise.

Throughout the Southeast Asian region, the success of the firms rested on a mutually beneficial relationship with immigrant Asians who had more or less settled in the region. Chinese and Indians served in various capacities, as labourers, agricultural moneylenders, and brokers in commodity trade, while Europeans and Anglo-Asians were preferred as administrative staff. However, in the early years of colonial rule, immigrant

---

[6] *Burma Recollections*, Memoirs of Sir Arthur Bruce, Commercial Adviser to the Government of Burma, 1944. European manuscript in India Office Archives, London: 21.

Asians competed with Western companies, particularly in rubber and tin mining. Chinese had long dominated the tin mining industry in Monthon Puket, Siam, to the consternation of British interests trying to break into the industry. With a steady supply of Chinese labour and a well-entrenched alliance with Malay chiefs, Chinese immigrants successfully controlled the tin and rubber industries up to the 1890s.

Once established, Western firms found that collaboration with immigrant Asians was not only useful but easy. The latter were available (certainly greater in number than Europeans), less costly (European salaries were steep) and, having been long-time residents of the place, spoke the local languages and were more familiar with the people and culture, often intermarrying with local women. Though foreign, Chinese and Indians were nevertheless viewed by the local populace as less alien than Europeans, whose residence in the colony was intermittent or brief, and distant from Southeast Asian cultures and lifestyles. Thus, in practice, Chinese and Indian immigrants bridged the local peasant economy (and community) with the larger export and import trade (and world) represented by Western firms.

Among the various roles of Asian immigrants, finance and brokerage had the greatest impact on the agricultural population. Because foreign banks did not extend credit to farmers, Chettyar and Chinese moneylenders financed agricultural and mining operations, from the purchase of land in some cases, to the processing and distribution of commodities. If the Burmese borrower had no land but owned paddy, the Chettyar would lend money on the security of paddy itself, up to two-thirds or three-quarters of the value of paddy to be bought, provided the Chettyar had his own watchman and lock on the godown.[7] Even local millers were financed by Chettyar and other private moneylenders at interest rates of 18 to 24 per cent or higher (English 1919: 664). Chinese and Chinese mestizos in central and northern Luzon applied a type of loan called *pacto de retroventa* (resale contract), whereby they held on to the land of the cultivator who had the option to buy it back at the price of the loan plus encumbrances added onto the property by the creditor. Unable to prove he had the option (since contracts were rarely notarized), or failing to repurchase the land, the borrower would lose it altogether to his Chinese creditor, who would, in turn, rent it out, sometimes to the original owner-cultivator (Wickberg 1965: 99).

---

[7] *Report of the Burma Provincial Banking Enquiry Committee 1929–30*, Vol. 1, 1930, Superintendent, Government Printing, Rangoon, 106.

'FREE TRADE' VERSION ONE

Among the frequently touted blessings of civilized rule, colonial officials cited freedom of trade as a fundamental requisite of economic development. Notwithstanding the legal and institutional arrangements supportive of Western enterprise, a case was often made for non-interference by the state in the operations of private industry. Southeast Asian colonial experiences suggest at least two interpretations of 'free trade': the absence of a monopoly, and the absence of trade barriers such as duties and quotas.

In 1923, the British minister of agriculture told the Burma Legislative Council, 'The whole of the Government's policy for many years has been to prevent the acquisition of a monopoly by any particular firm'.[8] Though said in reference to the forest industry, other British administrators made similar statements with respect to the rice trade. Yet, the fact is that the major export industries operated as cartel-like organizations, either to mitigate the effects of world crises in particular products or to obtain steady access to crop supplies at prices favourable to Western firms. A good example of the first is the sugar industry in Java. Following the 1884–5 (international) sugar crisis and the consequent fall in the world price of sugar, the General Syndicate of Sugar Producers in the Netherlands Indies was formed, consisting of resident managers of sugar factories in Java, most of whose owners lived in the Netherlands. In 1917, the Association of Owners of Netherlands Indies' Sugar Enterprises in Holland declared that the situation called for a sellers' cartel of all producers. This led to the creation of the United Java Sugar Producers with a representative in Surabaya, Java. Owing to labour unrest in 1918–21, the Syndicate established a separate Java Sugar Employers Union to set a common policy regarding labour unions. In 1932, the sugar export monopoly was awarded to the Netherlands Indies' Association for the Sale of Sugar, thereby supplanting the Syndicate. Their roles were then divided between the Syndicate, as sugar factory managers, and the Association, as exporters in full control of sugar (Boomgaard 1988: 162–3).

The second purpose of a cartel, to control supplies (and prices), is best exemplified by the Bullinger Pool, a combination of British rice millers and exporters formed in Burma in 1921 for the purchase and sale of rice and paddy. The four—Steel Bros and Co., Bulloch Bros and Co., Ellerman's Aracan Rice and Trading Co., and Anglo-Burma Rice Co.—had a combined share of only 10.3 per cent of the total number of rice mills in the colony in 1917 and 4.9 per cent in 1931. But these were large mills, their size (in terms of number of employees) averaging about nine to ten times

---

[8] *Report of the Burma Legislative Council Proceedings* (*BLCP*) 1, 2, 15 March 1923: 73.

that of all other mills.[9] Compared to 'the little smacks and trawlers of the rice milling industry with their output of ten, twenty, fifty, one hundred tonnes a day,' (Clark 1941: 38), the Steels mill in Kanaungtoe alone had a daily capacity of 1500 tonnes of paddy and produced 1000 tonnes of rice a day (Clark 1973: 19).

So powerful had the Pool become that barely two years after its founding, it had become the subject of debate in the Legislative Council. Was it true, asked a Burmese representative, that the European millers had 'formed a combination to depress the price of paddy' purchased and milled by them for export?[10] In 1929, on the eve of the depression, another Burmese representative proposed the creation of a committee to investigate the rice and paddy trade in general and 'the freights, the actions of the Bullinger's Pool'.[11] In its interim report, the Committee explained that its purpose was to investigate the fall in prices, 'especially in view of the belief widely current in Burma that it was due to the manipulations of the market by a group of millers in Rangoon'.[12] Not surprisingly, the Committee concluded that:

No mercantile firm can be expected to work without profit.... The Pool is an organization devised in the need for self-preservation in the fight with the too numerous mills that have been constructed. We could wish ... that a compromise could have been reached, under which the mills in excess both small and big would have been closed down and the supply of paddy divided at a fair rate corresponding to the world-price of rice among the continuing mills. But in the absence of such a compromise ... it does not seem right to scrutinize too closely the tactics in a fight for existence. The Pool has no legal advantage. It has no monopoly. It rests on its commercial reputation, its business skill and its financial backing. It is our opinion that in all the circumstances no case has been made out for Government interference.[13]

In the eyes of the Committee, therefore, matters would have been worse without the Bullinger Pool. Paddy prices would have soared uncontrollably, given the competition in the rice-milling sector. Cultivators would have benefited, but only temporarily because mills would end up working at a loss, thus leaving room for others to organize a monopoly.

[9] *Large Industrial Establishments in India, 1917 and 1931*, 1917, Superindent, Government Printing, Calcutta and Manager of Publications, Delhi, *Annual Report on the Working of the Indian Factories Act, 1917 and 1931*, Superindent, Government Printing, 1917 and 1931, Rangoon.

[10] *BLCP* 2, 1, 26 November 1923: 29.

[11] *BLCP* 13, 4, 18 February 1929: 154–69.

[12] Government of Burma Revenue Department Resolution, 23 November 1931, *Rangoon Gazette Weekly Budget*, 30 November 1931: 2.

[13] *Rice and Paddy Trade Interim Report*: 26–7.

Ultimately, according to the Committee, the paddy grower would have been worse off.[14] It was better, then, to have 'regulated' competition than one that operated freely. The same was true of the teak industry. As noted by the colonial legislature,

> It is obvious as regards the larger and more distant forests, that only a big firm can be in a position to work these in such a manner as to work out properly the stock of timber ripe for extraction and to secure to Government the revenue to which it is entitled for its forest produce. It is and has for many years been the intention of Government to see that adequate areas are left available for the extraction of forest produce by small traders.[15]

'FREE TRADE' VERSION TWO

The second type of 'free trade' was established by the American government in the Philippines. In 1906, the Payne–Aldrich Act allowed the free entry of US and Philippine goods into each other's countries, but with restrictions on the volume of Philippine sugar and tobacco that could enter the US free of duty (the quotas, though, were generous). However, no counterpart restrictions were imposed on American products. The law also set a ceiling of 20 per cent on the foreign (non-Philippine and non-US) content of Philippine-made goods that could enter the US duty-free. Rice was, in addition, exempted from duty-free treatment. Filipino leaders objected to free trade on the grounds that it would 'in the long run, be highly detrimental to the economic interests of the Filipino people' and turn the Philippines into an American dependency, thereby posing a threat at the time of independence (Salamanca 1968: 127). This fear was not without basis for one effect of free trade was the removal of all foreign competition (notably British) from the import and export trade, thereby giving the US a nearly 80 per cent share of the total foreign trade of the Philippines by the time of independence.

Free trade arrangements continued after the Philippines obtained independence. The Philippine Trade Law (1946), which was enacted as a condition for the grant of war rehabilitation funds from the US, guaranteed that duty-free quotas would be given to the same companies (mostly American) that had dominated the pre-War trade. As Shirley Jenkins (1954: 68) points out, the 'prolonged period of preferential trade ... encouraged the re-establishment of specialized agricultural production, which had been disrupted during the Japanese occupation. Trade preferences

---

[14] Solomon (1974), *Rice and Paddy Trade Interim Report*: 26.
[15] *BLCP* 1, 2: 73.

Southeast Asia / 189

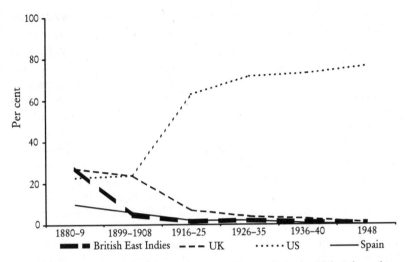

Figure 7.1 Philippine Foreign Trade: Share of Trade with Selected Countries, 1880–1948

Source: Jenkins 1954: 171.

and privileges to American investors tended to encourage the development of extractive industries, such as mining, rather than manufacturing for the domestic Philippine market'. Worse, the law required an amendment of the Philippine Constitution, which had restricted the development and use of natural resources to Filipino citizens and Philippine-owned corporations, so as to allow Americans 'equal' rights. The 'parity' amendment to the 1935 Constitution reads: 'The disposition, exploitation, development, and utilization of all agricultural, timber, and mineral lands of the public domain, waters, minerals, coal, petroleum and other mineral oils, all forces and sources of potential energy, and other natural resources of the Philippines, and the operation of public utilities, shall, if open to any person, be open to citizens of the United States and to all forms of business enterprise owned or controlled, directly or indirectly, by United States citizens' (Jenkins 1954: 67–8).

The amendment and free trade (with an annual decline in duty-free quotas) remained in force until 1974.

If the Southeast Asian agriculturist suffered from free enterprise, colonial governments offered at least some consolation: the cultivator's lament was common throughout the region. As a British colonial official put it, 'In regard to agricultural produce the complaint that the farmer receives only a small share of farm produce is general. It belongs to no particular country nor to any particular generation'.[16] It was also expected, as an official document noted.

The origins of the trouble lie in the position of the farmer as a small and isolated unit for whom the main day-to-day concern is production. His venture into the business of marketing the fruits of his labour are intermittent and have come to be regarded as subordinate. It is therefore not to be wondered at that in his dealings with those to whom buying and selling are fulltime occupations he often comes off a poor second.[17]

As colonies became increasingly intertwined into the world economy, peasants became more vulnerable to the vicissitudes of trade. The Great Depression in the 1930s was felt in the region, from rice in Burma, Siam, and Cochinchina to Javanese sugar, rubber in Malaya and Indo-china, and tin. The only exception perhaps was the Philippines, which (ironically) was protected by free trade. Brown argues, however, that even in the worst-hit areas, cultivators were able to resort to the evasion of rent, tax, and debt payments, or to shift from production for the market to production for home use as a means of coping with the crisis (Brown 1997: 52–3). While some diversification took place as a result of the depression (for example, the Java weaving industry), the Saya San rebellion in Burma in the early 1930s and the rise of mass-based ideological movements in Viet Nam and Indonesia during the same period challenge the efficacy of these self-defensive measures. The problem with Brown's thesis is his assumption that if, 'during the decades of export expansion, the material condition of the cultivating populations in Southeast Asia had worsened, the implication must be that cultivators had been coerced, in some way, into large-scale market production' (Brown 1997: 141). And since coercion by the state or the force of local circumstances seems an unlikely explanation for the tremendous growth of farming for export, and '[g]iven the sheer scale of the expansion, the huge numbers of cultivators involved, and the back-breaking nature of this work, it may be more realistic to argue that the agriculturist, pushing the frontier of cultivation outwards, was motivated principally by a reasonable prospect that he and his family would thereby profit' (Brown 1997: 141).

Brown's conclusion, therefore, is that peasant conditions were not as dismal as they have been made out to be. However, even if one were to assume that agriculturists had freely engaged in export production, can one rightly infer that their lives invariably improved (or did not

[16] *Market Section Bulletin* No. 3: Marketing Improvement, 1939, Superintendent, Government Printing, Rangoon, 1.

[17] *Market Selection Bulletin* No. 3.

progressively decline) as a result? Moreover, it cannot be denied that the demands of colonized peoples for control over their resources were expressed again and again in the region, with the awareness of colonial officials. In 1922, for instance, the Forest Administration of Burma reported that '[p]ublic opinion increasingly desires that a larger proportion of the timber trade should be in the hands of the natives of the country'.[18] In some instances, this demand was a parcel of the larger demand for political independence. Salud Algabre, who joined the Sakdal uprising in Central Luzon in 1935, explained that the problem of poverty, which had led to the rebellion, was not simply a matter of land tenancy or abuses by landowners. 'Freedom,' she said, 'was the solution.... There was no other answer to the abuses and the poverty. With independence the leaders would cease to be powerful. Instead, it would be the people who were powerful. The people would have their freedom. We would have our own lands; they would no longer be the monopoly of the *proprietarios* and of the government officials. As it was, we had nothing' (Sturtevant 1976: 291).

SPECTRE OF THE PAST

To this day, a good number of Southeast Asians subsist on very little. Unfinished projects, ongoing struggles, persistent colonial forms, structures and a mixture of traditional and new relations are still in evidence and they hound Southeast Asian peoples to the present. Consider, for example, the lament of Spanish importers and residents in the Philippines and their families in Spain during the currency crisis in the 1880s and 1890s. Reeling from the fall of the Mexican peso, which they called *aguila* (eagle), they blamed the central government for its failure to solve the monetary problem. Although the circumstances were different from those which Southeast Asia has faced recently—it was a bimetallic world then— the effects felt in the late nineteenth century[19] sound all too familiar today: weightless coins, decline in real wages, and so on. Analysing the economic state of the colony over a hundred years ago, Lopez-Jaena began with this observation: 'The Philippines is penniless; she does not have a cent. This is sad but it is true' (Lopez-Jaena 1974: 111). Given the staggering and growing foreign debt of the country today, his lines could well describe the present.

[18] *Report on Forest Administration in Burma*, 1922, Superintendent, Government Printing, Rangoon, 47.

[19] Q., 'La Cuestion Monetaria', *La Politica* IV, 101, 18 December 1894: 330; Tom-tit, 'Fisica Recreativa,' *Manililla* VIII, 340, 27 October 1894: 349.

The prolonged past continues to find itself in popular memories that surface every now and then, but most visibly in times of threat. When word leaked out from US defence officials that American combat troops would conduct their joint military exercise in 2003 in Jolo, the southernmost tip of the Philippines and home to the *Bangsa Moro* movement, Governor Farouk Hussin of the Autonomous Region of Muslim Mindanao warned: 'The Tausug, when they lull their babies to sleep, do not sing "Summertime" or "Hush, Little Baby". They sing ballads like, "Go to sleep so you'll be strong so you can avenge the atrocities committed on your father"'[20]— a reference to the US military campaign against the Tausug in Jolo in 1906 that resulted in the massacre of more than 600 Tausug men, women and children. Hussin added, 'They do not want a situation where these sad memories will be rekindled.'

But rekindled the memories are. After Washington retracted its statement, US Ambassador to the Philippines, Francis Ricciardone assured the Filipino people that: 'The US respects the Constitution of the Philippines. You are our ally, for heaven's sake.' He continued, 'We would not violate your laws or your Constitution. If we come, we come as invited allies working under your law, your rules and your commanders' lead. We will not come in as alien invaders.'[21] Yet, the assurance sounds ominously familiar. Soon after the Second World War, during the deliberations of the American Congress on the Philippine Trade Act, Congressman Walter Lynch asked if a law would be passed superseding the Philippine Constitution since some of the provisions of the bill ran counter to the Constitution. The sponsor, Congressman Jasper Bell, replied, 'Of course, we would not contemplate that the Philippine people would do anything contrary to their Constitution, but would contemplate that they, as a people, have the power to amend their Constitution, and, if there should be anything prohibiting this sort of agreement, they would undertake to make such amendment as might be necessary' (Jenkins 1954: 57). And indeed, the amendment was made.

For many Southeast Asians then, the long past and the extended present have come to mean similar things.

REFERENCES

Anderson, Benedict, (1983), *Imagined Communities: Reflections on the Origin and Spread of Nationalism*, Verso Books, London.

---

[20] *Philippine Daily Inquirer* (PDI), 27 February 2003.
[21] *Philippine Daily Inquirer* (PDI), 26 February 2003.

—— (1998), *The Spectre of Comparisons: Nationalism, Southeast Asia and the World*, Verso Books, London.

Aphornsuvan, Thanet, (1998), 'Slavery and Modernity: Freedom in the Making of Modern Siam', in David Kelly and Anthony Reid (eds), *Asian Freedoms: The Idea of Freedom in East and Southeast Asia*, Cambridge University Press, Cambridge.

Bonifacio, Andres, (1956, reprinted 2002), 'Ang Dapat Mabatid ng mga Tagalog', (What Filipinos Should Know), in Teodoro A. Agoncillo (ed.), *The Revolt of the Masses*, University of the Philippines Press, Quezon City.

Boomgaard, Peter, (1988), 'Treacherous Cane: The Java Sugar Industry between 1914 and 1940', in Bill Albert and Adrian Graves (eds), *The World Sugar Economy in War and Depression, 1914–40*, Routledge, London.

Braund, H. E. W., (1975), *Calling to Mind*, Pergamon Press, Oxford.

Brown, Ian, (1997), *Economic Change in South-East Asia, c. 1830–1980*, Oxford University Press, Kuala Lumpur.

Cady, John, (1958), *A History of Modern Burma*, Cornell University Press, Ithaca.

Carter, Paul, (1995), 'The Road to Botany Bay: An Essay in Spatial History', in Bill Ashcroft, Gareth Griffiths, and Helen Tiffin (eds), *The Post-colonial Studies Reader*, Routledge, London.

Clark, J. R., (1941), 'Burma and her Rice Export Trade', *Steels House Magazine*, 3(3), October.

—— (1973), 'The Wonder that is Rice', *Steels House Magazine*, December.

del Pilar, Marcelo H., (1974), 'Monastic Supremacy in the Philippines', (La Soberania Monacal en Filipinas), in Teodoro, A. Agoncillo (ed.), *Filipino Nationalism, 1872–1970*, R. P. Garcia Publishing Co., Quezon City.

Drabble, J. H., (1973), *Rubber in Malaya 1876–1922*, Oxford University Press, Kuala Lumpur.

Duiker, William J., (1976), *The Rise of Nationalism in Vietnam, 1900–1941*, Cornell University Press, Ithaca.

Emerson, Rupert, (1979), *Malaysia*, University of Malaya Press, Kuala Lumpur.

English, A. E., (1919), Oral Evidence Before the Indian Industrial Commission, 1918, in *British Parliamentary Papers* 20.

Furnivall, J. S., (1939, reprinted 1967), *Netherlands India, A Study of Plural Economy*, Cambridge University Press, Cambridge.

Ileto, Reynaldo C., (1979), *Pasyon and Revolution: Popular Movements in the Philippines, 1840–1910*, Ateneo de Manila University Press, Quezon City.

Jenkins, Shirley, (1954), *American Economic Policy toward the Philippines*, Stanford University Press, Stanford.

Lamb, Helen B., (1972), *Vietnam's Will to Live*, Monthly Review Press, New York.

Legarda Jr, Benito, (1999), *After the Galleons: Foreign Trade, Economic Change and Entrepreneurship in the Nineteenth-Century Philippines*, Ateneo de Manila University Press, Quezon City.

Lopez-Jaena, Graciano, (1974), 'The Philippines in Distress: Causes', in T.A. Agoncillo (ed.), *Filipino Nationalism, 1872–1970*, R. P. Garcia Publishing Co., Quezon City.

Marr, David G., (1981), *Vietnamese Tradition on Trial, 1920–1945*, University of California Press, Berkeley.

McCoy, Alfred W., (1982), 'A Queen Dies Slowly: The Rise and Decline of Iloilo City', in Alfred W. McCoy and Ed C. de Jesus (eds), *Philippine Social History: Global Trade and Local Transformations*, Ateneo de Manila University Press, Quezon City.

Morehead, F.T., (1944), *Burma Pamphlets No. 5: The Forests of Burma*, Longmans, Green & Co., London.

Moscotti, Albert D., (1974), 'British Policy and the Nationalist Movement in Burma, 1917–1937', *Asian Studies*, 11, University of Hawaii.

Nartsupha, Chatthip and Suthy Prasartset (eds), (1981), *The Political Economy of Siam, 1851–1910*, Sangroong Printing, Bangkok.

Quioquiap, (1894), 'El giro con Filipinas', *La Politica de España en Filipinas*, 4 (89), 3 July.

Reid, Anthony, (1998), 'Merdeka: The Concept of Freedom in Indonesia', in David Kelly and Anthony Reid (eds), *Asian Freedoms: The Idea of Freedom in East and Southeast Asia*, Cambridge University Press, Cambridge.

Roff, William R., (1967), *The Origins of Malay Nationalism*, Yale University Press, New Haven.

Salamanca, Bonifacio S., (1968), *The Filipino Reaction to American Rule, 1901–13*, The Shoe String Press, Connecticut.

Schurman, Jacob, George Dewey, Elwell Otis, Charles Denby, and Dean C. Worcester, (1900), 'To the People of the Philippine Islands', in *Report of the Philippine Commission to the President*, Vol. 1, Government Printing Office, Washington DC.

Solomon, E. H., (1931), 'Note of Dissent', *Interim Report of the Committee Appointed to Enquire into the Rice and Paddy Trade*, Superindent, Government Printing, Rangoon.

Stanley, Peter W., (1974), *A Nation in the Making: The Philippines and the United States, 1899–1921*, Harvard University Press, Cambridge.

Sturtevant, David R., (1976), *Popular Uprisings in the Philippines, 1840–1940*, Cornell University Press, Ithaca.

Wickberg, Edgar, (1965), *The Chinese in Philippine Life, 1850–1898*, Yale University Press, New Haven.

Wong Lin Ken, (1965), *The Malayan Tin Industry to 1914*, University of Arizona Press, Tucson.

8

India in the Long Twentieth Century

Sumit Sarkar

India's location within the three historical 'moments' that can be taken to comprise the 'long' twentieth century was both central, and, in many ways, rather specific. The South Asian subcontinent was the 'brightest jewel' in the 'Empire on which the sun never set', during the apogee of Western colonialism from the last quarter of the nineteenth century till the First World War. It then became the locus of one of the most powerful anti-colonial nationalist mass movements that ultimately destroyed the old forms of colonialism during the succeeding half-century. Its Indian part pioneered projects of non-alignment and autonomous Third World capitalist development during the Nehruvian era, through state initiative, with a degree of planning and a socialistic language. In recent years, its dominant groups have largely succumbed to the conjoint pressures and attractions of the current resurgence of modified forms of neo-colonialism, operating under the banners of 'globalization' and 'liberalization'. As in many other parts of the world, such surrender has been accompanied by a deepening stress on chauvinistic and majoritarian religious–cultural nationalism, that today seriously threatens the democratic and secular principles of the Constitution adopted in 1949.

If India then has been very much a part of wider, global currents, its history also has specificities with which it might be convenient to begin, to avoid the not uncommon danger of blurring important distinctions between the experiences of colonialism and anti-colonialism in different parts of the erstwhile 'Third' World. What distinguished the subcontinent was the combination of long and stable colonial domination (across centuries during which Britain and the West also underwent decisive changes), immense physical and demographic size, and the presence of pre-colonial societies that were exceptionally hierarchical and diversified. The subcontinent never became a settler colony, and the vast disproportion in numbers between the expatriate rulers and the indigenous peoples necessitated a shifting pattern of partial accommodations and alliances—unequal, but not entirely one-sided—with sections of Indians.

The latter occasionally involved the emergent stratum of English-educated middle-class Indians, but more often consisted of princes, landlords, traders, and other locally influential strata. Despite strong elements of racist discrimination, British rule, in other words, could not afford to remain a pure externality, but rested on adjustments with already existing power structures within indigenous society. The rhetoric of 'civilizing' Westernization has perhaps been taken too literally by its apologists and critics alike (notably by many of today's post-colonial theorists). Colonialism in India had both a 'Westernizing' as well as an 'Orientalizing' face, and on the whole, for much of the time, the second tended to predominate.[1]

A second preliminary point concerns the complexities of late-colonial Indian history. This has been interpreted for long through a single grid of colonial / anti-colonial conflict. Such a binary, of course, remains relevant, but with context-specific variations in degrees of centrality. This is becoming clearer as, pressed often by contemporary developments (notably the rise of right-wing Hindu chauvinism, the increasing political visibility of subordinate castes, and the emergence of feminist practice and theory), scholars are obliged to give greater attention to the history of identity formations around dividing-lines of religion, gender, and caste, interacting with, but not reducible to the simple binary beloved of nationalists, old or new.[2] And surely, only a framework that admits the possibility of multiple

[1] For a brief exposition of this argument, which is becoming increasingly influential among both Western and Indian historians in recent years, see Washbrook (1999: 395–421). I need to add that my argument is not that such a dualism was peculiar to India alone; it was, in fact, a fairly common imperialist strategy, expressed for instance through attempts at 'indirect rule' through 'native' 'chiefs' in many parts of Africa, right down to apartheid. But in India, there was both much more time, and greater need, for this to become more stable and effective.

[2] That binary had already been complicated by Left-nationalist, Marxist, and then Subalternist perspectives, highlighting the autonomy and importance of class conflicts and pressures of subordinated strata. But there has been a persistent tendency towards evaluating the significance of subaltern affirmations primarily in terms of their 'contributions' towards deepening anti-colonial movements. I have tried to elaborate this argument in Sarkar (2002).

narratives can begin to make sense of the more long-term dimensions of the extremely contradictory processes that have characterized post-colonial India.

Two clarifications are called for at the outset. Reasons of space and personal capacity alike have led me to confine the post-colonial narrative to India alone, omitting Pakistan and Bangladesh, even though the territories making up the latter will, of course, enter into my survey of British-ruled India. I should add that a curious anomaly of Indian historical scholarship has been its tendency to end its narratives (and teaching courses of 'modern' Indian history) with the conjoint coming of Independence and Partition in 1947. My disciplinary attainments and limits might contribute to a similar overbalance of the earlier phase in this account.

The dominant feature of late-nineteenth century developments in India was the thrust towards all-round centralization and integration of the subcontinent on a quite unprecedented scale. Crucial here was a thoroughgoing communications revolution, epitomized by the Suez Canal (1865–9), telegraph lines and a submarine cable, the replacement of sailing ships by steamers, and the pace of railway construction (432 miles in 1859, over 5000 a decade later, and around 25,000 by 1900)—as well as the spread of mechanical print. All these helped to weave more tightly together the various levels of British Indian administration (Secretary of State in London, the Viceroy and Executive Council in Calcutta and then in Delhi from 1911, the provincial governments) into a structure that was fundamentally autocratic, thinly veiled by an ideology of paternalistic benevolence and occasional talk of trusteeship and training towards self-government. Effective centralization went along with systematization of information-collection, through a hierarchy of official reports and an impressive battery of decennial census operations (from 1871), gazettes, and numerous other forms of documentation.

Arguably, it was only then, in the decades succeeding the suppression of the 1857 Rebellion, that a distinct colonial kind of 'modernity' began to manifest itself in many spheres of Indian life, with clear ruptures from pre-colonial times. But these were also the years, in India as well as in many other parts of the world, of large-scale 'inventions of tradition' on an unprecedented scale. The panic of 1857—when a section of erstwhile indigenous rulers and landlords had combined with rebel soldiers and disaffected peasants in a major effort to drive out the foreigners—led to efforts to conciliate and develop alliances with indigenous elites, in particular, the 662 surviving 'native princes' (most of them both highly despotic and increasingly loyal to the British) and landed elements. The 'Raj', consequently, tried to dress itself in 'oriental' and 'feudal' clothes, borrowing ceremonials in highly transmuted manner from the Mughals as well as medieval Europe. Queen Victoria, for instance, was proclaimed 'Empress of India' (Indianized as 'Kaiser-I-Hind') in a grandiose 'Imperial Assemblage' in 1877, amidst much of what the British imagined to be authentic 'oriental' ceremonial. Official architecture followed a similar conglomerate track, juxta-posing 'Indo-Saracenic' with Victorian Gothic.

In a speech to British owners of coalmines in India, an unusually frank Viceroy (Lord Curzon) declared in 1903: 'My work lies in administration, yours in exploitation—but both are aspects of the same question and the same duty'. (McLane 1977: 37). By the late nineteenth century, imperial control was certainly crucial for the effective integration of India into the capitalist world economy as supplier of foodstuff and raw materials to, and as a market for manufactured exports of, the industrialized West and, most notably, of Britain. Britain was far and away the largest supplier of Indian imports (over 60 per cent in 1913), and the subcontinent provided a captive market (there were no protective tariffs till the 1920s) for its cotton textiles, iron and steel, and engineering products at a time when these were facing increasing competition and tariff walls in Europe and America.

There was also a vital balance of payments dimension, for India maintained a trade surplus with these other parts of the capitalist world through exports of foodgrains, raw jute, jute manufactures, raw cotton, oilseeds, and hides and skins—precisely with the countries with which British deficits were increasing. And so, 'Britain's visible and invisible payments surplus with India enabled her to make good between two-fifths and one-third of her deficit with the other industrialized nations, and to continue to perform as an economy with a worldwide balance of payments surplus long after her trading position had declined'.[3]

The other major and undeniable benefit of Britain through its Indian Empire was military. The manpower resources of its colony, extracted easily for military service through poverty, compensated for Britain's own deficiencies in terms of a big standing army. Maintained at the cost of Indian revenues, the British Indian army was repeatedly sent on colonial adventures far removed from Indian borders, and later participated on a very big scale in the two World Wars.

Export of capital, which has figured so prominently in many theories of imperialism, was possibly a less significant dimension of the Indo-British colonial connection. British investments were significantly more in Latin America, USA, and Canada, with 51 per cent of portfolio investments

---

[3] Tomlinson (1979: 6) here is summarizing the findings regarding the balance of payments question worked out by Saul (1960: chapters 3, 8).

between 1865 and 1914 going to the Americas, as against only 14 per cent to Asia. Investments in India went mainly to government loans, railways, export-oriented tea and coffee plantations, mines, and jute mills. With the funds coming mainly from ploughed-back profits and savings of European residents in India, there was little real transfer of resources from Britain to India. Railway costs, in particular, were met in significant part from Indian revenues, through a system of 'guaranteed interest', by which a floor-level of profits was ensured to British investors at the expense of Indian taxpayers.

Late colonial India was under a free trade regime, with its British rulers claiming to follow economic policies of laissez-faire (shot through in practice, though, by numerous acts of special privilege and patronage to British entrepreneurs). There was a consistent export surplus, and the conditions might have seemed appropriate for the manifestation of the alleged fruits of 'market-driven' or 'export-led growth', beloved of old and new orthodox economic theorists. Yet, there was ample evidence of massive, and possibly growing, Indian poverty. There were major famines in many regions in the 1870s and the 1890s (the latter coinciding with plague epidemics), and even the obviously interested estimate of per capita annual national income made by Lord Curzon in the budget debate of 1901–2 amounted to Rs 30 (two pounds sterling), as against a figure 26 times higher for Britain (Bagchi 1972: Chapter 1).

The theme of Indian poverty became the starting point for a systematic critique of the economic consequences of British rule, which was the main achievement of the first generation of Indian nationalists. Starting with Dadabhai Naoroji from the 1870s, they argued that the export surplus in goods was being continually 'drained' away to Britain through official and unofficial remittances. British manufactures (notably Lancashire textiles), meanwhile, were destroying unprotected Indian handicrafts, excessive revenue demand was leading to rural impoverishment, while the commercialization of agriculture brought about by improved communications primarily benefited foreign export firms and shipping interests, while for peasants, it was often a 'forced' and harmful process. Textile mills owned by Indians had started emerging in Bombay and Ahmedabad, but the emergent Indian industrial capitalists were being hamstrung in diverse ways by the colonial state in the interests of British entrepreneurs.

The nationalist critique set off a debate that still goes on, into the details of which we cannot enter here. But three tentative generalizations might be permitted. First, there can be few doubts that the nationalist theories, formulated well over a century back, were guilty of simplifications and inadequacies. The amount of the 'drain of wealth', and, more important, its importance in macroeconomic terms, might well have been exaggerated. 'De-industrialization' was neither as cataclysmic nor as total as was often suggested: many handicrafts were able to adapt themselves to changed circumstances, survive, and at times (by the twentieth century, at least) even prosper.

The consequences of intensified commercialization, for artisans and peasants alike, varied considerably across regions, times, and by type of industry or crop. Relations between Indian business groups, their British counterparts, and the colonial state were not uniformly conflicting. The rapid growth in the export–import trade with the West, progressively drawing in more and more internal regions, meant significant profits for large numbers of Indian merchants, even though the commanding heights long remained beyond their reach. The steel plant started by the Tatas in the early twentieth century received state patronage, for the British were eager to keep out other European competitors, while even the growth of rivals to Lancashire textiles in western India meant gains for British textile machinery exports.

Yet, there can be little doubt either about persistent Indian mass poverty, or the reality of many points of acute tensions and disaffection, grounded in material conflicts, between foreign rule and large numbers of its subjects. These were frequently exacerbated by instances of racist discrimination and violence, which could occasionally unite the highest in 'native' society with the lowest, in a common sense of deprivation and injustice.[4] The excesses of 'revisionist' near-apologias need to be avoided as much as nationalist exaggerations.

In some ways current thinking has even added to the chargesheet against colonial rule, notably by the very significant recent focus on environmental history. The need to control and 'rationally' exploit forest resources, above all timber for railway construction, led the colonial state to impose a rigid regime of forest laws, by which age-old customary uses of forests for a variety of everyday purposes—by hunting–gathering, pastoral, and poorer sections of peasant communities—were suddenly blocked

---

[4] Amiya Bagchi (1972) elaborates, in convincing detail, the multifarious ways through which informal connections between European officials and businessmen often hindered the growth of indigenous commerce and industry. The emerging educated 'middle class' increasingly felt the presence of a 'glass ceiling' beyond which they could not rise, with respect to government jobs and professions alike. Respectable gentlemen not infrequently found themselves insulted or thrown out by whites from first class railway compartments. For the poor, racism took the cruder form of kicks and blows and shooting 'accidents', as the 'sahib' disciplined the 'coolie' in domestic service or tea plantations or bagged a native by mistake while out hunting. White-dominated courts regularly awarded ridiculously low punishments for such incidents.

and transformed into 'crimes'. The resultant conflicts run right through the colonial and post-colonial eras, and remain a central theme of contemporary environmentalist and other 'social' movements. State ownership of forests (the Forest Department eventually came to control about one-fifth of the land mass of British India) went along, however, with the consolidation of private property in cultivated land.

Colonialism simultaneously needed expansion of settled agriculture, for that was considered indispensable both for exports as well as for the stability of British rule (the 'unsettled', migrant peoples of the forest and waste generally being considered both unproductive and dangerous). Private property rights were therefore consolidated, initially for landlord groups and later, for a peasant upper stratum. 'Sedentarization' went along with dispossession, of food gatherers and pastoral groups as well as of poorer peasants hit hard by tighter notions of property and alienation through debt.

Highly-oppressive, at times near-servile, methods of extraction of labour from such dispossessed strata through a system of indenture-based migration were widely used to work plantations within India (notably, the tea gardens of Assam) as well as in other overseas colonies.[5] By the late nineteenth century, the same catchment areas had started providing cheap labour, through methods often nearly as oppressive, for the plantations, mines, and factories owned both by the British, and increasingly by Indian entrepreneurs. Colonialism, thus meant significant gains for some sections of Indians, and enhanced suffering and discontent among many more.

Any assumption, however, of straight-line, unmediated connections between material discontent produced by foreign rule, and the course of late-colonial Indian history, is bound to remain unsatisfactory—and that not only because of the differential consequences that have just been mentioned. British rule, in many ways, did help to constitute its own anti-colonial nationalist 'grave-diggers'. Administrative and political pressures and opportunities, the communications revolution, and a unified home market, the rapid spread of vernacular print culture, access to modern Western notions of liberalism and equal legal rights, all helped to constitute

[5] Statistics of Indian overseas labour emigration provide striking confirmation of the centrality of India for the entire system of British and, indeed, world imperialism. Between 1834 and 1924, around 6.5 million emigrated, primarily to British colonies in the West Indies, South and East Africa, Southeast Asia, and the Pacific, but also French and Dutch territories. Among them, around one and a quarter million went on indentures that have been characterized as a 'new system of slavery'. Indian indentured labour constituted no less than 85 per cent of the total flow of such enforced emigration between 1834 and 1920 (Northrup 1999: 89–91).

'public spheres'—regional and then, increasingly countrywide. Through these, nationalist ideologies and practices could spread, initially among educated, professional, middle-class groups, but then to expanding segments of peasants, workers, and business strata.

But it has to be emphasized immediately that what was emerging was not just a single, all embracing, 'Indian nation', rooted in a common sense of alienation from a racist and exploitative foreign domination, but a variety of intersecting and often mutually conflicting identities. And here, once again, colonial structures and policies were often crucial, through the logic of institutional practices as well as occasional 'divide and rule' strategies. Two instances will have to suffice.

The British Indian legal system carved out separate realms for 'Hindu' and 'Muslim' personal and family law, where cases were supposed to be decided in accordance with religious texts as interpreted by indigenous experts of the two communities. Combined with an unprecedented centralization of the entire legal system through a countrywide appellate structure, this led to a much sharper sense of an uniform Hindu–Muslim disjunction in numerous matters of everyday living than had probably been present earlier. A similar sharpening of distinctions between ethnic, linguistic, and religious communities (as well as within the latter in the case of Hindus, along lines of caste) was brought about through the institution of the decennial Census from 1871, for enumeration demanded clear-cut definitions, assumptions of firmly bounded, rather than relatively fuzzy, communities.

The late-colonial era thus meant the more or less simultaneous hardening of a multiplicity of identities. It is noteworthy, for instance, that the fifty years or so between the 1870s and the 1920s–30s were marked by the emergence of associations claiming to represent an enormous range of 'communities': 'Indian', 'regional' or linguistic, religious, caste, class, gender.[6] But 'hardening' went along, often with a potential fragility, for the identities could not but intersect with each other, producing conflicting and shifting loyalties, while the spread of notions of individual rights could also threaten many of the emergent putative solidarities.

Dominant or leading groups within the varied communities tried to control such potentially fissiparous tendencies through building up powerful

---

[6] Thus, the Indian Association was floated in 1876, the Indian National Congress in 1885, the Muslim League in 1906, the Hindu Mahasabha, c.1915. There were also a large number of provincial associations, numerous caste-based organizations, as well as the All India Trade Union Congress (1920), the All India Kisan Sabha (1936), and several women's organizations by the 1920s and 1930s.

enemy images.[7] The 'Other' might be the British for nationalists, but Hindu or Muslim for the two main religious groups, as well as high and low castes, landlords and peasants, capitalists and workers, for each other. A tightening of conservative or revivalist forms of both Hindu and Muslim religious solidarities, for instance, was a marked feature of the closing two decades of the nineteenth century.

This was, probably, in part a reaction to a preceding era of 'social reform', initiated by educated 'middle-class' men, but focused on gender-related issues of women's education, the ending of widow immolation, the lifting of the legal ban in Hindu law on widow remarriage, and raising the age of marriage. Hindu community solidarities also needed to be refurbished in the context of the beginnings of movements among lower castes with an anti-Brahminic slant. Related to both subversive tendencies was a slow expansion of the new print culture based public sphere, initially overwhelmingly high caste (or elite Muslim) male, but spreading out increasingly to some women and lower-caste men.[8]

Self-conscious anti-colonial nationalism began in the last quarter of the nineteenth century among small elite groups of English-educated middle class (generally high-caste Hindu) men.[9] These 'moderates' developed a powerful critique of many aspects of British rule, and demanded specific reforms in economic policies (reducing the 'drain of wealth', for instance), more jobs for Indians in the services, and a measure of representative institutions. The basic method was one of trying to win over public opinion in Britain through memorials and petitions, not mass agitation in India. The latter could threaten their own position as men of often considerable property and privilege, and was, in any case, beyond their resources and reach. An early twentieth century turn towards more aggressive imperial policies (notably Viceroy Curzon's decision in 1905 to partition Bengal, a region marked by a developed sense of linguistic–cultural unity among its predominantly upper-caste Hindu landed-cum-

[7] For an exposition of the complexities of the simultaneous hardening and fragility of identities, see Pradip Kumar Datta (1999: Chapter 1).

[8] For possible connections between public sphere development, gender reform initiatives, and an incipient discourse of individual rights, see Tanika Sarkar (2000: 6–7).

[9] Plebeian protests and confrontations with specific aspects or policies of British officialdom long preceded such self-conscious nationalism. With the significant exception of the 1857 Rebellion, however, these tended to be localized, and often directed against the immediate oppressors, who in most cases would be other, more privileged Indians. The British would get involved as the ultimate protectors of the latter, but could also at times play the part of distant, apparently impartial, superiors. Thus, a powerful peasant movement in the eastern part of Bengal (Pabna district) in 1873 raised the demand for being the tenants of Queen Victoria alone: anti-landlordism could go along with faith in the justice of British rule.

professional groups) stimulated moves towards more 'extremist' aims and strategies, anticipating, to some extent, the later methods of Gandhism.

Extremists in some parts of the country initiated a boycott of British imports, tried to promote indigenous enterprise, organized autonomous 'national' schools, and elaborated theories of peaceful 'passive resistance'. But the mass, particularly peasant, mobilization needed for the efficacy of such methods proved beyond the reach of this generation of nationalists. The extremists tried to compensate for their failure to elaborate any meaningful populist–agrarian programme through a combination of Hindu-revivalist rhetoric, with a degree of upper-caste gentry bullying of their predominantly lower-caste or Muslim tenants. The consequences included a quick collapse of the putatively 'mass' phase of this 'Swadeshi' movement, and the turn towards methods of terroristic individual violence on the part of the more militant extremist middle-class activists, aimed at frightening the British into giving concessions or, hopefully, independence. Extremist Hindu nationalism also tended to oppose reform endeavours by or on behalf of women and lower castes. Such 'social' change, in their opinion, could be divisive and require assistance from the foreign government: they should be postponed till the achievement of the 'political' objectives of the nationalists. Not surprisingly, the Swadeshi and immediate post-Swadeshi years were marked by the rapid development of both Muslim and lower-caste identity-based politics with a sharply anti-extremist slant, while the decline of open extremist agitation seems to have coincided also with some revival of interest in gender-related reformism after a period when these had been firmly excluded from public sphere activities.

A sea change came about in virtually all spheres of subcontinental life during the quarter-century following 1919–20, through the conjoint impact of a series of world developments (notably the two World Wars, anti-colonial nationalist and socialist upsurges inspired by the Russian Revolution and initial Soviet achievements, and the consequences of the Great Depression of the 1930s) and the advent of Gandhian nationalism. Building on his experience of fighting white racial discrimination of Indians in South Africa, and incorporating, in modified form, some of the earlier extremist techniques (like boycott and national education), Gandhi was able to evolve a remarkably effective praxis of all-India mass struggle that he tried to keep firmly disciplined and strictly non-violent.

Gandhian techniques progressed from withdrawal from all forms of participation in the structures of foreign rule ('non-cooperation', the key strategy tried out during the 1919–22 upsurge), to peaceful violation of select state laws ('civil disobedience', hallmark of the second round of countrywide struggle, this time aimed explicitly at complete independence, in 1930–4). The emphasis throughout on suffering and sacrifice—remaining totally non-violent in the face of brutal police assaults, mass courting of arrests by tens, sometimes hundreds of thousands, of men and women drawn from all strata and regions of the country, occasional no tax campaigns despite the risk to property—all made considerable sense in the context of a totally disarmed population. Such methods imparted courage and self-confidence to otherwise humble people, and bred among them the sense of a rare kind of moral superiority over their rulers.

In addition, the Gandhian amalgam of mass, yet controlled, struggle fitted in well with the interests and inclination of large numbers of his followers, particularly the business groups, the relatively better-off peasant strata, and the urban or small-town lower middle-class strata. Landholding peasants, and indigenous capitalists were, in fact, the two basic sections which nationalism under Gandhi was able to mobilize significantly for the first time—the latter perhaps largely because the Congress, quite suddenly, now appeared to be emerging into a position where it might be able to deliver the goods in terms of economic concessions, maybe ultimately opening up the prospects of independent capitalist growth.[10] In between the big movements, Gandhians in the countryside sought to retain and enhance peasant support through programmes of 'constructive' village-level work. These did not attempt any basic change in landlord–peasant or peasant–landless labour relationships, but did, at their best, achieve locally significant, though ultimately marginal gains in income and quality of everyday life for the poor (through encouraging hand-spinning and weaving, notably).

The basic Gandhian principles of *ahimsa* and *satyagraha* (roughly connoting the pursuit of Truth through strictly non-violent means) implied determined efforts to ultimately reconcile differences between mutually hostile identities, and this was applicable, both to relations with foreign rulers, and vis-à-vis the multiple identity formations among Indians themselves. The effort, in other words, was to achieve peaceful conflict resolution through weakening the walls between identities and, as such, came to attract considerable, and nowadays growing, attention and sympathy in many parts of the world.

[10] The Indian bourgeoisie itself came of age during these decades, taking advantage of the world trade disruptions through War and Depression reducing foreign competition. By the 1930s, for instance, the indigenous cotton textile industry, centred around Bombay and Ahmedabad, had been able to virtually drive out Lancashire from the home market. Capitalists could now afford to flex their muscles, giving considerable financial assistance to the Congress, while never burning their bridges entirely with the British.

In the context of anti-colonial nationalism, the programme implied evolving for the Congress an umbrella-like function, ideally unifying the entire country through smoothing over a variety of differences and hierarchies, but not seeking the subversion of these through any radical ruptures. Thus, it sought to subsume emergent linguistic–regional sentiments by reorganizing the Congress, early on in the Gandhian era, on the basis of language-based regions—with the implied promise of linguistic reorganization of provinces after acquisition of power. Landlord–peasant, and capitalist–worker conflicts were to be reconciled through modification in the direction of a 'trusteeship' relationship, but unrestrained class struggle and take-over of private property had to be avoided.

Caste hierarchy, similarly, was to be humanized, in particular through a trenchant rejection of its most obvious evil, untouchability, and the opening of temples to lower castes. But Gandhi, on the whole, retained a softness for the 'ideal' caste system as allegedly a valuable form of division of labour and functions. Gandhian mass movements were able to draw in women participants on a quite unprecedented scale, with many among them braving police violence and courting arrest. In regard to caste and gender alike, a measure of social change was thus reincorporated into nationalism after its expulsion in the Extremist era. Overall conceptions of feminine roles in family and society, however, remained fairly traditional.

Most significantly, perhaps, all his life, Gandhi sought to combine the personal beliefs and practices of a devout Hindu with a passionate advocacy of the value and indispensability of Hindu–Muslim brotherhood. The combination seemed brilliantly effective for a brief while in 1919–22, through an alliance with the Khilafat movement of large numbers of Muslims protesting against the erosion of authority of the Ottoman Sultan-Khalifa by the victorious Entente states. And, of course, in the end, he became a martyr to that cause (generally described as 'secular' in the sense of anti-'communal', in the distinctive usages of these terms that have become standard in India), being murdered by an activist of a right-wing Hindu-chauvinist formation in January 1948.

The achievements of Gandhian nationalism remain remarkable, in terms both of extent of mass politicization and practical gains. By the mid-1930s, the British had been forced into making major concessions, with Congress ministries running a number of provincial administrations and changes in the central government, and even independence in a not-too distant future, clearly becoming increasingly difficult to avoid. Yet, its limits cannot be ignored, and here, radical, Marxist, and Subalternist historiography has made a major contribution, highlighting the problems of collapsing the entire history of anti-colonialism in India into a narrative focused on Gandhian nationalism alone. The effort to combine mass mobilization with maintenance of Gandhian restrictions, and more generally, the conception of the Congress as unified umbrella which in practice often seemed to tilt in the direction of property and privilege, repeatedly stimulated into existence alternative, more radical strands. These became most obvious during the troughs between the big Gandhian upsurges.

There was for instance, a significant emergence of militant trade union activities in major industrial centres like Bombay, Calcutta, Madras, or Kanpur, and the six-month-long strike of the Bombay textile workers under Communist leadership in 1928 certainly deserves a place in the history of the international labour movement. Outside Ahmedabad, where Gandhi had personally led a strike in 1918 and then helped to set up an effective Majdoor Mahajan wedded to his principles of trusteeship, Gandhian ideas had little appeal for industrial workers, who often seemed to prefer the Communists despite the consistent official and capitalist repression the latter had to face.

Socialist ideas were, in fact, entering the country in significant ways during the inter-War decades, attracting attention and sympathy from considerable sections of the Congress itself, and producing, by the 1930s, a distinct Left group within the national movement. Nehru, in particular, became for some years a powerful advocate, and proclaimed himself to be 'a socialist and republican, and ... no believer in kings and princes ... or ... the modern kings of industry' as President of the Lahore Congress of 1929. He combined this, however, with an abiding personal and political loyalty to Gandhi. Autonomous 'kisan' or peasant associations also began proliferating in many parts of the country by the 1930s, led by socialist or communist activists. With the exception of some scattered groups who had already developed connections with the Comintern from the early 1920s, the Left alternatives emerged from among participants in the Congress movements themselves. Many were disillusioned by Gandhi's hesitations about anti-landlord no-rent campaigns (as distinct from no-revenue, directed against the British government), as well as by his habit of abruptly and unilaterally calling off movements when they seemed to many to be still advancing, but appeared to be going beyond the non-violent boundaries the Mahatma was determined to maintain.

There was also the problem of roughly one-third of the country ruled theoretically by 'native' princes, who with rare exceptions, combined utter servility to their British overlords with forms of despotism vis-à-vis their subjects often in excess of British Indian practices. Yet, the Congress leaders for long remained reluctant about extending the nationalist struggle for civil and political rights into the princely states. At another level,

Gandhi's halfway house concerning caste oppression appeared quite unsatisfactory to many subordinate castes or, notably, untouchable (dalit) people, and by the late 1920s, a powerful alternative leader had emerged among the latter, in the figure of Ambedkar. A partly autonomous women's movement was also emerging, rather elitist in its composition and techniques still, but raising issues like votes for women and family law reform.

The strength of Congress nationalism was revealed, however, by the skill its leaders repeatedly displayed in partly accommodating many of these diverse pressures and dissident groups, through concessions that remained largely at the level of programmatic statements and rhetoric, but were still far from insignificant in historical perspective. It was through such openings towards radicalism—described in some later scholarship in terms of the Gramscian category of 'passive revolution' (Chatterjee 1986)— that the content of Congress objectives came to be broadened considerably in the course of the 1930s, to be partly enshrined later in independent India's Constitution in 1950. Abolition of princely rule, democracy grounded on universal franchise, secularism, federalism, a measure of 'social justice', embodied notably in a structure of 'reservations' or affirmative action for dalits and other underprivileged groups—had not at all figured in the early programmes of the Congress, or indeed before this radicalization under pressure, mounted, above all, by Left-leaning strata of various kinds. It is in terms of the richness of such, often extremely sharp, internal differences and debates that the ultimate significance of anti-colonial nationalism in India needs to be evaluated.

Other colonies had to face much more brutal repression, and so perhaps needed to display greater heroism, but few nationalist leaders or thinkers elsewhere revealed the capacity to look beyond nationalism, even question many of its ideals and forms, of the kind one notices at times in Tagore, Gandhi, and Nehru. It is a pity, and a sign of degeneration of a nationalism in power, that during the post-colonial era it is precisely these differences and debates that have tended to be slurred over in the quest for a simplistic saga of untarnished national heroism and glory.

The major and, it seems, abiding failure was of course on the question of 'communalism', both Muslim and Hindu—the Indian English term since the early twentieth century for a religion-based identity politics that assumes a state of inevitable and total conflict between such communities. Tensions, quite often bursting forth into violent riots, between Hindus and Muslims became a recurrent feature of many parts of the country from the 1920s onwards. In the context of responsible government and, eventually, independence beginning to appear an increasingly possible and not too distant objective, leaders claiming to represent the Muslim minority wanted protection via a more decentralized polity where the Muslim-majority provinces could enjoy autonomy from a centre bound to be dominated by Hindus.

Congress plans for the future, however, tended to emphasize a greater degree of unitary central control. Here there was often a convergence between Hindu-chauvinist groups within the national movement dreaming of a majoritarian-Hindu 'Bharat', and secular, even radical-Left strands that felt such unity would be essential for political independence and economic growth. Matters were not helped by princely pressures for autonomy within a loose federal structure, quite often backed by the British. This became what the Muslim League leader, Jinnah, would term the crucial 'parting of the ways', and in 1940, the League formally adopted what would come to be called the 'Pakistan resolution', demanding separate Muslim-ruled state or states in the north-western and eastern part of the country where Muslims were in the majority.

While what Indian nationalists often termed 'Muslim separatism' has usually predominated in conventional Indian accounts of late-colonial times, the significance and reach of Hindu communalism should not be underrated, even for these years. Such tendencies and ideological influences operated both within the Congress, despite the insistence of its leadership, particularly from the 1930s, on 'secular' principles (meaning, operationally, not rejection or even indifference towards religion, but repudiation of all forms of communal hostility in the cause of a unified 'nation'), and outside its fold, through organizations like the Hindu Mahasabha and, more crucially, the Rashtriya Swayamsevak Sangh (RSS). The latter, founded in 1925, by men some of whom had been extremist nationalists, was a semi-martial, all-male body dedicated towards spreading—through unostentatious 'cultural' indoctrination—a message of total hostility towards Muslim (as well as, sometimes Christian) minorities. It believed that only 'Hindus' (as defined and remoulded by them) could be truly 'nationalists', for only Hindu religion and culture had originated within the country: Muslims, Christians, secularists, Leftists were all suspect in that respect. Through a curious displacement, RSS thinking and practice thus replaced British rulers by Muslims as the principal target for Hindu nationalist hostility.[11]

---

[11] The historical literature on anti-colonial nationalism is immense, making referencing virtually impossible within a brief essay. But see the attempt at a comprehensive, though by now somewhat dated account in Sumit Sarkar (1983), the essays of David Hardiman, Gyanendra Pandey and Partha Chatterjee and, for a valuable brief account of Gandhian ideas and practices, see David Hardiman (2003).

British rule came to an end in August 1947, after five incredibly crowded and violent years that culminated in an independence that was also simultaneously the partition of British India into the sovereign states of India and Pakistan. In August 1942, the Congress—many of whose leaders probably felt that Britain was going down in the war against Germany and Japan—launched its 'Quit India' movement, which in some areas became quite violent. Meanwhile one important nationalist leader, Subhas Bose, had escaped from the country to strike an alliance with Japan, recruiting his 'Indian National Army' from among British Indian prisoners of war who had been captured by the Japanese during their headlong advance through Southeast Asia in early 1942. Militarily, the INA did not amount to much, and the British were also able to suppress the 1942 movement with enormous violence. But such blatant repression made the persecuted Congress more popular than ever before, erasing memories of its often dubious, compromising policies during the preceding years of running many provincial governments. 1942 also badly split the erstwhile Left alternative to the dominant Congress leadership, for socialist groups were in the forefront of the Quit India movement and often sympathetic towards Bose, while the Communists, believing that solidarity with a Soviet Union imperilled by Nazi invasion had the highest priority, condemned Bose as a 'Quisling', and called for an anti-fascist peoples' war.

By 1945–6, however, the situation had changed considerably. Communists were once again in the forefront of the anti-imperialist struggle, leading a massive strike wave, organizing powerful peasant movements, and actively supporting a mutiny by the Royal Indian Navy ratings in Bombay, in what they hoped would be a 'final bid for power' under the banner of Congress–Muslim League–Communist unity. This was not to be, however. By then the Congress leaders were busy negotiating a 'peaceful' transfer of power with a much weakened Britain ruled by a reasonably sympathetic Labour government, while the Muslim League insistently demanded Pakistan (though, just possibly, as a bargaining counter), in August 1946, in an act of brinkmanship, which seems to have gone badly out of control. Calcutta and then more and more parts of the country exploded in communal violence on a quite unprecedented scale, in the wake of a Muslim League call for a 'Direct Action Day'. In the summer of 1947, the Congress reluctantly agreed to Partition, despite Gandhi's deep and visible unhappiness.

What followed was a further escalation of violence from both sides, amounting to a religious civil war which left anything from several hundred thousand to several millions murdered, raped, or driven from their homes in what in today's terms would amount to ethnic cleansing on a colossal scale. Searing memories of the holocaust naturally persist, and have been repeatedly dredged up in later times by interested, quite often ruling groups in both Pakistan and India as convenient instruments for diversion of attention from internal problems. And Kashmir has continued to remain a persistent problem, claimed by Pakistan on the strength of its Muslim majority, and by India on the ground of the voluntary accession of its ruler in August 1947, backed up, at that point, by what was then a firmly secular–nationalist regional movement closely allied with the Congress.[12]

Given such highly unpropitious beginnings, the achievements of the early 'Nehruvian' years of the Indian Republic perhaps deserve somewhat greater recognition than many are prepared to accord them nowadays. A stable, liberal–democratic parliamentary structure was established, in significant contrast to the vicissitudes undergone by the other state created by Partition, Pakistan (which has seen several spells of military dictatorship), as well as many other newly independent ex-colonial countries. Widespread revulsion at the murder of the Mahatma led to the discrediting, for a number of years, of the Hindu Right, and Hindu–Muslim communal riots, while still happening occasionally, seemed to be under control, and secularism firmly in the saddle.

The main alternative to Nehru's broadly centrist policies appeared to be posed by the Left, within which a still-united Communist movement was the principal force. Initially, during 1948–51, it plunged into what was later accepted to have been the 'Left-sectarian' error of attempting armed insurrection through urban revolt and then peasant-based guerrilla action against a regime still basking in the main in the aura of having led a successful freedom struggle. But then, the Communists shifted to parliamentary politics, and began to periodically win elections and form governments, singly or through coalitions. In a couple of states, notably Kerala and West Bengal, fairly strong trade union movements had emerged in the main industrial centres, though there was also a vast unorganized casual labour sector both in the towns and the countryside, to which little attention was usually paid. As in the 1930s, the Congress under Nehru (and later, in the early years of his daughter, Indira Gandhi) was able to maintain overall control through occasional judicious adjustments and openings—which during these years tended to be towards the Left.

[12] Later Indian governments, however, have managed to dissipate much of that earlier support through excessively centralizing policies.

Communist militancy, even in defeat, played a seldom recognized role in undermining autocratic–feudal regimes in the erstwhile princely states, for the latter came to feel that integration into the 'Indian Union', sweetened by the generous 'privy purses' offered by India's tough (and bitterly anti-Communist) Home Minister, Sardar Patel, was certainly preferable to peasant revolution.[13] Containment of the Left also demanded a measure of land reforms through abolition, with compensation, of big landlordism and some redistribution of land through ceilings on the size of farms (though, grossly diluted in implementation, in most states).

From the mid-1950s, the state embarked on development of heavy industries (notably steel and heavy engineering, the latter totally absent under colonialism, as well as other infrastructure necessary for private capitalist advance, but too unprofitable for private investors) through an expanding public sector, a degree of planning, and protectionist policies. There was considerable deployment also, particularly at election times, of a populist–'socialist' rhetoric. Combined with an uneven, but not negligible advance in agricultural production that ended the initial post-independence dependence on food imports (the last years of British rule, it needs to be remembered, had been marked by the terrible Bengal Famine of 1943), the first two or three decades after 1947 saw India emerging as an independent economy with a broader industrial–technological base than most of the Third World (though not, it seems, Communist-ruled China, despite the latter's abrupt and sometimes disastrous oscillations in policy).

The early 1950s also saw reforms in Hindu family and personal laws, improving significantly the legal status of women—though the more radical proposals were considerably diluted under pressure from conservative Hindu elements both within and outside the Congress.[14] Nehruvian foreign policy enormously raised India's international reputation for some years, on the basis of non-alignment combined with sympathy and support for anti-colonial liberation struggles. A close relationship was established with the post-Stalin Soviet Union, which helped India build its first public sector steel mill after credit had been refused by the Western powers, and there was also an initial friendship with Communist China.

[13] The biggest princely state, Hyderabad, which initially refused to accede to India, was sufficiently weakened by a major Communist-led peasant insurrection in its Telengana region, directed against landlords and effectively redistributing land in some areas, to succumb easily in August 1948 to an Indian 'police action'. The Indian army was then used to smash the Communist guerrillas.

[14] The dalit leader, Ambedkar, who had been invited by Nehru to join his first Cabinet and who had drafted a more radical Hindu Code Bill, was deeply disappointed by what he felt were Nehru's compromising ways, resigned, and went back into Opposition to the Congress.

Things began to come apart from the early 1960s, with the quarrel and military clashes with China in 1959–62, that was itself related to the Sino-Soviet split smashing the dream of a united socialist third of the world. The border confrontations stimulated nationalist frenzy, and gave a major shot in the arm to so far dormant right-wing Hindu nationalist formations. The most effective of the latter, the RSS, had in any case continued throughout to carry on unostentatious propagation of its violently communal Hindutva ideology, through an expanding chain of schools and the training of cadres, drawing recruits mainly from small-town petty bourgeois elements. The Communists, in contrast, came to be badly, and permanently, divided in the fall-out of the international communist ruptures of the 1960s, breaking up by the late 1960s into three major strands—Communist Party of India (CPI), CPI(M) (for Marxist), CPI(ML) (for Marxist–Leninist), as well as a growing number of splinter groups. They still seemed to be advancing in some regions, even while spending much of their energies in mutual, quite often violent, quarrelling. The late 1960s and early 1970s were marked by what came to be called the 'Naxalite' rebellions in some of the more underdeveloped parts of the country, a return to methods of peasant armed struggle inspired by the then radical message of China, but drawing principal sustenance from the continued and sharpening tensions in a rural society where oppressive landed groups were still very much in power. But there was also the development, more considerable in some areas than in others, of a rich farmer strata, rendering the digits of the older kind of radical–Left agrarian strategies at times difficult to sustain.

The problems and contradictions of the Nehruvian path were also becoming clearer at many other levels. The basic developmental thrust was of a technocratic–bureaucratic kind, breeding corruption (what came to be termed the 'licence–contract raj') and inefficiency, with the burdens falling heavily on the poor. The massive enhancements in military expenditure from the 1960s onwards, in the context of the new problems with China and the perennial tensions and occasional brief wars with Pakistan, added enormously to the strains. Another problematic dimension, that only began to attract wider attention later, was the very widespread assumption equating progress with the 'conquest' of nature. (This was then also much in evidence in the countries of 'actually existing' bureaucratic socialism.) It found dramatic expression in the huge multipurpose hydroelectric projects that Nehru famously described as 'the temples of modern India'. These largely ignored possible ecological problems and, till protests gathered strength in recent years, remained blind towards the plight of large numbers of mostly poor people, expropriated from age-old common property resources of forests, rivers, and pastures 'for the greater common good'.[15]

The mounting unpopularity of the ruling party, now entering its third decade of virtually uninterrupted power, expressed itself through major electoral reverses and splits within the Congress itself in the late 1960s. For some years, Indira Gandhi appeared able to stage a revival, once again, through, some left-inclined dramatic gestures (notably, bank nationalization, abolition of privy purses for princes, and the promise of bits of land for dalit agricultural labourers) and, above all, a successful war with Pakistan in 1971 that enabled the formation of the breakaway state of Bangladesh. But soon, charges of rampant corruption, fears of a permanent 'dynastic' rule by the Nehru family, and ruthless government suppression of a countrywide railway strike, briefly brought together elements from right and part of the left opposition in a brief tacit alliance against a centre feared to be turning authoritarian. The point of unity was provided by the highly respected figure of Jayaprakash Narain, famous militant leader of 1942 and a life-long socialist who now seemed willing to cooperate even with the RSS. Indira's response was the Emergency of 1975–7, an onslaught on civil liberties, the unpopularity of which was vastly enhanced in its closing months by the enormous powers amassed by her son Sanjay, notorious for his policy of controlling population growth through forced sterilization. The Congress faced a countrywide rout in the elections after the Emergency was lifted in early 1977, and a non-Congress coalition came to power in the centre for the very first time. But a quick revival of tensions that had been subordinated in the common fight against Indira Gandhi's Emergency led to a break-up of this uneasy alliance within two years and a Congress return to power in 1980.

It seemed to be a rather different Congress though, making overtures towards the right as well as right-leaning policies of its own, in place of the earlier, broadly center–left trajectory. The RSS, now functioning electorally through the Bharatiya Janata Party (BJP), along with a proliferating chain of affiliated organizations collectively making up its 'family' (the Sangh Parivar), had in the end been the principal beneficiary of the Emergency and its aftermath. Indira, and then her successor Rajiv Gandhi, tried to take the wind out of the sails of this Hindu right by itself projecting a somewhat Hindu-nationalist image, in what proved both opportunistic and counter-productive.

---

[15] The telling, obviously ironic phrase used by the well-known writer and social activist Arundhati Roy in a recent essay denouncing the displacements of what she estimates to have been around 50 million people since Independence through such 'developmental' projects.

This turn was related to what was perceived as the growth of various regional 'separatist' trends, notably among Sikhs in the Punjab in the early and mid-1980s, but also among tribal groups in the North-east and some other parts of the country. In the immediate post-1947 years, the centre had been resilient enough to be able to partly accommodate some similar tendencies, notably the Dravidian movement in Tamil Nadu. The responses to the Sikh 'Khalistani' movement, which itself turned to terrorist ways, was much more repressive and authoritarian, and a vicious circle of violence and statist counter-violence raged for some years after the killing of Indira Gandhi in 1984 was followed in Delhi by several days of wholesale massacres of Sikhs in then-unprecedented state-sponsored genocide. Kashmir, as throughout, remained a running sore, with considerable elements of incitement from Pakistan, which has consistently claimed it on the strength of the region having a big Muslim majority. Centralizing, authoritarian, and increasingly Hindu-nationalist tendencies of the Indian state have, however, sharpened the problem enormously, particularly over the last decade. Tendencies advocating greater autonomy within a more meaningfully federal structure have been regularly suppressed as much, and sometimes more than Muslim-communal separatist or pro-Pakistan groups.

The other major, and eventually still more far-reaching change was in economic policy, where the Nehruvian digits started getting abandoned in the new world climate of 'structural adjustment', 'liberalization', and 'globalization'. There was a sharp turn away from the emphasis on public sector investments and planning, more and more concessions were given to private business, both Indian and foreign, and the whole process was speeded up enormously following the collapse of the Soviet Union, India's principal economic partner for more than a generation, and growing pressures from US-dominated institutions like the World Bank and the IMF. The consequences, as virtually everywhere, have included both apparent gains for upwardly-mobile urban middle-class groups—increasingly living a 'globalized' life and wallowing in the new atmosphere of rampant consumerism—and sharpening misery for much wider sections of society.

Worst affected perhaps have been the industrial workers, for capitalists since the 1980s (particularly following the heroic, but ultimately unsuccessful textile labour strike in Bombay in 1982–3) have been shifting their investments towards smaller units in the so-called unorganized sector, which do not have the kinds of protective laws which several generations of labour struggles had won for workers in factories. Once again, the pattern would be a familiar one: as elsewhere, trade unions have lost much of their earlier power and influence over the past generation, so much so that a recent fine study by an Indian labour historian of the rise and decline of the workers' movement in Kanpur has chosen, as its title, the phrase *Lost Worlds* (Joshi 2003).

Since the late 1980s, the Sangh Parivar has progressively taken over and immensely accelerated the rightward political, cultural, and economic shifts initiated by the Congress, so much so that the very foundations of the post-colonial polity are now under serious threat. The turning point was the 'Ramjanmabhoomi' movement, that began in the mid-1980s, aimed at destroying a sixteenth-century mosque in Ayodhya, which the Sangh Parivar claims had been built after demolishing an ancient Ram temple, and which was allegedly the precise spot where that epic hero had been born. The campaign advanced through an escalation of anti-Muslim riots, which accompanied the countrywide 'Rath Yatra' on the issue in the autumn of 1990 led by L.K. Advani (India's Deputy Premier cum Home Minister from 1998 to 2004), and followed the wanton destruction of the Babri Masjid on 6 December 1992. The Sangh Parivar advance since then has had its ups and downs, while a BJP-led coalition was in power in New Delhi from 1998 till its unexpected electoral defeat in May 2004.

Governance has not proved to be the BJP's strong point, but this is periodically compensated for by onslaughts on one or other religious minority. Thus, attacks on Christians around 1998–9 culminated with the burning alive of Dr Staines, an Australian missionary serving lepers, together with his children, in an Orissa village, while the prospect of a possible electoral defeat in Gujarat stimulated the ghastly state-organized anti-Muslim massacres in that province in early 2002, the worst on the subcontinent since the Partition riots. Meanwhile, cultural indoctrination in the values of aggressive, majoritarian, and obscurantist Hindu-nationalism goes on with state backing, including the 'rewriting' of school history textbooks, occasional censorship attempts directed against secular writers and artists, and the attempt by the Union Minister in charge of higher education to introduce courses on astrology in universities. And religious-cultural nationalism is accompanied by a vastly speeded up, very often blatantly corrupt, sale of public sector enterprises, concessions to multinationals, and a sharp turn in Indian foreign policy in a pro-US direction.

It would be unbalanced, however, to conclude without mentioning certain possible counter-points, though none of them, either singly or collectively, as yet amount to an effective total challenge to the right-wing shifts I have been summarizing. Their presence, however, goes some way towards explicating the appeal of Hindu nationalist ideology and policies to the more conservative sections of Indian society. The organized Left, in diverse forms, is still more of a force, though often a rather stagnating one, in some parts of the country than in most other parts of the post-1991 world. The CPI(M) has now governed West Bengal uninterruptedly for more than a quarter-century, while there remain pockets of extreme-Left insurgency in several states, drawing sustenance from the most oppressed segments of rural society despite enormous state repression as well their own occasionally brutal ways.

There have also been a series of largely novel developments over the past generation: including a proliferation of grassroots activists connected to an expanding chain of 'non-governmental organizations', very diverse in their programmes and ways, but often with remarkably innovative ideas; the emergence of numerous kinds of environmental activism, the best known among them being the Narmada Bachao Andolan, energizing peasants and tribals against the displacements caused by the construction of dams, which often seem to be directly related to the interests of businessmen and contractors; and the spread of self-consciously feminist groups, along with some moves towards gay and lesbian organization. Many among these diverse formations have been actively opposing the processes of globalization and liberalization in their own ways.

At the more obviously political level though, the national, yet far from unproblematic, alternative to the BJP still seems to be the Congress: it remains to be seen how far the present policies will be radically reversed if it does manage to return to power in the next elections. Much hope has been placed sometimes in what is, next to the rise of the Hindu right, the most remarkable of the political changes of the last two decades—the new prominence of intermediate-caste and dalit parties. These certainly represent some empowerment of the underprivileged, and it is significant that the implementation, under the pressure of the first Mandal Report, of extensions of reservations in government jobs to these 'Other Backward Castes' was probably the immediate occasion for the 1990 campaign by Advani, with the BJP seeking to rebuild high-caste-led Hindu unity which it felt was on the point of being undermined by ruptures along caste lines. But subordinate caste politics so far has tended to remain stuck in the grooves of fairly narrow forms of identity-based politics, leading to repeated splintering and opportunist manoeuvres, not excluding temporary alliances with the BJP at times.

This brings me to my last, and a somewhat general, point. Post-colonial Indian history, particularly in more recent decades, has been remarkably full of paradoxes. Foremost among these, perhaps, is that democratic institutions, on the whole, have been advancing, in the sense of their actual spread to lower levels of society and, yet, they have come to be widely discredited, very often branded as invariably corrupt, and are increasingly under threat of subversion or overthrow by fundamentally anti-democratic Hindutva forces. The early years had seen the establishment of the formal structures of a liberal parliamentary regime, equal civil and political rights, and the rule of law. These were notable achievements whose value is perhaps more obvious today for many earlier radical critics of such merely 'bourgeois' freedoms now that they are under threat. But it remains true that during the first couple of decades or so after Independence, politicians and leaders, including those on the Left, still tended to be drawn over-whelmingly from the educated, largely upper-caste strata. Since then, there has been a definite shift downwards in the composition of this 'political class' in most parts of the country. For instance, few could imagine in those years that a dalit woman leader would be ever able to become the chief minister of India's biggest and, in some ways, most high-caste dominated state, Uttar Pradesh. There has also been the spread of a varying, limited, but not insignificant measure of village self-government (the so-called panchayats). Inevitably, given the skewed and hierarchical nature of rural society in terms of class and caste alike, these have been usually dominated by the locally powerful; but it still represents a degree of spread of popular participation. And we have already noted the proliferation, in recent years, of grassroots organizations autonomous of both the state and party organi-zations, and their contributions to popular empowerment

Yet, throughout, such democratization has gone along with, and probably been outstripped by, the growing strength of the state apparatus, and the readiness, really cutting across all political lines, of those in power to use it quite ruthlessly against opponents. The Indian state now has, at its command, military, paramilitary, and police resources that exceed what the British ever had in India and it has to be admitted that on the whole, these have proved more trigger-happy against unarmed civilian dissenters than an alien government functioning through indigenous subordinates could generally afford to be. A number of Indian political theorists in recent years have sought to explain this paradox of greater authoritarianism accompanying the widening of democratic spaces in terms of the contin-ued weakness of institutions and 'civil society'. The question then be-comes why these have remained weak, despite a high level of mass political interest and awareness indicated by the phenomenon of the poor generally voting in much larger numbers than the rich, and regularly exercising their power of electorally throwing out the government in power in what has come to be termed the 'incumbency factor'.

The convenient explanation, in terms of the persistence of structures of colonial bureaucratic authority, would not really do, as we have just mentioned. Sudipta Kaviraj (2001: 314–21) has suggested what amounts to a precisely opposite explanation. Nationalists in opposition to colonial rule had tried to defend and extend elements of civil-society barriers to state power. The post-Independence 'rare combination of power and utter dominance over the moral imagination of its people', however—particularly effective, we might add, in a country like India, with a long history of peaceful mass anti-colonial struggle—led to nationalist elites dominating both the state and incipient elements of civil society. The latter, therefore, became less and not more of a check on the state apparatus than in colonial times, for it was now easy to brand the more dangerous kinds of opposition as anti-national.

But what has deepened the problem, Kaviraj suggests, is the kind of oppositional forces that have developed, particularly in recent decades and given the overall stasis of the Left. These have occasionally been described in favourable, 'communitarian' terms, as fitting into a post-Enlightenment state/indigenous community model—an approach fairly widespread some years back within the Subaltern Studies school of historians. Kaviraj, evidently disagrees. For him, what are usually termed identity-based formations—so common, almost ubiquitous, both in religious and caste-based modes, and posing either the danger of majoritarian authoritarianism or helping to fragment opposition to such tendencies—need to be explored in terms of Tonnies' famous category of *Gemeinschaft* as contrasted to 'modern' voluntary associations of the *Gesselschaft* kind. Not that the first variety can be, in any full sense, 'traditional' or 'pre-modern'; we have mentioned, in passing, that both religious and caste-based 'hard' identities have been products of late-colonial situations and structures in today's India in many ways. But the point is that they can be plausibly presented, and accepted, as somehow more 'natural', 'traditional', or 'ascriptive', and so, command deeper allegiance than 'modern' ideologies. Right from the beginning of universal franchise-based elections, for instance, as well as earlier, of course, political parties, irrespective of ideologies, even those on the far Left, have regularly taken due cognisance of such caste or religious affiliations while choosing their candidates for particular constituencies. Notions of individual rights of dissent, even against one's own community, and the consequent ability to freely and rationally deploy private reason on public matters irrespective of inherited affiliations—the Habermas model of the modern public sphere, in other words—thus remain underdeveloped (Kaviraj 2001: 314–21).[16]

---

[16] For another view, which to my mind still leans overmuch towards vestiges of a communitarian approach, see, in the same volume, Partha Chatterjee (2001: 165).

REFERENCES

Bagchi, Amiya, (1972), *Private Investment in India, 1900–1939*, Cambridge University Press, Cambridge.

Chatterjee, Partha, (1982), 'Agrarian Relations and Communalism in Bengal, 1926–1935', in Ranajit Guha (ed.), *Subaltern Studies, Volume 1*, Oxford University Press, Delhi: 9–38.

—— (1983), 'More on Modes of Power and Peasantry', in Ranajit Guha (ed.), *Subaltern Studies, Volume 2*, Oxford University Press, Delhi: 311–50.

—— (1984), 'Gandhi and the Critique of Civil Society', in Ranajit Guha (ed.), *Subaltern Studies, Volume 3*, Oxford University Press, Delhi: 153–95.

—— (1986), *Nationalist Thought in the Colonial World: A Derivative Discourse?*, Oxford University Press, Delhi.

—— (2001), 'On Civil and Political Society in Post-colonial Democracies', in Sudipta Kaviraj and Sunil Khilnani (eds), *Civil Society: History and Possibilities*, Cambridge University Press, Cambridge.

Datta, Pradip Kumar, (1999), *Carving Blocs: Communal Ideology in Early Twentieth Century Bengal*, Oxford University Press, Delhi.

Hardiman, David, (1982), 'The Indian "Faction": A Political Theory Examined', in Ranajit Guha (ed.), *Subaltern Studies, Volume 1*, Oxford University Press, Delhi: 198–232.

—— (1984), 'Adivasi Assertion in South Gujarat: The Devi Movement', in Ranajit Guha (ed.), *Subaltern Studies, Volume 3*, Oxford University Press, Delhi: 196–230.

—— (2003), *Gandhi in His Time and Ours*, Permanent Black, Delhi.

Joshi, Chitra, (2003), *Lost Worlds: Indian Labour and Its Forgotten Histories*, Permanent Black, Delhi.

Kaviraj, Sudipta, (2001), 'In Search of Civil Society', in Sudipta Kaviraj and Sunil Khilnani (eds), *Civil Society: History and Possibilities*, Cambridge University Press, Cambridge.

McLane, John R., (1977), *Indian Nationalism and the Early Congress*, Princeton University Press, Princeton.

Naoroji, Dadabhai, (1962), *Poverty and Un-British Rule in India*, Government of India, Delhi.

Northrup, David, (1999), 'Migration from Africa, Asia, and the South Pacific', in Andrew Porter (ed.), *The Oxford History of the British Empire, Volume III: The Nineteenth Century*, Oxford University Press, Oxford.

Pandey, Gyanendra, (1984), 'Encounters and Calamities: The History of North Indian Qasba in the Nineteenth Century', in Ranajit Guha (ed.), *Subaltern Studies, Volume 3*, Oxford University Press, Delhi: 231–70.

Roy, Arundhati, (1999), 'The Greater Common Good', in Arundhati Roy (ed.), *The Cost of Living*, Flamingo, London: 7–114.

Sarkar, Sumit, (2002), *Beyond Nationalist Frames*, Permanent Black, Delhi and Indiana University Press, Bloomington.

—— (1983), *Modern India, 1885–1947*, Macmillan, Delhi.

Sarkar, Tanika, (2000), *Hindu Wife, Hindu Nation: Community, Religion and Cultural Nationalism*, Permanent Black, Delhi.

Saul, S.B., (1960), *Studies in British Overseas Trade, 1870–1914*, Liverpool University Press, Liverpool.

Tomlinson, B.R., (1979), *The Political Economy of the Raj, 1914–47: The Economics of Decolonization in India*, Macmillan, London.

Washbrook, David, (1999), 'India, 1818–1860: The Two Faces of Colonialism', in Andrew Porter (ed.), *The Oxford History of the British Empire, Volume III: The Nineteenth Century*, Oxford University Press, Oxford: 395–421.

9

Lenin's Theory of Imperialism Today

Prabhat Patnaik

The significance of Lenin's *Imperialism* arises not so much from the details of its content or the data it provides; nor does it arise from the sheer fact that it 'explains' imperialism and the World War. The book is significant because it provides the steel frame for a grand reconstruction of Marxism (within which the 'explanation' for wars is located) that became the basis for revolutionary praxis for the rest of the twentieth century. Lenin did not just happen to develop a theory (of imperialism) and put it down on paper, as is usually the case with other authors and books. Rather, he saw the need for a grand reconstruction of Marxism and the outline of what such a structure should look like, and then set out to erect the steel frame for it. In other words, the inspiration for the book came from the crisis of praxis that had engulfed the working class movement upon the outbreak of the First World War, rather than from some sudden blinding 'illumination' regarding the nature of imperialism per se. Lenin saw the theoretical void whose filling was essential for revolutionary praxis, and filled it with a work which made use of whatever data happened to be available. The profundity of this work would not have changed an iota if he had put in half or twice as much data. Let us begin therefore by recapturing briefly the historical conjuncture in which it was written and which gave rise to the theoretical confusion (or what I have called 'theoretical void') underlying the crisis of praxis.

THE CONTEXT OF LENIN'S THEORY

Almost at the very moment when Marxism succeeded in establishing its theoretical sway over the European and in particular, the German working class movement, it was confronted with an altogether new challenge. This challenge came not from the followers of Bakunin, or of Proudhon, or of Lassalle, but from within its own ranks. Eduard Bernstein, a friend of Engels since 1888 and a prominent member of the German Social Democratic Party, argued in 1901 for an extensive 'revision' of Marxism (which is the origin of the term 'revisionism'). The Marxist perception of the need for a revolutionary overthrow of capitalism, he argued, derived from the view that it was a historically doomed system, or that it was moving towards an economic breakdown anyway. But since such a breakdown had neither occurred nor was anywhere in sight, the agenda for the revolutionary overthrow of the system should be shelved in favour of struggles within the system for the economic betterment of the working class. The proletariat, in other words, should give up its revolutionary socialist programme, and settle down to peaceful trade unionism within the system.

What is more, since the 'will of the majority' prevails in a democracy, the introduction of political freedom, democracy, and universal suffrage in bourgeois society removes the basis for believing any longer that the state is an organ of class-rule. Bernstein's position was summed up by his remark: 'The movement is everything, the ultimate aim is nothing'. To remain occupied exclusively with the empirical day-to-day activity of trade unionism and petty politics with the aim of gaining advantages of the moment, and to forget about the basic features of the whole capitalist system, about the direction of its evolution, and about the primary goal of bringing in socialism: such was Bernstein's advice to the working class.

Bernstein was not alone in suggesting a 'revisionist' programme; and the programme too was comprehensive, not confined only to the sphere of economic and political activity, but encompassing the realm of theory as well, both philosophy and political economy. Indeed, Lenin saw the comprehensiveness and the pervasiveness of revisionism as a positive development reflecting an objective trend towards overcoming heterogeneity.

Even though the revisionist tendency was sharply attacked within each Social Democratic Party, it made deep inroads into the working class movement. When the First World War intervened, the extent of the sway of revisionism, which found expression in the form of 'social patriotism' and 'social chauvinism', became apparent. Three distinct positions emerged within European Social Democracy on the question of war. The first was the straightforward social-chauvinist position which was held by the majority of the leadership in most parties.[1]

The Second, was a 'centrist' position—held by Kautsky, Longuet, Turati, Ramsay Macdonald, and Martov among others—which, while opposing social-chauvinism, did not wish to break with the social-chauvinist elements within Social Democracy and, while opposing the war, wanted to fight for peace, rather than revolution. In Lenin's words, 'The "Centre" all vow and declare that they are Marxists and internationalists, that they are for peace, for bringing every kind of "pressure" to bear upon the governments, for "demanding" in every way that their own government should "ascertain the will of the people for peace", that they are for all sorts of peace campaigns, for peace without annexations, etc.—*and for peace with the social-chauvinists*. The "Centre" is for unity, the Centre is opposed to a split' (1977a: 76).

The third position, held by Lenin, Liebknecht, Luxemburg, Radek, and others, was summed up by the title of Liebknecht's pamphlet, *The Main Enemy is Within the Country*. It believed that 'the problem of war can be solved only in a revolutionary way', that since the war is an imperialist war for a division of the 'spoils', to talk of a war against war is meaningless unless it is directed against 'one's own' imperialist bourgeoisie. The proletariat therefore should convert the imperialist war into a revolutionary civil war to overthrow the imperialist bourgeoisie. This third position wanted a complete break from social-chauvinism and, hence, from 'Centrism' (since the latter was unwilling to break from social-chauvinism), and setting up a new International of revolutionary Marxists.

The positions articulated in *Imperialism* had already been part of the understanding and the programme that Lenin, as the leader of the authentic internationalist section of the Socialist movement, had been advocating for some time. But, while putting together positions that had already been aired for some time in a single comprehensive document, *Imperialism* gave these positions theoretical roots, by locating them within the corpus of Marxist political economy.

The difference between the character of Luxemburg's and Lenin's books on imperialism (without going into the contents of the two books) is quite marked in this respect: Lenin's book is overwhelmingly, insistently, passionately concerned with praxis, while Luxemburg's is an incisive tract on abstract theory. But as Lukacs once remarked: 'The

---

[1] Its adherents within Russia included such stalwarts as Plekhanov, Zasulich, and Potressov.

highest level of development of theory is when theory bursts into praxis' (1970). Lenin's *Imperialism* is, indeed, theory bursting into praxis.

WIDENING THE SCOPE OF REVOLUTIONARY PRAXIS

While the crisis of praxis facing the European workers' movement in the context of the War might have been the immediate provocation behind *Imperialism*, the theory advanced in the book did much more than merely provide a solution to this crisis. Indeed, the hallmark of *Imperialism* lies in the fact that while providing a theoretical answer to the problem of praxis of the European working class movement, it widened the scope of revolutionary praxis itself to cover the oppressed nations as well. The theory it put forward permitted the linking up of the two main currents of revolutionary struggle in the twentieth century. The International it helped to found was an International the like of which had not been seen till then. It was an International in the true sense of the term, where delegates from India, China, and Viet Nam would hobnob with those from Germany, Britain, and France.

Even though Marx and Engels had been preoccupied with the proletarian revolution in Europe, the question of revolution in the colonies had made fleeting appearances in several of their letters and journalistic writings. In his 8 August 1853 article in the *New York Daily Tribune*, Marx had written: 'The Indians will not reap the fruits of the new elements of society scattered among them by the British bourgeoisie till in Great Britain itself the now ruling classes shall have been supplanted by the industrial proletariat, or till the Hindoos themselves shall have grown strong enough to throw off the English yoke altogether.' And Engels, in a letter to Kautsky on 12 September 1882, had written: 'India will perhaps, indeed very probably, produce a revolution.... The same thing might also take place elsewhere, e.g. in Algiers and Egypt, and would certainly be the best thing *for us*'.

Lenin not only brought this subterranean stream of thinking into the open—he not only placed the question of revolution in the East as much on the agenda as the revolution in the imperialist countries, but, what is more, he made the revolution in the East as much a business of the Communist International as that in the imperialist countries. It is in this respect that he broke completely new ground. And the theoretical expression of this perception that the two revolutions were dialectically related, that one could not talk of the one without being concerned about the other, was contained in *Imperialism*. In his preface to the French and German editions of *Imperialism*, Lenin himself clarified this composite picture of dual oppression in the following words: 'But as a matter of fact, the capitalist threads, which in thousands of different intercrossings bind these enterprises with private property in the means of production in general, have converted this railway construction into an instrument for oppressing *a thousand million* people (in the colonies and semi-colonies), that is, more than half the population of the globe that inhabits the dependent countries, as well as the wage-slaves of capital in the "civilized" countries'. The fact that these 'thousand million' people were now brought to the centrestage of revolutionary theory—on par with the wage-slaves of 'civilized' countries which, till then, had been the exclusive focus of attention—is a fact of enormous significance.

Seeing the revolutionary potential of these 'thousand million' people was not just pious hope or wishful thinking. It was a reading of what was actually happening. Lenin (1975: 246) had noted that '1905 was followed by revolutions in Turkey, Persia, and China, and that a revolutionary movement developed in India'. He had commented on the fact that the arrest of Tilak had been followed by a General Strike of workers in Bombay. He had also noted both the enormous leap in the consciousness of the colonial people and the growth in their capacity to use arms ('a very useful thing') that had come about as a result of their employment as cannon fodder in the imperialist war. In other words, Lenin saw the revolutionary process in the colonies and dependencies actually acquiring much greater vigour in the pre-War and War years.

Soon, he would place even greater reliance on the struggle of the oppressed peoples than he had done in *Imperialism*. As the prospects of a European, especially German, Revolution receded, Lenin increasingly pinned his hopes on the revolutionary struggles in the East. 'In the last analysis', he wrote in 1923, 'the outcome of the struggle will be determined by the fact that Russia, India, China, etc., account for the overwhelming majority of the population of the globe. And during the last few years it is this majority that has been drawn into the struggle for emancipation with extraordinary rapidity, so that in this respect there cannot be the slightest doubt what the final outcome of the world struggle will be. In this sense the complete victory of socialism is fully and absolutely assured' (Lenin 1975: 725).

This, however, was to come later. *Imperialism* still hoped for an imminent revolution that could break out *anywhere*. The immediate hurdles were supposed to be the 'corrupt' social-chauvinist leaders and their 'spineless' social-pacifist camp followers, from whose influence the proletariat had to be emancipated.

THE PERSPECTIVE ON REVOLUTIONARY STRATEGY

Lenin not only linked the two most powerful revolutionary streams of the twentieth century, but also gave a definite shape to the strategy to be followed within each of them. In particular, he outlined the strategy to be followed in the struggle for national liberation in the colonies and the semi-colonies. He insisted, of course, on a concrete analysis of the situation in each country and a differentiated set of tactics to be pursued across countries depending on the concrete conditions. But he set out the overall perspective on this question at the Second Congress of the Communist International.

This perspective, inter alia, had two important components. First, the Communist International and the Communist Parties must support the 'bourgeois-democratic liberation movement' in the colonial and backward countries, but only on the condition that the independence of the proletarian movement, 'even if it is in its most embryonic form', is upheld under all circumstances. Second, special support must be given to the peasant movement 'against the landowners, against landed proprietorship, and against all manifestations and survivals of feudalism', and every effort should be exerted to 'apply the basic principle of the Soviet system in countries where pre-capitalist relations predominate—by setting up "working people's Soviets", etc.' (Lenin 1975: 376).

At the Second Congress, as is well known, M. N. Roy objected to Lenin's thesis on supporting 'bourgeois–democratic' national movements on the grounds that 'a certain *rapprochement* had developed between the bourgeoisie of the exploiting countries and that of the colonies, so that very often the bourgeoisie of the oppressed countries, while it does support the national movement, is in full accord with the imperialist bourgeoisie, that is joins forces with it against all revolutionary movements and revolutionary classes'.[2] As a result, the final report, which was adopted unanimously, represented a compromise where the term 'bourgeois-democratic' was replaced by the term 'national–revolutionary'.

This compromise, it has been argued, had 'the effect of blunting the sharp edge of Lenin's thought and of bridging disagreement by resort to a potential ambiguity' (Carr 1966: 256). In any case, the question of the Communist movement's attitude to the bourgeoisie in the colonial and dependent countries was to become a vexed question which occupied the Communist International for long, and on which the International's position went through several twists and turns (during the Sixth and the

---

[2] This is the way Lenin summed up the criticism against his position; see Lenin (1975: 406).

Seventh Congresses). What is more, all the issues of the Second Congress debate, namely, the attitude to adopt towards the bourgeoisie, the possibility of bypassing the capitalist phase of development in newly liberated countries, were to emerge once again in a new incarnation after decolonization. Indeed, they are still with us.

As regards the advanced countries, Lenin's *Imperialism* posed the question: why was it that when world revolution had come on the agenda, some of the greatest luminaries of social democracy, not to mention significant sections of the working class in these countries, were taking revisionist, and even downright social-chauvinist positions? Lenin had already attempted once before to explain revisionism. His explanation had been as follows: 'A number of new "middle strata" are inevitably brought into existence again and again by capitalism. These small producers are just as inevitably being cast again into the ranks of the proletariat. It is quite natural that the petty-bourgeois world outlook should again and again crop up in the ranks of the broad workers' parties' (Lenin 1977b: 55).

This explanation, offered in 1908, would have certainly appeared inadequate after the outbreak of the war. In *Imperialism* therefore, Lenin provided an altogether different explanation for the phenomenon, namely the fact that monopoly super-profits were used in the imperialist countries to bribe a 'thin upper stratum' of the working class, the 'workers' aristocracy', and certain trade unionists and leaders of the workers' movement. Lenin's theoretical inspiration for this position came from certain remarks that Engels had made in two of his letters. And Lenin's own position has, in turn, been the springboard for a vast literature on 'unequal exchange' that has developed since his time to explain the dwindling revolutionary influence within the working class in the advanced capitalist countries.

MISCONCEPTIONS ABOUT LENIN'S THEORY

Imperialism is one of Lenin's most misunderstood works as regards its central argument. The reason for this misunderstanding is, in my view, the following: it is generally taken for granted that a theory of imperialism must be a functional theory. It must have a particular form, where it first shows why capitalism in the absence of imperialism cannot be sustained within the metropolis, and then demonstrates how imperialism specifically rescues capitalism from these insurmountable contradictions. Although Lenin's theory is not of this genre, a theory of this genre has been almost invariably read into Lenin. This has resulted not only in a distortion of his views, but also in the levelling against him of a whole range of illicit criticisms.[3]

The most common theory of such nature read into Lenin is under-consumptionism; no less a person than John Strachey (1959)—for long the leading British Communist Party theoretician—provided such an interpretation of Lenin after he abandoned communism. The under-consumptionist argument runs as follows: the emergence of monopoly capitalism implies a shift of income distribution away from the workers, the non-capitalist petty producers, and the non-monopoly capitalist producers, towards the monopolists. Since the propensity to consume of the monopolists is lower than that of the strata from whom such income distribution shifts occur, these shifts entail a reduction in consumption demand relative to what it would have been under competitive capitalism for an identical level of social output. Other things being equal, this, in turn, means that the shift to monopoly pushes the economy into an over-production crisis. True, such a crisis would not occur if investment could increase to compensate for the reduction in consumption, but there is no reason why this should happen at all. On the contrary, if the economy does face an over-production crisis, then its level of investment would get further lowered compared to what it otherwise would have been. In short, the transition from competitive to monopoly capitalism (or any further increase in monopoly profit margins in conditions of monopoly capitalism itself) would, other things remaining the same, push the economy towards generalized over-production.

A specific form of the under-consumption argument which is of some historical relevance, is the following: in the transition to monopoly capitalism, the shift in income distribution in favour of the monopolists and away from the petty producers would take the form of an adverse shift in the intersectoral terms of trade for primary producers, since petty producers, in the form of the peasantry, are likely to be producing primary commodities for ultimate processing in a manufacturing sector that is typically dominated by the monopolists. The fact that the peasants consume a larger proportion of their income than the monopoly capitalists, would in such a case entail a decline in exports from the manufacturing to the primary commodity sector without an offsetting increase in the internal demand of the manufacturing sector for its own output. This, other things remaining the same, would give rise to a crisis of over-production.

If we focus on the world economy as a whole, then this income shift from the petty producers to the monopoly capitalists would show as a

---

[3] For a somewhat more detailed discussion of the issues of this section, see Patnaik (1986).

secular shift in the terms of trade against primary producers, and in favour of manufacturing, as far as international prices are concerned. The tendency towards over-production in this case would show itself as a sluggishness of exports (other than what is financed by loans and other forms of capital exports) from the metropolitan countries taken together, which are the manufacturing centre of the world economy, to the primary commodity-producing Third World countries which suffer terms of trade losses, without a spontaneous offsetting increase in the domestic demand in the metropolitan countries.

Finally, the tendency towards an over-production crisis can also arise for a reason that is altogether different from under-consumption. In the transition from competitive to monopoly capitalism, even if the magnitude of consumption relative to output remains unchanged, the magnitude of investment relative to output is likely to decline. This is because many investment projects expected to fetch the average rate of profit in the economy, would not be taken up by the monopolists who earn a higher-than-average rate of profit. A shift in income distribution from the non-monopoly to the monopoly capitalists therefore would, other things remaining the same, reduce the level of investment below what it would otherwise have been and hence give rise to generalized over-production on account of what one might call 'under-investment'.

To say all this does not of course mean that over-production would actually happen. The tendency towards over-production, immanent in the transition from competitive to monopoly capitalism, can be offset by imperialism if it entails an export surplus financed by capital exports. In other words, a logically consistent theory of imperialism can be built which sees imperialism as functionally necessary for capitalism as it moves into the monopoly phase. Not only is such a theory logically consistent, it is historically plausible as well.

Indeed each of the different lines of argument advanced above can stand the test of historical scrutiny. The secular decline in the terms of trade for primary producers from the onset of monopoly capitalism until the Second World War has been attested to by a host of writers (for example, Lewis 1978), starting from Raul Prebisch (1950). The fact that this decline was because of the rise in the 'degree of monopoly' (to use Kalecki's term) in the era of monopoly capitalism, and was not an accidental phenomenon, has been argued by several economic historians (for example, Hobsbawm 1969). The fact that this was a cause of the sluggish export growth of Britain (leaving aside exports financed by capital exports) has been argued by Arthur Lewis (1949). It is also significant that the period of the inter-War years, when capital exports dried up owing to uncertainties of exchange rate movements (or, some[4] might say, the 'closing of the frontier', since much of the capital exports were to the temperate regions of white settlement), also saw the greatest depression in the history of capitalism: it can be argued that the over-production crisis, which had been suppressed through capital exports till then, suddenly burst forth.

Not only are all these historically plausible arguments, but they have actually been made by a host of Marxist or progressive economists and economic historians. They deserve serious attention from any student of capitalism. But the important point is this: neither under-consumption nor under-investment constitutes a part of Lenin's argument. There may be a tendency towards generalized over-production under monopoly capitalism, either from under-consumption in any of the ways suggested above (as a host of Marxist writers from Kalecki to Baran and Sweezy were to argue later), or from under-investment (in the manner outlined above). But Lenin's theory does not invoke any such tendency because it is not a functional theory of imperialism at all. Let us now look briefly at his argument.

The competition between capitals, which is the hallmark of capitalism, takes the form of rivalries between large monopoly combines, aided by their respective nation-states, in the era of monopoly capitalism. As part of this rivalry, each monopoly combine tries to acquire for itself as much 'economic territory' as possible, as sources of raw material, as markets, as destinations of capital exports, and quite often, for no reason other than to prevent that 'economic territory' from falling into the hands of its rivals. Imperialism, in other words, is not some specially designed policy to serve a functional necessity. It is endemic to monopoly capitalism. It is not a thing apart, but simply the way monopoly capitalism behaves, which is why distinguishing it from monopoly capitalism is misleading.

POST-WAR DEVELOPMENTS IN CAPITALISM

There can be scarcely any doubt that Lenin's prognostications in *Imperialism* were resoundingly vindicated during the period 1914–45. The real question, however, is: what is the relationship between the Leninist perception and the post-Second World War developments when capitalism is supposed to have 'changed'?

Capitalism emerged from the Second World War badly bruised. The balance of class forces in the advanced capitalist countries had shifted quite

---

[4] This group would include J. M. Keynes (1919).

significantly in favour of the working class, which had made immense sacrifices during the war. And the tide of the national liberation struggle in the colonies had swollen to a torrent. In this situation, capitalism pursued a two-pronged strategy for its immediate survival: isolation and repression of the revolutionary forces, notably the Communists, on the one hand; and concessions to and compromises with the demands of the domestic working class and the colonial movements. The Cold War, the rise of McCarthyism, the suppression of the revolutionary struggles in Greece and Malaya, the attempted suppression of the struggles in Viet Nam and Korea (and through the latter the attempt to hit back at China where the imperialist-supported Kuomintang had proved unequal to the task of defeating the Communists), the removal from the post-War coalition governments of the French and the Italian Communists who had acquired immense popularity because of their role in the Resistance, and the string of military bases set up all over the world by the US, were all examples of the first track of this two-pronged strategy. There can be little doubt that an important element underlying the successes that imperialism had on this front was the fact that the US had emerged relatively unscathed from the war, while the Soviet Union had borne the brunt of the war and had been its worst sufferer.

It is the second track of this strategy, however, that concerns us here. That involved decolonization by handing over power, wherever possible, to the emerging Third World bourgeoisie; the introduction of Keynesian demand management policies to achieve near-full employment at home; and the provision of a host of welfare measures (though much of it was paid for by the working class itself) (Patnaik 1986). These concessions together created a conjuncture that proved highly favourable to growth, and the capitalist world experienced the most impressive boom in its history during the decades of the 1950s and the 1960s.

Three elements went into this boom: first, the high levels of demand sustained through Keynesian demand management and, in particular, the large US budget deficits, incurred inter alia for financing the massive military expenditure bill, ensured that investment and, with it, the growth rate, was kept up. Second, the stock of innovations not introduced during the inter-War period marked by Depression, was available for introduction now, together with a host of new innovations that resulted in part from the wartime technological advances (Lewis 1978). And these kept up the rate of productivity growth, owing to which the workers could obtain significant wage increases in the prevailing conditions of high employment. Third, in their bid to step up the pace of industrialization through the imports of capital goods, the newly-independent Third World countries vied with one another to push out primary commodity exports, so that notwithstanding decolonization, the terms of trade for primary commodities deteriorated vis-à-vis manufacturing. This contributed to keeping inflation rates low in the metropolis and, hence, prolonging the boom.[5]

In the course of the boom, the working class in the metropolis, therefore, made significant gains in terms of its living standards. The Third World, as a whole, also grew much faster than ever in its history. Within the Third World, moreover, some countries, which for geo-political reasons (as 'frontline States' in the fight against Communism) were accorded generous market access by the metropolitan countries, grew particularly rapidly. Both these phenomena created the impression that capitalism had 'changed'. Henceforth, it was argued, we would have the reign of 'welfare capitalism' in the metropolis within which the working class would continue to prosper. As regards the Third World, being 'linked' to the metropolitan countries, such as the East and Southeast Asian countries were linked, no longer appeared to constitute a barrier to economic advance (contrary to the formulation of the Sixth Congress of the Comintern, which was widely accepted by even non-Marxist Third World nationalists).

In retrospect, however, the entire period of the post-War boom, 'welfarism', and successful diffusion of industrial capitalism to the Third World, which appeared to negate Marxist prognostications, seems like an exception, a discontinuity, a displacement of the system brought about by the exigencies of the post-War situation rather than the 'normal' functioning of the system. Indeed, the very tendencies of capitalism highlighted by Lenin, notably the centralization of capital, operating through the boom years, have brought about not only the end of this phase of capitalism, but even a rolling back of the achievements of the metropolitan working class and Third World peoples. Capitalism since the 1970s has acquired an altogether different, though more familiar look (in terms of its predatory nature, its inhumanity, and its attempt to dominate). This, of course, does not mean that we have a return to the conjuncture that prevailed in the pre-War period, captured so well by the Leninist vision. It means the unfolding of a new conjuncture, some words on which may be in order.

THE NATURE OF CONTEMPORARY FINANCE CAPITAL

The centralization of capital today has proceeded much beyond what Lenin had written about. What is more, it has not proceeded within the

[5] For a detailed discussion of this last argument as well as data and explanations in the terms of trade movements, see Patnaik (1997).

parameters of the world described by Lenin, but by transcending those parameters. It is not the case that German capital *qua* German capital has got more centralized, or British capital *qua* British capital has got more centralized, and that each has remained locked in rivalry with the other in the manner described by Lenin. Rather, the centralization of capital within each has been accompanied and overlaid by a process of 'globalization' of capital (in a specific sense that I shall describe shortly) that has transcended these rivalries themselves. Centralization has not meant mere quantitative changes in a world frozen in the same mould as in Lenin's time. It has meant a qualitative transformation in the world itself.

Of course, globalization of capital per se is not a new phenomenon. There was globalization of capital in Lenin's time as well, since imperialism necessarily entails such globalization. Contemporary globalization, however, has certain specific characteristics that emerge with sharper relief when we compare it to what was happening at the turn of the century. In the heyday of capital exports prior to the First World War, Britain, the leading capital exporter of that time, ran a current account surplus of between 5 and 10 per cent of her GNP for over four decades, averaging 8 per cent over the two decades prior to the War. By contrast, the largest capital exporter of modern times, Japan, has run current account surpluses averaging only 2.8 per cent of her GDP during the decade 1984–93 (Ghosh and Sen 1998). What this shows is *not* that capital flows today are relatively less important than earlier, but that such flows are largely detached from the current account of the balance of payments, that is, they pertain largely to the capital account of the balance of payments. Now, direct foreign investment, or other long-term capital flows generally give rise to concomitant commodity movements as well, which are reflected in the current account of the balance of payments.

On the other hand, short-term financial flows, which represent pure shifting of funds from one form of asset holding to another, do not generate concomitant commodity movements (except when they precipitate a crisis). The fact that contemporary capital flows are associated with relatively small current account surpluses by the leading capital exporters indicates therefore that much of this capital movement represents short-run speculative capital flows. Direct confirmation of this is provided by the fact that only about 2 per cent of cross-border capital flows are on account of trade-related transactions. In short, 'globalization' today is not accompanied by any significant relative increase in long-term capital flows; it represents predominantly a globalization of finance in the form of 'hot money' flows. It is not the mobility of capital-in-production that has increased in relative terms, but the mobility of capital-as-finance. When we talk of finance capital today we refer to an entity that is quite different from the finance capital of Lenin's days.

At least three differences need to be noted. First, Lenin had talked about nation-based, and hence nation-state aided, finance capital; what we have today is finance that, though drawn from particular nations, is neither amenable to the control or discipline of any nation-state, nor engaged in promoting any definable 'national interest'. Second, and correspondingly, we do not have the coalescence of industry and finance (both based in a particular nation and aided by the particular nation-state) that Bukharin had talked about and Lenin had endorsed. Instead, what we have is finance pursuing its objectives, which predominantly amounts to making speculative gains through 'hot money' flows. Third, this finance operates not in the context of intense inter-imperialist rivalries, but rather in the context of very noticeable unity among the leading capitalist powers. This is not to say that rivalries among them do not exist; of course they do, and could even flare up some day. But, as of now, their rivalries (notwithstanding the differences over the attack on Iraq) remain muted.

These differences from Lenin's picture of finance capital are not matters for mere cataloguing. They are themselves interrelated; and they conjure up an altogether different totality. For example, globalized capital as a bloc cannot be too closely tethered to industry based in a particular imperialist country: the very fact of its being globalized implies that it has to spill out of the narrow confines of industry and pursue a whole lot of activities in search of quick gains, which make it predominantly speculative in character. Likewise, its very global character is an important factor that keeps inter-imperialist rivalries in check. Any fragmentation of the world into separate 'spheres of influence', which would happen under intensified inter-imperialist rivalry, would put barriers in the way of global movements of finance. In other words, the traits we have underscored fit into one another, and they define an altogether new entity.

At the same time, it must not be forgotten that this globalization of finance is based on and itself represents an enormous unprecedented centralization, a carrying forward of precisely the process that Lenin had emphasized. In fact today, not only do we have centralization of finance capital in the usual sense of financial institutions controlling and deploying enormous amounts of funds, but also in the additional sense of their being able to stimulate 'herd behaviour' among others in response to their own actions, so that they also influence the decisions of finance that is not under their direct control. The entire globe is the theatre of operation of this gigantic bloc (in the sense of being inclined to move synchronously) of finance, which, though drawn from specific countries, is no longer, in any narrow sense, 'tied' to the 'national interest'. In the sphere of finance, we thus have globalization accompanying centralization, which has reached such a level that a single credit-rating agency, or a single George Soros, can wreck an economy within hours by causing capital flight out of it.

Emphasizing this aspect of globalization of finance should not give the impression that the centralization of capital in the sphere of production, in the form of multinational corporations (MNCs), and their global activities is of secondary importance. But much is written about the MNCs that have also been with us for a long time now. Globalization of finance, by contrast, is a relatively more recent phenomenon of great consequence, and hence, deserves special attention.

The consequences of the process of centralization-cum-globalization of finance capital are quite far-reaching. First, it is one contributory factor to the prolonged slowdown in the advanced capitalist world and the high unemployment rates that prevail (on which cyclical crises are additionally superimposed). No doubt, the impact of this slowdown has been uneven across the advanced capitalist countries, with Britain and the US doing rather better than the rest (on which more later). No doubt there are other important contributory factors to the slowdown, but the role of this particular factor cannot be underestimated.

It restricts the scope for demand management by the nation-state, undermining Keynesianism directly. Financial interests within any country, as Keynes and Kalecki had argued, tend to be hostile to demand management: when finance is *international*, this hostility acquires a spontaneous effectiveness. Any effort by the state to expand economic activity makes speculators apprehensive about the imminence of inflation, of exchange rate depreciation, and, more generally, of political radicalism, and finance flows out of the country. This precipitates actual depreciation and inflation, forcing the state to curtail activity to the level that speculators feel comfortable with. Putting it differently, state intervention presupposes a 'control area' of the state over which its writ can run; 'globalization' of finance tends to undermine this 'control area'.

The fact that a host of left-wing governments in the advanced capitalist countries, elected on the promise that they would increase employment, have signally failed to do so, underscores this objective constraint on state intervention. This constraint also explains the decline of all ideologies of social change, from social democracy to Keynesianism to Third World nationalism: since all of them see the nation-state as the agency of intervention, 'globalization' of finance, by restricting the state's capacity to intervene, has undermined their coherence. Indeed, the decline of the Soviet Union too is not unrelated to this phenomenon of 'globalization' of finance, since even the Soviet system had, towards the end, lost its immunity to capital flight.

The levels of activity and employment in the advanced capitalist world as a whole would not be so low, even without state intervention in demand management in individual countries, if the US state could boost aggregate demand for all of them. One would normally expect that with the dollar being the strongest currency, even without the *imprimatur* of the Bretton Woods system, the US would play this 'leadership' role for the capitalist world as a whole by enlarging its fiscal and current account deficits. But since the US economy has a high propensity to import, any such expansionary policy would benefit other economies more than it would the US. In pursuing such policies, in short, the US would be enlarging foreign claims upon itself for the sake of increasing employment in other countries, which it is not 'altruistic' enough to do.

Second, this new context has resulted in the unleashing of a major imperialist offensive against the Third World, in the form of the imposition of 'liberalization'. The prising open of Third World markets for goods and services, and the prising open of Third World economies for unrestricted movements of international finance capital have grave consequences for the Third World. Let us look at these closely.

THE CONSEQUENCES OF 'GLOBALIZATION' FOR THE THIRD WORLD

Imperialist propaganda tries to mask the consequences of liberalization and globalization for the Third World, but these are seriously adverse. At least five of them are relevant here. First, liberalization entails a drastic squeeze on the living standards of the workers and peasants in the Third World. Trade liberalization has the effect of de-industrializing these economies and pushing them into export agriculture, which is both detrimental to their food security and exposes the peasants to the vicissitudes of sharp price fluctuations on the world market. Getting caught in the vortex of international finance has the effect of trapping them into being perennially concerned about retaining the 'confidence' of international speculators; for this, government expenditure has to be restricted, subsidies lowered, the economy deflated and workers' rights curtailed. The net effect of all this is stagnation, higher unemployment, and a regressive shift in income distribution, which together accentuate poverty.

Second, it abrogates the economic and political sovereignty of these countries. The unhindered operation within these countries of international capital, that is dominated by and mediated through the metropolis, requires such an abrogation, since protection for such capital has to be arranged by metropolitan states, and agencies like the IMF controlled by them, by subverting the autonomy of the Third World states. But holding these countries under the thraldom of IMF conditionalities, which is the obvious mechanism for subverting autonomy, is usually supplemented by other mechanisms. As a part of the measures to retain 'investors' confidence', key positions in government have often got to be handed over to pro-imperialist politicians and bureaucrats. Personnel from the Fund and the Bank are deployed in the Economic Ministries which, in turn, are given greater autonomy on the plea of preventing them from being hamstrung by the caprices of the 'politicians'. (Autonomy of the central bank of course is insisted upon as a part of financial liberalization itself.) All these measures ensure that economic decision-making cannot be undertaken in an autonomous fashion by the domestic state.

Third, associated with the effort to retain 'investors' confidence' is a progressive transfer of natural resources and assets, especially of the public sector, to foreign hands at throwaway prices, a process of what one may call 'de-nationalization'. 'Privatization', in any case, is imposed on these economies as part of IMF conditionalities, and the beneficiaries of it are, eventually, if not immediately, the MNCs. In addition, whenever the caprices of international speculators threaten capital flight, the government, in desperation, resorts to de-nationalization of valuable assets, as a means of checking it.

Fourth, since the abrogation of sovereignty, the squeeze on the working people, the transfer of precious domestic assets 'for a song' to foreign hands, cannot be effected without reducing the political power of the people, there is necessarily an attenuation of democracy. There are several mechanisms for this, including some that have been mentioned above. But a very powerful mechanism consists in the following: different bourgeois and petty bourgeois political parties, afraid of triggering off capital flight, swear allegiance to the same set of policies of liberalization, so that the people are denied any effective political choice. In short, satisfying the caprices of international speculators on the one hand and respecting the will of the people on the other, are mutually incompatible; once the economy, and by implication, the polity, gets oriented towards satisfying the former, it has to find ways of circumventing the latter.

Finally, these countries become inevitably enmeshed in ethnic conflicts, secessionist movements, communal conflagrations, and fundamentalist threats once they 'liberalize' their economies and get caught in the vortex of international financial flows. Deflation and unemployment are conducive to the growth of exclusivist and chauvinist movements of various kinds, as the break up of Yugoslavia has clearly demonstrated. Such internecine struggles not only engulf Third World societies once they have adopted the imperialist-dictated policies, but are particularly useful from the point of view of imperialism: they act as a barrier to the emergence of revolutionary challenges to imperialism by dividing the people; they permit an effective whittling down of democracy; and permit imperialism to intervene, whenever it likes, in the name of 'preventing human rights abuses'. (Under the 'Bush doctrine', of course, which was explicated in the context of Iraq, the US has now abrogated to itself the right to intervene anywhere in the world that it wishes to.)

'GLOBALIZATION' AND SUPER-IMPERIALISM

The emergence of international finance capital, therefore, is associated with a new epoch that differs in very significant ways both from the epoch that Lenin had written about, and from the immediate post-War period of capitalist boom and welfarism. While the first difference would be appreciated by many, this second difference is less appreciated up to now. But we shall be concerned here with one implication of the first difference itself.

Different state systems correspond to different phases of imperialism. The phase that Lenin had written about was marked by rivalry among different finance capitals and correspondingly, the different imperialist states were locked in armed conflict. But if inter-imperialist rivalries are muted today, and if finance capital is international in the sense outlined earlier, then it follows that the state system supporting its operation must also be different: it would have to be a surrogate world state, towards which the existing state system would tend to move.

Such a surrogate world state could be created through what Karl Kautsky had called 'ultra-imperialism', where 'internationally united finance capital' was engaged in a joint, and relatively peaceful, exploitation of the globe. Lenin, however, had criticized Kautsky on the grounds that any such peaceful partition of the world could, at best, be a temporary truce reflecting the relative strengths of the rival finance capitals; with uneven development, which is endemic to capitalism, these relative strengths would necessarily change, giving rise to a renewed burst of inter-imperialist rivalry and a forcible re-partitioning of the world among the imperialist powers.

But what neither Kautsky nor Lenin had visualized was the possibility of a third, and altogether different, trajectory: if the strength of one of the imperialist powers exceeds that of its rivals by more than a critical margin, then this difference would tend to persist and even increase, leading to a state of 'super-imperialism', which could be quite stable, not in the sense of being necessarily long-lived, but in the sense of having considerable capacity to manipulate its contradictions. To be sure, 'super-imperialism' is nominally a form of 'ultra-imperialism', since it must also be based on some sort of an agreement among imperialist powers: the difference lies in the fact that in the case of 'super-imperialism', this agreement is dictated by the super-imperialist power itself.

There can be little doubt that the US today has emerged as a super-imperialist power. It has now acquired access to the massive Iraqi oil reserves that would strengthen its currency, enable it to borrow internationally to finance further military actions, and use those actions, in turn, to enlarge access to critical commodities that would further strengthen its currency. In short, the US has acquired the capacity to manipulate its contradictions, at least in the sense of being able to ward off challenges from rival imperialist powers.

To talk of 'super-imperialism' does not, of course, mean that nation-states disappear. Rather, 'super-imperialism' is exercised *through* the system of nation-states, by decimating *independent* nation-states, and by ensuring that all the remaining nation-states are either 'allies' (such as Blair's Britain), or 'client-states' (such as Turkey), or 'puppet-states' (such as Hamid Karzai's Afghanistan). Imperialism operates, as mentioned above, through state systems. Imperialism in Lenin's time operated through a certain state system; contemporary imperialism is bringing into being its own specific state system, the state system of super imperialism.

The term 'super-imperialism' has been used in the past to describe the post-War situation when the US was the exclusively dominant power among the imperialist countries; but then, it was restrained by the presence of the Soviet Union and other socialist countries, and faced a certain degree of hostility from the newly decolonized countries, many of whom had relatively autonomous bourgeois states and were grouped in the non-aligned movement. Today's world—where one of the 'super-powers', the Soviet Union, has collapsed, where the socialist challenge has been beaten back for the time being, where the non-aligned movement is in shambles, and where enforced 'globalization' under the aegis of imperialism has undermined the independence of several Third World nation-states—corresponds more closely to the concept of super-imperialism.

The fact that super-imperialism has considerable capacity to ward off challenges from rival imperialist powers does not mean that its contradictions disappear, or that it can manipulate them to ward off all challenges. In particular, as mentioned earlier, this epoch is marked by deflation, stagnation and recession. There is, therefore, a basic difference between the current era and the period of the 1950s and the 1960s, for which the term super-imperialism had been used, and in the context of which many authors, like Herbert Marcuse, had also argued that imperialism could manipulate its internal contradictions. That was a period of Keynesian demand management, and an associated long boom, but the current epoch is one of stagnation and unemployment in the metropolis, and impoverishment, de-industrialization, and adverse terms of trade for the periphery, a *denouement* that is associated inter alia with the rapid radicalization of the Third World peasantry, as happened in the 1930s.

THE RELEVANCE OF LENIN

The precise shape that the unfolding anti-super-imperialist struggle may take, however, is a matter that need not be gone into here. What is clear is that the aim of any such struggle in the Third World must be the building of an independent nation-state. This requires an alternative class base for the struggle (since the Third World bourgeoisie has shown itself to be utterly incapable of leading any anti-imperialist struggle any longer); an alternative economic programme which 'rolls back' globalization, retreats from the trajectory of capitalist development that led to 'globalization', and activates the state to pursue a broad-based egalitarian development path; and an alternative agenda that promotes decentralized decision-making and protects the democratic rights of the people.

This conclusion, which emerges from the perception of the current phase of imperialism outlined earlier, is different in certain crucial ways from Lenin's, which may prompt the question: what relevance does Lenin's theory have in today's world? The answer lies in the fact that even when the perception is different from Lenin's, it is arrived at by using Leninist concepts, by adopting the Leninist approach, and by pursuing the Leninist *problematique*. Even when we demarcate today's world from that of Lenin's, we do so by taking Lenin as our point of departure. Lenin's work, in other words, represents a *practical* engagement with imperialism, an engagement that produced a certain perception at that time. Even though our perception today may be different, our *practical* engagement can only be along the theoretical route charted by Lenin.

REFERENCES

Carr, E. H., (1966), *The Bolshevik Revolution*, Volume 3, Penguin, Harmondsworth.

Ghosh, Jayati and Abhijit Sen, (1998), 'Capital Flows and Macro-Economies: A Historical View', in Deepak Nayyar (ed.), *Economics as Ideology and Experience: Essays in Honour of Ashok Mitra*, Frank Cass, London.

Hobsbawm, E. J., (1969), *Industry and Empire*, Penguin, Harmondsworth.

Keynes, J. M., (1919), *The Economic Consequences of the Peace*, Macmillan, London.

Lenin, V. I., (1975), *Selected Works* (in three volumes), Volume 3, Progress Publishers, Moscow.

—— (1977a), *Collected Works*, Volume 24, third printing, Progress Publishers, Moscow.

—— (1977b), *Selected Works* (in three volumes), Volume 1, Progress Publishers, Moscow.

Lewis, W. A., (1949), *Economic Survey, 1919–1939*, Allen and Unwin, London.

—— (1978), *Growth and Fluctuations, 1870–1913*, Allen and Unwin, London.

Lukacs, Georg (1970), *Lenin*, New Left Books, London.

Patnaik, Prabhat, (1986), 'On the Economic Crisis of World Capitalism', in Prabhat Patnaik (ed.), *Lenin and Imperialism*, Orient Longman, Delhi.

—— (1997), *Accumulation and Stability Under Capitalism*, Clarendon Press, Oxford.

Prebisch, Raul, (1950), *The Economic Development of Latin America and Its Principal Problems*, United Nations Economic Commission for Latin America, Santiago.

Strachey, John, (1959), *The End of Empire*, Gollancz, London.

Index